The Great Pulp Heroes

THE GREAT PULP HEROES

by

Don Hutchison

illustrations by
Frank Hamilton

POPULAR PUBLICATIONS • 2025

Text © 2025 Don Hutchison. All rights reserved.
Illustrations by © 2025 Frank Hamilton. All rights reserved.
Authorized and produced under license.

No part of this book may be reproduced or utilized in any form or by any means,
electronic or mechanical, without permission in writing from the publisher.
Visit popularpublications.com for more books like this.

TABLE OF CONTENTS

THE GREAT STORY EXPLOSION 1
THE SHADOW'S SHADOW 11
DOC! 35
G-8'S WEIRD WAR 63
THE SPIDER'S WEB 77
PRE-WAR PARANOIA: OPERATOR #5 99
TWENTY YEARS OF MURDER 117
BLACK BATS AND GREEN GHOSTS 139
G-MEN 157
CALLING CAPTAIN FUTURE 173
CLOUDLAND CAVALIERS 189
TRAIL OF THE RIO KID 209
JUSTICE, INC. 219
MASTERS OF MENACE 233
LOST CITIES AND HIDDEN JUNGLES 267
THE ROAD TO ZERO 285
CORRESPONDENCE 297

THE GREAT STORY EXPLOSION

THEY WERE GAUDY. They were gory. They were glorious. And they were everywhere. Back in the thirties and forties, every newsstand in places big enough to have sidewalks harbored stacks of magazines bearing enameled covers that were designed to flypaper the eyes with circus-poster brilliance.

And what titles they had: *South Sea Stories! Black Mask! Adventure! Super Science Stories! Hollywood Detective! Magic Carpet! Doc Savage! Railroad Stories! The Spider! Northwest Romances! Famous Fantastic Mysteries! Jungle Stories! Western Raiders! Zeppelin Stories!*

The roll call is endless. They were called the pulps. By definition they were magazines of popular fiction, handling such staples as adventure, action, and romance. Between their birth in the first years of the last century and their demise in the middle fifties, they represented the greatest explosion of mass entertainment via the printed word that a thrill-seeking public ever experienced.

Variety was infinite. There were detective pulps, western pulps, science-fiction pulps, sports pulps, romance pulps, gang war pulps, horror pulps, spicy mystery pulps, jungle and desert adventure pulps, and *The Shadow*. There were straight aviation pulps with names like *Dare-Devil Aces* and *Sky Fighters*, as well as macabre variants like *G-8 and His Battle Aces*, which routinely ladled out titles like "Squadron of Corpses," "The Headless Staffel," and "Scourge of the Sky Beast." From railroad yarns to pirate stories, from the center of the earth to the farthest reaches of the universe, the gaudy, gory, glorious pulp magazines delivered on their promise: something for everyone.

How to explain the euphoria of the pulps? Perhaps you had to be there. You had to be young—at least in spirit. You had to be poor (most people were). You had to be part of that troubled, more innocent time. For armchair adventurers it was a Golden Age—before television, when imagination and a need for heroes were coupled with a world of vicarious wonders.

It is ironic that the most galvanic era in American popular culture was not that of the two Great Wars but the decade of the Great Depression, when the popular arts were fired with creative optimism. Middle- and lower-class workers—whose fear was that of the breadline—flocked to movies with titles like *Flying Down to Rio*, *A Night at the Opera*, and *Grand Hotel*. And hero-hungry readers, anxious to buy an hour's anodyne, poured mountains of dimes across newsstand counters to find new worlds of adventure printed on cheap pulp paper sandwiched between eye-searing covers. Whole forests were leveled to supply the insatiable demand for dreams that mere pennies could buy. And the word merchants were there to make sure that demand never exceeded supply.

At a penny a word—sometimes more, but often less—you had to sell a lot of words to make a living. Even so, a few pulp scriveners discovered gold in them thar thrills. In the depths of the Great Depression, it was rumored that a fictioneer named Frederick Faust (aka Max Brand) earned $80,000 a year on pulp writing alone. He wound up living like a Medici in a castle in Italy, surrounded by a retinue of servants.

As the audience for pulp thrills grew, the magazines became

an enormous market for would-be wordsmiths as well as for familiar names. By the twenties and thirties, the mass-market pulps were into a Golden Age of creativity, with new and exciting writers commanding armies of devoted fans.

The fantasy pulps developed such names as Robert E. Howard, H.P. Lovecraft, and Edgar Rice Burroughs. The detective story was elevated to a fine—and peculiarly American—art form by the gargantuan talents of Dashiell Hammett, Raymond Chandler, and Cornell Woolrich. The Western pulps had Max Brand, Walt Coburn, and Ernest Haycox, among others, and the adventure fiction field boasted too many famous names to enumerate.

Possibly the only fictional category invented by the pulps was that of science fiction, beginning as early as 1910, adventure titles like *Argosy* and *All-Story Magazine* had featured what they called "scientific romances," stories of lost races and adventure on other planets. But it took a man named Hugo Gernsback to begin a new magazine, *Amazing Stories*, that would deal exclusively with this new breed of story as a genre. Gernsback's discovery led the way to other pulp titles that attracted the early works of Ray Bradbury, Isaac Asimov, and Robert Heinlein.

It was a literary Gold Rush, but for the few who struck pay dirt (Hammett, Burroughs, Erle Stanley Gardner), hundreds of others found the panning tough. In his book *The Pulp Jungle*, author Frank Gruber confided:

> *There were in existence, at this time, some 150 pulp magazines, solidly established. A vast market for stories. But these were still Depression days, and the competition was fierce. It was a literary*

jungle, and every writer was a tiger. You had to be brash, you had to be tough, you had to claw your way into the jungle and fight for your life every minute you were in it. There were more writers than there were magazines. All were hungry writers.

Storytellers have always existed, of course, from caveman practitioners who spun tales to keep the clan together and the demons at bay, through Dumas and Dickens to twentieth-century writers like Edgar Wallace who could, and did, churn out a novel a week and in between find time to dash off a play and a few short stories. But never before and never again did there exist a market for wordsmiths like that of the fabulous pulps. Each month, brightly colored covers shrilled the names of hundreds of writers as familiar as household brands. To their fans, they were names that crackled with the thrill of lightning: Dashiell Hammett, Carroll John Daly, H. Bedford Jones, Cornell Woolrich, Max Brand, Raymond Chandler, Robert E. Howard, A. Merritt, Edmond Hamilton, H.P. Lovecraft, Hugh B. Cave, Talbot Mundy, Johnston McCulley, and legions of others.

While the pulp magazine was a twentieth-century publishing sensation, the history of cheap fiction for the masses can be traced as far back as the Industrial Revolution. When more leisure time for workers was combined with universal education and the invention of the steam printing press, a new reading public was created. Inevitably, a new type of literature arose to meet demand—a literature that did not attempt to educate or uplift but existed simply to entertain. Freed of the patronage of the well educated and the wealthy, it was a literature conceived as a branch of show business, produced for a mass audience that wished to be excited and amused.

What we now call "pulp" fiction was produced as early as the 1840s, when publishers decided that one way to lower costs, and thus price, was to use newspaper presses and cheap newsprint paper. A news sheet, doubled to make four pages, made a reasonable book-like format. The product of this discovery was something called the family story paper. Such story papers as *The Corsair* and the *Yankee Privateer*, although called newspapers and enjoying special newspaper postal rates, were really collections of fiction that ran novels in serial form.

Then came the revolution. In 1860, a firm called Beadle & Adams published a paperbound novel for ten cents, titled *Malaeska: The Indian Wife of the White Hunter*. The dime novel had arrived. Small wonder that the first dime novel was a homespun western, or that the most popular series characters would be frontier icons like Buffalo Bill Cody, Kit Carson, and Jesse James. (The dime novel dream parade also included such fictitious buckaroos as Red River Bill, Headshot Dave, Young Wild West, and the marvellously alliterative Roaring Ralph Rockwood, the Reckless Ranger.)

For the next forty years, dime novels (later reduced to a nickel) would pour from the presses by the millions. They would be much criticized and reviled, but generations of children gobbled them up. They found that beneath their lurid paper covers were even more lurid stories chock full of blood, bullets, heart-stopping suspense and relentless, frantic action. The dime-novel shocker introduced and defined many pulp fiction staples: western stories, war stories, pirate stories, romance stories, detective stories, and even continuing-character series.

By the turn of the nineteenth century, the appeal of the dime novel had waned. Its characters, style, and action-oriented plots were soon transferred to the pulps, so called because a publisher named Frank Munsey had begun to print an all-fiction magazine titled *The Argosy* on cheap pulpwood paper. Munsey had the idea that the story was more important than what it was printed on. He must have guessed correctly because the lowly pulp magazine went on to become the most popular form of reading material in America between World War I and the end of World War II.

Street & Smith, a dime-novel giant, began converting paper-covered books into pulp magazines as early as 1903. Eventually, *The Buffalo Bill Weekly* dime-novel series was transformed into *Western Story Magazine*, with old Bill held over briefly in a series of new stories. Likewise, that resolute but fictitious detective, Nick Carter, became editor emeritus of the newly created *Detective Story Magazine*. Other genres—science fiction, love story, horror, war and aviation—soon followed.

What made the pulps different from the weekly story papers and dime novels was that they were true magazines, generous in both size and variety of content. They were all-permeating atmosphere, a delirious environment of irresistibly lurid covers, dynamic illustrations, worshipful letters, and breathless fiction. For only ten cents, or a little more—the price of a magazine containing novels, short stories, departments, and artwork—a reader could get lost in the violent lives of heroes and heroines as outsized and engrossing as any to be found in the great myths and legends.

As pulp publisher Henry Steeger once explained it:

> *Pulps were the principal entertainment vehicle for millions of Americans. They were an unflickering, uncolored TV screen upon*

which the reader could spread the most glorious imagination he possessed. The athletes were stronger, the heroes were nobler, the girls were more beautiful, and the palaces were more luxurious than any in existence; they were always there at any time of the day or night on dull, no-gloss paper that was kind to the eyes.

Not surprisingly, the heyday of the pulp heroes was the period of the "dirty thirties." The Great Depression had smashed into America with the ferocity of a hurricane. Unemployment became a way of life, creating a new "leisure class," as hundreds of thousands of rootless scarecrow figures shuffled through breadlines and soup kitchens, wan symbols of hard times. Pulp-paper fiction was the cheapest thrill around, and tattered copies of *Detective Fiction Weekly* and *Dime Western* were passed from hand to hand or left behind in boxcars and hobo jungles. To most citizens, the NRA acronym stood for National Recovery Act, but pulp fiction publishers proudly carried the familiar NRA blue eagle on their covers, stating that it promised "New Reading Appeal."

As the Roaring Twenties marched to a cataclysmic market crash, many North Americans had learned to accept organized crime (created by Prohibition) as "big business" and gangsters as a form of barbaric royalty. But the glorification of gang rule took an abrupt turn in the Great Depression when Americans awoke from their paralysis of fascination and began looking for new heroes who did not reflect the rule of force over ideals. As usual, the pulps were there to supply what the public desired.

Pulp avengers—individuals of strength, speed, brains, and stamina—arose to do battle with working-class America's perceived enemies: gangsters, bankers, punks, fiends, lawyers, politicians, and threatening foreign hordes. The most famous of these avengers, The Shadow, leaped into the fray in 1931 as the first titular hero of his own magazine. He proved that a magazine built around the exploits of a single character was an idea whose time had come. The Shadow took off like a flashfire, causing scores of new "character" titles to pop up on the newsstands, ranging from outright imitations to new departures. There were aviation heroes (the Lone Eagle and Bill Barnes), masters of disguise (Secret Agent X and the Phantom Detective), western heroes (The Rio Kid and The Lone Ranger), adventure heroes (Doc Savage and The Skipper), and even a science fiction hero (Captain Future). Ironically one of the most famous of all pulp-hero creations, Johnston McCulley's Zorro ("the Robin Hood of California") never did have his own title, but he appeared regularly in the magazines from his inception in 1919 right up to the final gasp of the pulps themselves.

Much has been made of the pulp magazines as training grounds for serious literary authors ranging from MacKinlay Kantor to Tennessee Williams. The fact is that most of the pulps treasured by collectors today represent an unpretentious, calculatedly disposable literature that was too exciting to be respectable and too much fun to be taken seriously.

The series hero is older than Beowulf and Ulysses. No doubt conceived around the flickering glow of Stone Age campfires, the protracted adventures of heroic champions appeal to the child in all of us—the kid who is willing to have a good story repeated because he wants it never to end. In the tradition of such literary ancestors, the great heroes of the pulps were not conceived as carriers of substantive meaning; they were invented for fans of the preposterous, for connoisseurs of the outrageous—for the child that lurks in all of us.

Say what you will of the great pulp heroes, but they were a beguiling lot. With their narratives yoked to gut emotions, they brought messages of a limitless world of adventure and experience, a great shining universe that was full of color and juice, where heroes were not forced to do homework, mow lawns, go to bed early, or eat up their vegetables. It was all fantasy, of course—heroism rampant with seldom a dull or ugly moment—but it got a lot of readers through some hard times and filled their minds with hope, wonder, and even inspiration.

THE SHADOW'S SHADOW

Thundering automatics blasting red-tipped flame rumble in the night... answering blasts echo back... final volleys from automatics... silence. Then from the blackness behind automatics moves a deeper blackness—a shadow within a shadow—and disappears into the night. On the chill night air is born a peal of laughter.
The triumphant laugh of The Shadow!
"Who knows what evil lurrrrrks in the hearts of men? The Shadow knows! Hehhhhhhhhh-hehhhhhhhhh-hehhhhhhhh."

PROBABLY NO LINES in old-time radio or mystery fiction are as famous as that sonorous question and its echoing triumphant answer. Following his magazine debut in April of 1931, The Shadow led the fight against crime and boredom for almost two decades—on the airwaves, in his own long-lived magazine, and in comics and movies, as well as toys, games, and all the other paraphernalia associated with a commercially created folk-myth idol. No wonder he was always laughing.

Of all the mystery men of pulpland, none was more popular or more influential than The Shadow. For legions of fans, he was the uncrowned king of mystery. He was mystery personified.

If one were to ask, "Who is/was The Shadow?" a generation of radio buffs would intone, "The Shadow is, in reality, Lamont Cranston, wealthy young man-about-town who, years ago in the Orient, learned the hypnotic power to cloud men's minds so they could not see him." And another generation of pulp story enthusiasts would reply, "Not so." It seems that pulp readers were privy to more confidential disclosures. In the magazine stories, Lamont Cranston was but one of the disguises of the real Shadow, Kent Allard, an explorer-aviator-adventurer whose identity as the Master of Darkness is known only to two Xinca Indians sworn to eternal secrecy.

Unlike his radio counterpart, the magazine Shadow at no time "clouded men's minds to render himself invisible." Instead, he used a black cloak and black slouch hat to blend into the shadows of night, sometimes hiding in the gloom of an otherwise brightly lit room. In the glowering cover portraits by George Rozen, his cloak became crimson-lined with a crimson collar covering his mouth (pulp covers needed color!) leaving the "burning eyes" and "hawklike" visage prominently exposed. Other icons which appeared frequently on those amazing covers included his giant licorice-colored .45 automatics and a fire opal ring.

As another contrast to The Shadow of radio fame—who had only his "friend and companion, the lovely Margo Lane" to assist him—the pulp Shadow was supported by a veritable army of aides. They included Burbank, his mysterious contact man who spent his life at a switchboard; Harry Vincent, who acted as The Shadow's advance man and proxy; Rutledge Mann, an investment broker; Clyde Burke, a reporter on the *Classic*, who furnished The Shadow with inside information; Moe Shrevnitz, who transported the Crime Master to battle—in his taxicab; Cliff Marsland and Hawkeye, who posed as criminals to ferret crimedom's secrets; an expert lock-picker named Tapper; and the giant African, Jericho, whose terrifying physical strength was equaled only by his willingness to fight crime.

Whenever necessary, the Knight of Darkness dispensed with his fighting togs to assume the guise of Lamont Cranston, Henry Arnaud, or Fritz, the dull-mannered janitor at police headquarters. As wealthy playboy Cranston, he maintained a friendship with Police Commissioner Ralph Weston; as

Fritz he managed to keep an eye on Weston's right-hand man, Inspector Joe Cardona. Sometimes he appeared as a character named George Clarendon, sometimes as elderly Phineas Twambley, and once as the Rajah of Lengore. In one story, "The North Woods Mystery," The Shadow is revealed as Beaver Luke, an Indian character who is said to be establishing new beaver colonies for the Canadian government.

It can be argued that The Shadow, as a character, ranks among the great creations of popular fiction. Like Sherlock Holmes and Tarzan, he is greater than all the stories in which he appears, his weird and inexplicable nature appealing to some deep recess in the human psyche. Ironically, the character did not spring from any one man's imagination—deep and shadowy or otherwise—but instead was created by public appeal mated with blind luck. Foremost amongst the pulp publishers of the thirties was Street & Smith, the fabled fiction factory. The company sponsored a Thursday night radio program, one of whose functions was to promote their *Detective Story Magazine*. The "announcer" on the program was a mysterious character with a sepulchral voice known as The Shadow—purely a radio gimmick to lend an air of mystery to the proceedings. Surprisingly, the wickedly mirthful radio voice caught the public fancy. Acting quickly, the Messrs. Street & Smith decided to rush out something called *The Shadow, A Detective Magazine*, copyrighting the title to protect their new discovery.

In its dime-novel days, the company had created such fictional marvels as Nick Carter, Buffalo Bill, and Frank Merriwell. Street & Smith general manager Henry W. Ralston saw the new title as a way of reintroducing the concept of a single-character hero magazine. He even salvaged a leftover

Nick Carter manuscript with the idea of rewriting it to fit the new character. Propitiously, none of his regular writers fancied the task of reworking an antedated private eye into terminally weird, cloaked phantom.

In a move born of possible frustration, the job was eventually farmed out to a young newspaperman and part-time magician named Walter Brown Gibson, who just happened to drop by the company offices looking for writing assignments. Gibson was asked to turn out a 75,000-word story about a mysterious being called The Shadow. That was it. Nobody told him who The Shadow was because nobody knew.

Since the character did not belong to the writer but to the publisher, Street & Smith insisted that Gibson write the novels using a pen name. He utilized the names of two magic dealers, Maxwell Holden and U.F. Grant, to create the inspired pseudonym of Maxwell Grant.

The first story, appropriately titled "The Living Shadow," is not a typical example of pulse-pounding pulp action. Gibson was a journalist, not a fiction writer. Creating the adventures of The Shadow was an assignment that required learning on the job. He took as his model an old Horatio Alger dime novel, using it as a guideline to work out the number of chapters and words to a chapter to fashion it to the correct length. Nowhere in the book is the identity of The Shadow revealed; Gibson had not decided upon it at the time. The Shadow is merely a mysterious figure whose voice is heard on the radio, sometimes passing on coded clues to his operatives. This was before the dramatized radio series began and refers of course to the "voice" heard on the *Detective Story* program.

The proxy hero of "The Living Shadow" is young, handsome

Harry Vincent—destined to be The Shadow's top agent. As the story opens, the melancholic Harry is about to commit suicide by leaping off a fog-swathed bridge. He is snatched to safety by Gibson's sinister-looking protagonist who, in turn, demands a life of servitude.

> *"Your life is no longer your own,"* the cloaked stranger warns him.
>
> *"I shall improve it… But I shall risk it, too. Perhaps I shall lose it, because I have lost lives, just as I have saved them. This is my promise: life, with enjoyment, with danger, with excitement… Life, above all, with honor. But if I give it, I demand obedience. Absolute obedience."*

In the years to follow, on more than one occasion, Harry must have wished he had jumped.

Almost to everyone's surprise, the first issue sold out. A second one, featuring "The Eyes of the Shadow," introduced millionaire Lamont Cranston, a member of New York's exclusive Cobalt Club. It is strongly suggested that Cranston may be the identity of the mysterious Shadow. But only an issue later, in "The Shadow Laughs," Cranston is disqualified in the role by the real Shadow, who convinces the globe-trotting playboy to leave the country so that The Shadow can impersonate him in comfort. They alone share the secret, with the possible exception of Burbank, The Shadow's chair-bound contact man.

These first three stories are intricate, episodic narratives, brimming with atmosphere and clotted with incidental characters. What they lacked was the delirious action so beloved by pulp fans. This was partly because Gibson was blissfully ignorant of pulp stereotypes—his models were mainstream mystery novels of an earlier era—and partly because of an editorial vision that saw The Shadow as a living symbol for all that was mysterious and puzzling. As mystery enthusiast Chris Steinbrunner once explained:

> *Menacing figures dressed in black had long been popular character in mystery stories, films and plays... Gibson took this terrible dread shape that had hitherto been the hero's nemesis and made it the hero. The Shadow was both the force for good and lurker in the darkness.*

One of the places the cloaked phantom lurked was in his own New Jersey mansion, conveniently located close to New York City crime lords. His plush manse had a tower room outfitted as a wireless station from which he and contact man Burbank communicated with his army of dedicated aides. He had his own plane stationed at a nearby hangar and even an Autogiro, a prototype of the present-day helicopter, which could whisk him to perilous rooftop encounters.

When he wasn't using Moe Shrevnitz's souped-up cab, The Shadow was ferried around in an imported limousine driven by Cranston's imperturbable chauffeur, Stanley. The back seat of the limousine was witness to numerous magical transformations as the pseudo-Cranston slipped into something more comfortable:

> *A low, soft laugh came from the hidden lips of Lamont Cranston. The man half raised himself in the back seat. Something black enmeshed him; the folds of a somber garment fluttered*

toward the floor. Then the pallid face of Cranston disappeared as the shadow of a hat brim settled upon it. Invisible hands raised clinking objects from the suitcase. All was blackness in the rear of the limousine. A transformation had taken place, though even Stanley had not realized it. Lamont Cranston had become The Shadow!

Good old, dense Stanley. He never did twig to the fact that he served two masters. Sometimes The Shadow repaired to his sanctum—a blue-lit grotto in the Manhattan badlands. The eerie isolation of the mystic sanctum undoubtedly helped relieve pent-up tension; it was here that the clandestine crime fighter spent endless hours chortling to the four walls and/or writing cryptic messages to himself in invisible ink. It was all very strange, but nobody ever accused The Shadow of being mister average guy.

The Shadow was mystery piled upon mystery. Even his face was something of an enigma. In one novel, it is suggested that his true face is featureless. In another, "The Shadow's Shadow" (February 1, 1933), master criminal Felix Zubian stares into the countenance of The Shadow—not the disguised features of Lamont Cranston or Henry Arnaud—and he recoils in horror.

What did The Shadow really look like? Only The Shadow knew.

Readers must have adored the mysterious shenanigans. Within months The Shadow went from quarterly to monthly, and within a year or two it was selling more than 300,000 copies per issue. Gibson signed yet another contract. The magazine would appear twice a month; he was to produce twenty-four adventures per year, one 60,000-word novel every two weeks for as long as the popularity of The Shadow continued. That figure totaled more than 1,440,000 words per year.

The circulation soared. By living, thinking, even dreaming the life of The Shadow, Gibson was to chronicle the Master Avenger's activities for a hectic eighteen years. Keeping two dozen yarns ahead of publication, he sometimes turned out a fresh book in four to six days, often working all night to meet self-imposed deadlines.

Behind a typewriter, he was as superhuman as his own creation. He worked on a battery of machines. When one began to "get tired," he'd move on to another, and then to a third. He worked in a continuous flow, living the life of The Shadow as he typed, until his fingers began to swell, or the tips became bloody.

> *"By living, thinking, even dreaming the story in one continued process," Gibson revealed, "ideas came faster and faster. Sometimes the typewriter keys would fly so fast that I wondered if my fingers could keep up with them. And at the finish of the story I often had to take a few days off as my fingertips were too sore to begin work on the next book."*

An irrepressible raconteur brimming with energy, Walter Gibson was uniquely qualified to serve as The Shadow's personal biographer. While still a boy, he had taken to puzzles and sleight-of-hand and thought seriously of making magic his life's work. Instead, he became a reporter for the now-defunct Philadelphia *North American* and later moved on to the *Ledger Syndicate* where he wrote Sunday features and, with his "Puzzle a Day" column, helped to make the crossword puzzle a national craze. A friend and confidant of the century's greatest magicians—Houdini, Thurston, Blackstone—Gibson ghosted books for all of them as well as devising many of their illusions.

"Magic and mystery," Gibson once wrote, "are so closely

interwoven that it is hard to tell where one leaves off and the other begins."

Magic and mystery. Mystery and magic. These were the polarities of Gibson's existence, and they would become the secret of the special qualities that would raise The Shadow beyond the level of a mere pulp character.

While The Shadow was the first pulp hero to be awarded his own magazine, it should be noted in fairness that he reflected a long line of phantom avengers and dual-identity mystery men, some dating as far back as the previous century. These included such early characters as Fantomas, The Scarlet Pimpernel, Arsene Lupin, and the pulps' own Zorro.

One acknowledged inspiration for The Shadow was that of Jimmie Dale, alias The Gray Seal. Jimmie Dale was the hero of a series of books (and pulp serials) written after the end of World War I by a Canadian writer named Frank L. Packard. They are out of print now and are likely to remain so, but they formed a template that Walter Gibson and many of his imitators would follow.

Nearly two decades before the advent of the first pulp-hero magazine, Packard wrote of a hero who stalked the night in a black mask and slouch hat to aid the helpless and to bring criminals to justice. Like The Shadow, many of The Gray Seal's adventures occurred in a Chinatown setting—a sinister, pulp-style Chinatown where tong wars were declared, ghastly murders hatched, and where a man's life was worth the price of a little opium—or even less.

Although Jimmie Dale owned a luxurious Riverside Drive mansion and belonged to the exclusive St. James Club (surely a model for Lamont Cranston's Cobalt Club), as The Gray Seal he maintained an underworld "Sanctuary," deep in the heart of the east side Bad Lands, where no questions were asked so long as the rent was paid. The Sanctuary was where he kept his disguises, a change of clothes and weapons, and from which he emerged in his disguise as Larry the Bat, a stooped, gaunt underworld figure.

Disguise was also to be a way of life for the jolly illusionist who created and chronicled the adventures of The Shadow under the invented name of Maxwell Grant. As the fame of his character grew, Walter Gibson's anonymity must have proved frustrating. He began to inject characters with monikers like Blister Wagon, Wilton Barges, Lewis G. Barton, and Granite Bowles—all anagrams of his real name.

Under any name, Gibson's work brimmed with invention and novelty. Thanks to him, The Shadow did not remain fixed or static in character—and neither did his adventures. The two were always in a state of flux, as mercurial and energetic as the man who pounded them out in a creative fever. Most of the early exploits involved proxy heroes, with The Shadow remaining offstage as a nebulous figure of Gothic mystery, almost omniscient. As Gibson—and his readers—became familiar with the character, the image solidified into that of a sinister magician-wraith, confounding evildoers with a bag of tricks ranging from wall-hugging suction cups to finger-snapping explosive powders.

None of this was accidental. Gibson, Henry Ralston, and Shadow editor John Nanovic held regular story conferences, guiding The Shadow's destiny with the care and consideration of loving parents. The "think tank" approach helped Gibson keep the series fresh and ever changing. Unlike many of the pulp-hero magazines, one issue of The Shadow is not a carbon copy of another.

What made Gibson's contribution to the form unique was the combination of a magician's flair for misdirection and illusion with a journalist's respect for facts and accuracy. Gibson always stressed that no matter how fanciful his yarns might become, the descriptions of people, places, and things were accurate in essential details. Despite his mind-numbing work schedule, the reporter in him took the time to check on guns, gems, cults, wills, spies, ghosts, morgues, and all sorts of deadly devices that The Shadow might encounter. He briefed himself on unusual localities and strange legends that would intrigue readers.

"I always tried to keep the stories informative," Gibson said. "You pick up any of The Shadows and you read about something happening on the Limited between New York and Savannah, why you'll find it's running exactly according to the timetable of 1936 or whenever the story was written."

Because of the speed with which he had to work, combined with his lively interest in all things, many of the characters and details of The Shadow novels are like an ongoing record of Walter Gibson's life and enthusiasms. Almost everything was grist for his story mill.

As the author traveled, so did his creation. Gibson built a cabin in Maine and began to spend winters in Florida. Both locations became Shadow locales. "The London Crimes" and "Castle of Doom" were set in England. "Washington Crime" and "The Case of Congressman Coyd" took place in the nation's capital. "The Mardi Gras Mystery" reflected a New Orleans experience. "In Gangdom's Doom," The Shadow cleaned up

Chicago; once, in a story titled "Quetzal," he found himself on the wrong end of a Mexican firing squad.

In a conversation I once had with Walter Gibson, he revealed that the 1936 Shadow yarn, "The Northwoods Mystery," had been based on a trip into the Ontario Northland.

> *"You know, I was criticized for including a French-Canadian guide named Pierre," he confided. "Some people thought the character and his name were too much of a pulp magazine cliché or something. But darn it, I really did have a guide who was just like that character—and his name really was Pierre!"*

As the series progressed, important changes took place. Early Shadow novels had been written in the discreet nonviolent manner of the twenty's detective thrillers. All too often, The Shadow's foes were small-time hoods bearing such cheap names as Squint Preston, Nogger Tellif, and Konk Zitz. (If Mr. and Mrs. Tellif had given it any thought, they might have known that a name like Nogger would get their kid into hot water sooner or later.)

In those early stories, The Shadow's guns "blasted," "roared," and "boomed," sending demoralized punks "howling" and "cowering" back to their miserable rat holes, but he seldom if ever really killed anyone. Fortunately, things improved. The vaporous night creature of the early stories gradually solidified into an awesome figure of lethal jurisprudence. By 1933, he began cutting a bloody swath through the underworld, judging, condemning, and executing bulge-eyed crooks and killers—not neatly, but with an oversized .45 in both hands—and all the while, that low laugh! Atmosphere became charged with action. The newer, sterner Shadow didn't believe in justice—he was justice—implacable and inevitable.

> *There were no echoes to his sardonic laugh. The reverberations of The Shadow's mirth were drowned in the roar of his .45s as the controlling fingers loosed a stream of lead into the midst of the startled mobsters.*
>
> *Bodies thudded to the floor. Gasping oaths spattered from snarling lips that closed to speak no more. Shattered flashlights fell useless. With one fierce volley from his recoiling automatics, The Shadow cleared the way. Upon the floor lay the piled-up bodies of Gats Hackett's new band of killers—men who would never slay for their black-hearted chief.*
>
> *The automatics disappeared beneath The Shadow's cloak. He had used every cartridge. The hands emerged, bringing forth another pair of pistols. With a forward spring, the black-clad figure swept over the mass of bodies that cluttered the doorway to the hall.*

Readers loved it. They bought magazines. They mailed off dimes for Shadow pins and rubber stamps. They wrote idolatrous letters to his magazine.

By 1937, many of The Shadow's fan letters requested membership in his "Century Club," an honor list of readers who claimed to have read one hundred or more of his adventures. One Shadowholic went so far as to express his dedication with the threat of applied torture: "If Maxwell Grant ever quits writing The Shadow stories or runs out of ideas, he should be made to feel the soothing embrace of the Iron Maiden. No offense meant, Mr. Grant."

Numerous correspondents stressed fascination with The Shadow's criminal foes, who necessarily grew more monstrous as he disposed of their wimpy predecessors. Reacting to public enthusiasm, a roll call of master fiends arose in novels bearing their grotesque names: The Black Master, Charg Monster, Gray Fist, The Murder Master, The Creeper, and The Cobra. One Shadow novel titled "The Hydra" dealt not with a single super foe but with a criminal organization which put forth two new hoodlums whenever one was killed, much as the Hydra of legend sprouted two new heads each time one was severed.

Occasionally a villain would escape The Shadow's wrath long enough to make a return appearance. The first of these was Rodil Mocquino, the evil Haitian voodoo doctor, who led his zombie slaves in "The Voodoo Master" (March 1, 1936), "City of Doom" (May 15, 1936), and "Voodoo Trail" (June 1, 1938). Other recurring villains included The Hand, The Wasp, and the Prince of Evil.

From his beginning, The Shadow's favorite crime haunts were the so-called Chinatowns on both coasts, reflecting Gibson's admiration for Sax Rohmer's popular Fu Manchu novels. Known as Ying Ko to the Chinese, the Master of Darkness skulked through New York's Chinatown in The Living Shadow," "The Fate Joss," "The Chinese Disks," "The Living Joss," and "The Jade Dragon." San Francisco's Chinatown encountered him in "Green Eyes," "The Chinese Tapestry," "Six Men of Evil Teeth of the Dragon," "The Chinese Primrose," and finally in "Jade Dragon," the latter not to be confused with "The Jade Dragon" of 1942, which was set in Manhattan's Chinatown.

After numerous Chinatown combats, it was perhaps inevitable that The Shadow would eventually encounter an Oriental supervillain whose abilities and resources were the equal of his own.

As Walter Gibson explained it,

> *That was left for Shiwan Khan in "The Golden Master" of September 15, 1939. Since The Shadow in his early years had visited Tibet, there to acquire hypnotic powers that helped him to triumph over fiends of crime, it stood to reason that his nemesis—if he should ever have one—would have to come from that mystic land in order to challenge The Shadow on his home ground. Shiwan Khan not only came from Tibet, he claimed that he owned it, along with outlying territories, which made him formidable, indeed.*

Shiwan Khan, The Shadow's own Yellow Peril, stalked through four novels, along with his colorful retinue of Mongols, Chinese, Afghans, Tibetan wizards, and (shades of Sax Rohmer) Dacoit stranglers. Ironically, it wasn't super fiends who gave The Shadow sleepless nights but some of the Master Avenger's own imitators. By the mid-thirties, flamboyant rivals like Popular Publications' The Spider began cutting into sales. Suspecting that Gibson's intricate, atmospheric style might need boosting, Street & Smith decided to hire another "Maxwell Grant" to inject fresh input into the series. The idea wasn't to replace Gibson but simply to introduce the odd pulp-style action story to give the magazine variety. They found such a thrill doctor in a writer named Theodore Tinsley. A frequent contributor to the prestigious *Black Mask* magazine, Tinsley was a skilled craftsman who matched the familiar Gibson style while introducing his own brand of hardboiled, cliff-hanging suspense. His most significant contribution, however, was the introduction of scenes featuring females disrobing or having their clothing ripped strategically. This allowed cover artists to introduce mildly titillating situations—at least by Street & Smith's sedate standards. Sales bounced back, probably due to the liberated covers rather than the new author's excellent but unacknowledged contributions. (It was during the Tinsley era that George Rozen's powerful, symbolic covers gave way to Graves Gladney's more illustrative paintings.)

Over seven years, from "Partners in Peril" (November 1, 1936) to "The Golden Doom" (July 1943), Tinsley contributed twenty-seven novels to the series—roughly four a year. While Gibson's Shadow reflected the author's interest in magic, Tinsley's Shadow was never far removed from trains. One of his finest contributions was "The Pooltex Tangle" (October 1, 1937), a lightning-paced ode to steam-puffing chariots and the glimmering sweep of metal rails.

With his Shadow workload reduced to a mere twenty novels a year, Walter Gibson occupied his "spare time" with numerous other assignments. One of these was The Shadow comic book which Street & Smith originated to cash in on the juvenile market that had sprung up as an offshoot of the hero pulps. He wrote the comic book Shadow from the first issue on for six years, condensing highlights from specific novels into the required number of pages.

Small wonder that The Shadow's fame soon spread like wildfire into other mediums, the foremost of which were the classic radio adaptations that outlasted the magazine by five years. While the pulp novels were basically mystery stories

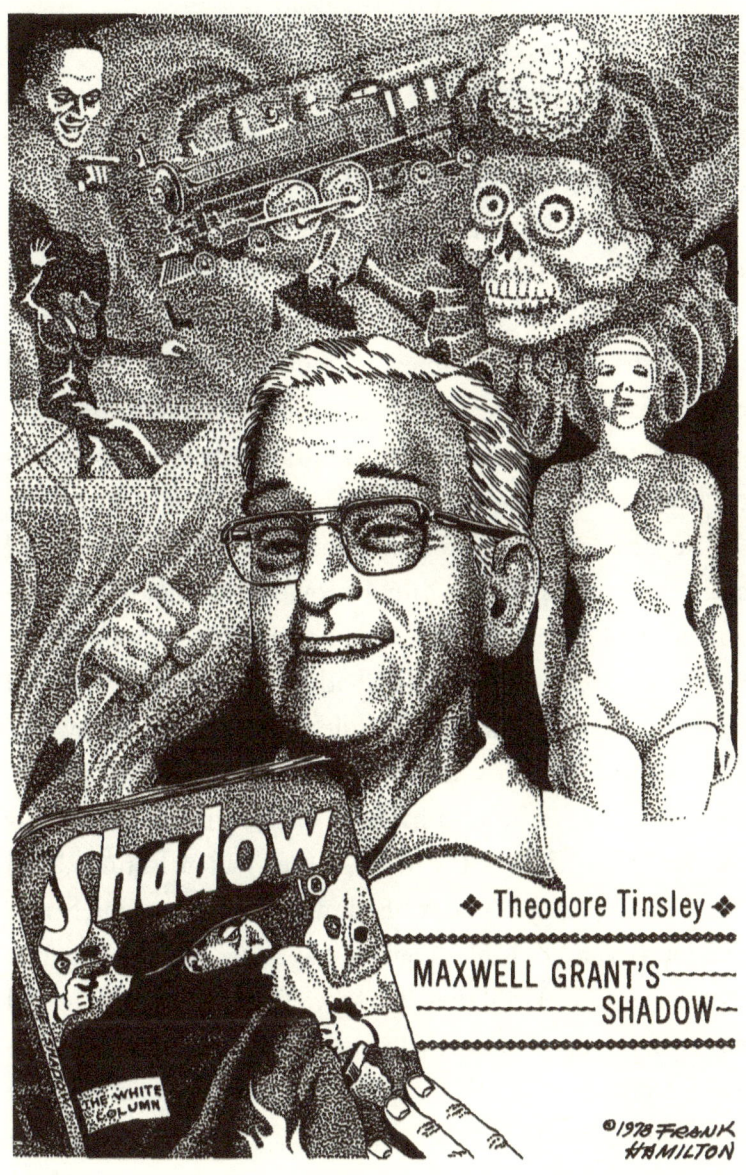

enriched with atmosphere and incident, the radio programs were outright melodramas, often luridly so. Episodes like "Isle of the Dead," "Tomb of Terror," "When the Grave is Open," and "The Gibbering Things" were commonplace, as were yarns about werewolves, ghouls, haunted houses, and other trappings of the Gothic spook story. The idea was to chill you a little so that the sponsor, Blue Coal, could warm you up with hearty messages concerning winter heating.

In addition to the comic book, there were Big Little Books, a syndicated daily comic strip, and a host of commercial tie-ins such as Shadow disguise kits, The Shadow Pencil Lite, Shadow masks, Shadow capes, games, stationery, etc. A 1940 issue of the magazine (carrying an illustrated ad for a plethora of Shadow-oriented games and gimmicks) admonished young readers to "Make it a Shadow Christmas!"

The Shadow was also the subject of one movie serial and seven feature films. Silent movie retread Rod LaRocque donned cape and black hat unenthusiastically in Grand National's 1937 turkey, "The Shadow Strikes." He returned in "International Crime" as a radio crime reporter known as The Shadow, sans cape and hat. In 1946, Monogram starred athletic Kane Richmond in three disappointingly facetious Shadow titles: "Behind the Mask," "The Shadow Returns," and The Missing Lady." A later Shadow feature, "Bourbon Street Shadows" (aka "Invisible Avenger") was produced by Republic Pictures in 1958. Until the 1994 special effects-laden Universal film starring Alec Baldwin, it was notable mainly as the only movie version in which Cranston/Shadow became invisible by "clouding men's minds." The serial, released by Columbia in 1940, was titled simply "The Shadow." To its credit, it drew inspiration from its pulp magazine source, even if The Shadow did use .38 revolvers instead of his trusty .45 automatics, and even if he did seem to miss every time. In the fifteen-chapter serial play, the burning eyes and hawk-nosed visage of actor

Victor Jory bore a startling likeness to the magazine covers, giving credence to his portrayal. Fans knew he wasn't the real Shadow, though, because he spent too much time getting knocked about by low-grade comic hoodlums.

It is ironic that, during the war years, the radio version of The Shadow maintained and even increased his popularity while his magazine counterpart began falling on leaner times—as did virtually all the pulp-hero titles. Loyal readers knew they were in trouble when Margo Lane, The Shadow's radio "friend and companion," joined the pulps and soon became his primary, and sometimes only, assistant. It was an entrance that would herald the beginning of a disheartening slide into mediocrity.

Walter Gibson continued turning out two Shadow novels a month until March 1943, when declining popularity, combined with wartime paper shortages, forced the magazine to publish only one issue a month. By the end of the year, the Street & Smith pulp chain was the first of its kind to adapt to the more "respectable" digest size. For The Shadow it was a reduction in spirit as well as content. In April of 1945 ("Death Has Gray Eyes"), Shadow fans were dismayed to discover that their hero had been relegated to the back of his own book, with a routine detective novel shoved up front.

In 1946, following a chain of editorial upheavals, Walter Gibson abandoned the series over a contractual dispute. A new "Maxwell Grant" was quickly hired. In the new look stories, ghosted by Bruce Elliott, The Shadow's cloak and hat were eventually left at home, and the uncostumed Lamont Cranston became little more than a glorified private eye in a series of modern detective settings. By this time the Shadow novels had been trimmed to little more than the length of short stories, bearing prosaic titles like "Death on Ice" and "Room 1313"—quite a come down from the glory days of "The Masked Headsman," "The Gray Ghost," and "The Creeping Death." Besides, who wants to read a Shadow magazine without The Shadow? In 1947, the magazine was reduced to a bi-monthly and in 1948 a quarterly.

Then, with the 1948 Fall issue, in a belated attempt to revive the pulp tradition (and circulation figures), the magazine was again published full size, sporting dynamic Rozen covers. Gibson wrote four final Shadow novels in the grand old style, including one in which he himself made a brief appearance. Alas, the attempted rejuvenation came too late. It was but a last hurrah before the world turned rotten and there was no room for pulp heroes anymore.

When The Shadow magazine folded in the summer of 1949 with its 325th issue, it appeared that time had accomplished what a score of master fiends could not. The Shadow's sinister laughter seemed permanently stilled.

Or was it?

Fortunately, many of the old Shadow radio programs were saved on transcription disks and tapes. They are still being played on many stations and are currently available on numerous Internet sites for sale on CDs or downloads. Of course, the comic book Shadow never did disappear for long. Various comic book companies, including DC, Dark Horse, and even Archie Comics have had a fling at interpreting the Master Avenger following the demise of Street & Smith's own long-running comic. Even the pulp stories have been recycled by various paperback companies, notably Bantam Books and Pyramid Books, during the sixties and seventies.

In 1963, Belmont Books even commissioned a string of original Shadow novels, the first one written by Walter Gibson himself—just for old time's sake.

When the magazine folded, old pro Walter Gibson simply turned to other writing. His career encompassed 149 other books of all types, thousands of newspaper and magazine pieces, comics, radio shows, puzzles, magic tricks, and other material under various pen names. Author J. Randolph Cox's monumental guide to the work of Walter Gibson *(Man of Magic and Mystery,* Scarecrow Press, 1988) is a staggering 328 pages long. Ironically, that which Gibson will be remembered for—his 283 Shadow novels—represents but a fraction of his total output.

Walter Gibson died in 1985 at the age of 88. He lived to see his Depression-era phantom attain folk-hero immortality. Endless revivals of The Shadow in paperback, hardcover, and comic book form had enabled him to climb out from behind the Maxwell Grant pen name. In his later years, he enjoyed increasing public recognition in newspaper and magazine articles, radio and television appearances, and as a guest at various conventions. He even made peace with his famous pseudonym and designed a signature in which the two names were intertwined.

In 1979, Walter Gibson was awarded a Master's Fellowship by the Academy of Magical Arts and Sciences, an award never given to a nonperforming magician. Another honor—the Lamont Award—was named after his creation and was bestowed at the annual Pulpcon gathering of pulp aficionados for outstanding effort in keeping alive the memory and spirit of the pulp magazine era.

In the final analysis, the greatest monument to Walter Gibson's memory is his own legacy. He accomplished that which only a few people in history have been fortunate enough to do.

He created a legend.

DOC!

There was death afoot in the darkness.

It crept furtively along a steel girder. Hundreds of feet below yawned glass-and-brick walled cracks—New York streets. Down there, late workers scurried homeward. Most of them carried umbrellas, and did not glance upward.

Even had they looked, they probably would have noticed nothing. The night was black as a cave bat. Rain threshed down monotonously. The clammy sky was like an oppressive shroud wrapped around the tops of the tall buildings. The naked beams were a sinister forest.

It was in this forest that Death prowled.

Death was a man.

THE FOREGOING PROSE is what is known in writers parlance as a narrative hook. It was the way pulp fictioneers began almost every story back in the golden age of the pulp magazines and was in fact the bait used to snag newsstand perusers of the March 1933 issue of *Doc Savage Magazine.*

The magazine's 60,000-word novel, "The Man of Bronze," was the opening salvo in a series of monthly adventures that would chronicle the hair-raising exploits of Clark Savage Jr., known to the world as Doc Savage. The circulation of the *Doc Savage Magazine* reached 200,000 soon after publication of that historic first issue.

Doc was a vivid splash of color in the emptiness of the Great

Depression. During the thirties and forties generations of youth grew up under the spell of his far-ranging exploits. For years they poured millions of grubby dimes across newsstand counters to follow the monthly adventures of their modern Galahad.

"A man of superhuman strength and protean genius, whose life is dedicated to the destruction of evildoers," Doc Savage was the original inspiration for literally hundreds of superhuman freaks who, in 1933, were yet to be imagined. There is much to indicate, for instance, that when teenagers Jerry Siegel and Joe Shuster created the comic book adventures of Superman, their model was Doc Savage, the Man of Bronze, who antedated the Man of Steel and his host of imitators by several years.

Doc could run faster than a horse, bite through nails, untie knots with his tongue, hold his breath longer than a South Seas pearl diver, scale any building that wasn't smoother than a sheet of glass, speak any language known to man, and a few others besides. A master surgeon, chemist, pilot, engineer, archaeologist—Doc was a walking compendium of mankind's total knowledge.

Like most of the great pulp heroes, the Man of Bronze supplied escapist entertainment for the Depression-era dispossessed. More important, he was a personification of American ideals at a time when those virtues were being questioned. For Doc Savage, the system had not failed. A self-made phenomenon, his power, wealth, and humanitarian exploits demonstrated to youthful readers that success or failure depended on the individual, that a man could still better himself with effort. Doc was not Superman. He was Super American. His physical and mental powers were not the result of being born on some alien planet; they were the culmination of extreme dedication combined with two hours of intensive mental and physical exercise each day, a regimen which had been instituted by his father when Doc was barely old enough to walk.

Young Clark was born on the schooner Orion off the island of Andros. His mother died some fourteen months later, and he was raised by his wealthy adventurer father to be a perfect human specimen. The boy's unconventional education was handled by experts ranging from Indian fakirs to Yale physicists, from circus acrobats to jungle trackers. He even had a specialty, that of surgery; he was the world's best, of course, and hence earned the sobriquet "Doc."

To bone up on the newest developments in all fields of science and world affairs, the Man of Bronze retired periodically to his mysterious Fortress of Solitude (later appropriated by Superman), a rendezvous built on a rocky island deep in the Arctic regions. This was one of the secrets of his universal knowledge, for his periods of concentration there were long and intense. Whether even a mental giant like Doc could handle today's information explosion is a matter of conjecture, but back in the thirties he more than held his own.

From the beginning, Doc Savage was handcrafted for success. The folks at Street & Smith publications had a runaway hit with pulpdom's first superhero, The Shadow. It was only natural that sooner or later they would attempt a sibling money earner.

For a while the publishers toyed with the idea of a character called the Phantom, but in 1933 Ned Pine's Standard Publications beat them to the punch when they published *The Phantom Detective* magazine. Street & Smith abandoned the idea of a direct Shadow imitation and instead decided to fashion a different type of hero altogether: a strapping adventurer who would use scientific gadgets as weapons.

The Shadow's godparents, Henry W. Ralston, editorial executive at S&S, and Shadow editor John Nanovic, developed the character and many of the basic concepts in a series of editorial sessions. They decided that the new superhero would be named Doc Savage and that he should combine "the clue-following ability of Sherlock Holmes, the muscular tree-swinging agility of Tarzan, and the scientific sleuthing of Craig Kennedy." They did not add, but could have, that he should have the morals of a saint. Doc was designed to be a hard act to follow.

According to Nanovic, Doc and his aides were all reflections of real people whom Ralston knew personally. Pulp researcher (and latter-day Doc writer) Will Murray has revealed that Doc was based on the character of Major Richard Henry Savage, an American engineer, author, lawyer, and soldier who fought in the Spanish-American War and served in the Egyptian Army. To the attributes of this authentic real-life character, Ralston added the superhuman moral, mental, and physical abilities of Nick Carter—Street & Smith's original paper hero.

Editor Nanovic handed a thirty-page outline for Doc Savage, *Supreme Adventurer*, to a dynamic twenty-eight-year-old freelance writer named Lester Dent. He had come to their attention through his work on their own *Top Notch* and *The Popular* magazines, and on request had pounded out an unpublished Shadow story as proof of his hero writer abilities.

Dent was six feet two and weighed in at around 200 pounds; if his black hair had been changed to bronze, he might have served as a model for Doc himself. Like Doc, he was a tinkerer and a gadgeteer as well as a world traveler with an explosive love of fun and adventure.

Street & Smith gave Dent the unprecedented offer of exclusive production rights to the Doc Savage novels. He was to write them under a house name, Kenneth Robeson, but he could, if he so wished, hire another writer to help out, then pay the other man out of his own salary. Furthermore, he was not restricted to work only on Doc Savage.

Dent was enthusiastic. What he did with the editors' outline was something even they could not have anticipated fully. In a vibrant style that blended globe-trotting adventure and science-fiction concepts with hardboiled prose and quirky humor, he made Doc Savage and his friends spring to life.

In "The Man of Bronze," a unique pledge is sworn by a group of six men meeting on the 86th floor of one of New York's tallest buildings: while a would-be assassin peers down at them from his steel eyrie, Doc Savage and his five aides—"the greatest brains ever assembled in one group"—meet to mourn the death of Doc's father, a man known throughout the world for his work in righting wrongs. The six unique men dedicate themselves to uphold the elder Savage's ideals, "to go here and there, from one end of the world to the other, looking for excitement and adventure, striving to help those who need help, and punishing those who deserve it."

Unlike most superheroes, Doc was no loner. He was aided in his worldwide crusades by his rough-and-tumble aides, the Amazing Five, and, on occasion, by his lovely bronze-haired cousin, Patricia Savage. Doc and his confederacy of globe-trotting do-gooders were described in the opening scenes of "The Man of Bronze." It was a description that would not vary greatly throughout the seventeen years to follow. Surprisingly, it was the portrayal of Doc himself that proved flexible. In the opening novel, Doc was six feet tall, but it seems he continued growing until in 1935 he stood nearly six-feet-six. Other than that, Doc remained agelessly constant. If not actually immortal, he was wondrously durable, possibly because of the medicinal properties of an age-retarding plant, silphium, involved in his adventures on the Caribbean Island of Fear Cay.

Doc's skin was of a permanent bronze color, a characteristic peculiar to the entire Savage clan. His features were so regular that they might be that of a man sculpted in hard bronze: "The lines of the features, the unusually high forehead, the mobile muscular, but not too-full mouth, the lean cheeks, denoted a power of character seldom seen." His hair was of a bronze a trifle darker than his skin, laying straight on his scalp like a metal skullcap. We are told that Doc's bronze hue had been kilned by the heat of tropic suns. This reference to the tropics may explain the exotic trilling sound which he uttered in those rare moments of unconscious stress: possibly the imitation of a jungle bird.

Above all else, Doc's eyes caught and held attention:

They were weird, commanding eyes, like nothing so much as pools of flake gold. They radiated a hypnotic quality, an ability to inspire fear or respect—to convey threat, domination or command. Even in repose, they glowed with the heat of an indomitable will.

Not exactly a description of your modern antihero! If Doc himself remained an impossible ideal for youthful readers, his five boisterous aides presented more human fronts as well as a variety of physical types for vicarious identification. Chief among his pals was "Monk" Mayfair, the amiable, apelike being who was described as one of the world's leading chemists, a millionaire with a penthouse laboratory near Wall Street, which was a setting in many of the Doc Savage novels.

The most common (as well as the most tiresome) running gag in the Doc Savage yarns was Monk's constant feud with Ham Brooks. Ham was the ying to Monk's yang. Slender, waspish, quick moving, Ham looked like what he was—possibly the most astute lawyer Harvard ever turned out. A dapper dresser, he carried a black walking stick that was, among other things, a sword cane. Those baddies fortunate enough to escape Monk's bristle-covered fists usually wound up on the wrong end of Ham's sticker.

Doc's other aides included John "Renny" Renwick, civil engineer, who was a big, somewhat gaunt man with a severe puritanical face; Major Thomas J. Roberts, an ectomorphic electrical wizard, also called "Long Tom"; and William Harper Littlejohn, called "Johnny," an archaeologist who had formerly been the head of the natural science research department of a famous university, an environment which perhaps had given him his penchant for big words. "Superamalgamated" was Johnny's favorite expletive, a word which could also be used to describe Lester Dent, the writer of the Savage opus.

In the world of the pulps there existed a curious relationship between the fictitious characters and their creators. Robert J. Hogan, author of the high-flying G-8 adventures was himself a World War I pilot—even if he did extrapolate some bizarre variations on his own experiences. The Shadow reflected many of the interests of his writer, Walter Gibson, an expert in magic and the supernatural; and Norvell Page, who for a decade chronicled the macabre exploits of the Spider came to identify so completely with his own creation that he took to wearing a black cape and black slouch hat in public.

As for Lester Dent—who wrote 165 of the 181 Doc Savage novels under the publisher-owned name of Kenneth Robeson—he was the kind of man who might have joined Doc's merry band of adventurers. As a boy, Dent traveled across Wyoming in a covered wagon. In his adult years, he made forays prospecting for gold in Mexico, Death Valley, and elsewhere, sailed his small schooner, the *Albatross*, on treasure-hunting expeditions, explored Mayan ruins and prehistoric Indian dwellings, toured Nazi-overrun Europe, invented electrical gadgets, and flew his own plane. As recognition of his travels, he was made a member of The Explorers' Club of New York.

But, according to Dent, it was the lonely life of a rancher's son that prepared him for later success as a storyteller. "I had no playmates," he explained.

> *I lived a completely distorted youth. My only playmate was my imagination, and that period of intense imaginative creation which kids generally get over at the age of five or six, I carried till I was twelve or thirteen. My imaginary voyages and accomplishments were extremely real. I almost think I learned at the time a form of self-hypnosis.*

As a young adult, happily married and working at a night telegraph job for the *Tulsa World*, Lester got deterred when he turned his hand to setting down some of his imaginative daydreams in the form of written adventure stories. His first thirteen stories gathered rejection slips from various pulp editors, but his fourteenth sold for $250. The story was titled

"Pirate Cay," and it appeared in Street & Smith's prestigious *Top Notch* magazine in the September 1st, 1929 issue.

Following several other sales, the young writer was stunned to receive a telegram from Dell Publishing Company of New York. The editor at Dell suggested that if Lester was earning less than a hundred dollars per week at his present job he should quit immediately and be taken under their wing. In return for writing exclusively for Dell, he would be given a five-hundred-dollar-a-month drawing account.

After checking on the editor's sanity, Dent and his wife Norma soon left for the Big Apple. While working at Dell, he learned the discipline required to turn out immense volumes of well-crafted fiction. Eventually, the magazines he wrote for folded, but by that time he was skilled enough to tackle the precarious life of the freelance writer.

Dent sold western romances, air-war thrillers, detective yarns, and straight adventure pieces to a variety of magazines. One series, the adventures of scientific detective Lynn Lash, presaged Doc Savage, right down to crime-fighting gadgets and the inclusion of an apish character named Monk. The young author's skill at characterization and plotting combined with his scientific knowledge and technical virtuosity soon brought him to the attention of the editors at Street & Smith, the fabled "fiction factory." They were looking for a writer who could handle Doc Savage. Lester Dent was born for the job.

For the next fifteen years, Dent was responsible for one Doc Savage novel a month, at $500 a story to begin with and later at $750 a crack. In his spare time, he knocked out the Click Rush series for *Crime Busters* as well as a variety of tales for such top pulp markets as *Black Mask* and *Argosy*.

A native of La Plata, Missouri (pop. 1400), Dent moved back to his hometown to continue churning out the monthly Savage adventures.

Because of Dent's own adventures, the Doc Savage thrillers were characterized by an authenticity of background. As for Dent's writing style, an anonymous Newsweek writer suggested that it read "as if he had a stopwatch in one hand and a thesaurus in the other." Certainly, the yarns were written in a bravura, hell-for-leather manner which carried youthful readers along in a phantasmagorical series of fights, chases, and escapes, all tied together with remarkably fluid transitions.

A successful pulp hero writer—and few were more successful than Dent—had to work fast and never look back. Dent's typewriter keys flew like machine-gun bullets. Sometimes he got carried away.

Longtime *Doc Savage* editor, John Nanovic, related how his own son would humiliate him by reading aloud a sentence from one of the stories: "Doc's arm drifted outward with lightning speed."

As Nanovic explained, "You had to be a Doc Savage fan to know that there was nothing wrong with that. If anybody could drift his arm outward with lightning speed, Doc could do it. And the way Dent wrote it, you believed it. It was just right."

Lester Dent's work was not rich in allegory or poetic symbolism. It was not intended to be. His stories were jolting, exotic, antic, throbbing with narrative drive and cliff-hanging suspense. They usually started with a stinger:

The man carried a .30-.30 rifle in one hand and two boxes of cartridges, both open, in the other hand. He acted as if ready to drop the cartridges and use the rifle any instant.

– or –

Five men were running across the golf links of the Widebrook Country Club. They kept in a compact group, and their manner was determined and sinister. Each carried a hooded golf bag. The hour was near midnight.

– or –

It was too bad that nobody saw what happened to the new army X-ship on its test flight. It happened that there were clouds that night, and anyway, the impossible thing occurred twenty thousand feet in the air.

Pulp writers knew how to set the scene quickly and get on with the mayhem.

Like most single-character series, the Doc Savage stories were written from a strict formula. Author Dent's own personal recipe for plotting high-powered adventure fiction appeared under his byline in a 1939 issue of *Writer's Digest*. The article was as unpretentious as Dent himself. Suspense, he opined, is the sugar that draws the flies. Among other things, he admonished the would-be writer to introduce the hero as quickly as possible and immediately swat him with a fistful of troubles; to introduce a menace strong enough to hang like a cloud over the hero; to have at least one minor surprise to a printed page; to keep shoveling grief onto the hero. "The idea," Dent wrote, "is to avoid monotony."

Dent did his best to avoid monotony. Turning out 200,000 words a month and selling every word, he often earned two to four thousand dollars a month—and this in the days of breadlines and hobo jungles.

The Savage novels flooded from his pen, each one bearing an evocative title: "The Land of Terror," "The Lost Oasis," "The Phantom City," "The Thousand-Headed Man," "The Squeaking Goblin," "Poison Island," "The Sargasso Ogre," "The Man Who Fell Up."

Doc and his boys went everywhere and did everything. Adventurers all, they discovered lost cities and forgotten races in the world's secret recesses. From the Valley of the Vanished to the oceans' depths, to a prehistoric world in the Arctic, they pitted brain, brawn, and super-science against such foes as The Sargasso Ogre, The Mind-Changing Monster, The Living Fire Menace, The Stone Man, The Vanisher, The Annihilist, The Mystic Mullah, and The Roar Devil. They stopped wars, prevented a new Ice Age, battled dinosaurs and ancient mummies, and saved humanity from one world-wrecker after another. Throughout it all raced the beguiling Savage mystique: eyes of flake gold. Muscles bunched like cordwood. That eerie trilling whistle.

Even the covers contributed to Doc's image. One of the greatest of pulp artists, Walter Baumhofer, was the initial Doc portrayer, and he set the standard for all to follow. Many of his paintings were really portraits of Doc frozen in the middle of some adventurous situation. One such cover ("Quest of Qui," July 1935) was only a close-up study of Doc, refuting the pulp belief that action and action alone sold copies.

To millions of young readers, Doc Savage assumed the

proportions of a real-life hero. Street & Smith did nothing to shatter the illusion. The magazine carried a Doc Savage credo, a Doc Savage Club, Doc Savage portraits, Doc Savage lapel pins, and a gold Doc Savage award that went to deserving nominees.

Doc's daily calisthenics were such an important part of his adventures that Street & Smith began to publish a series of articles on the various exercises. These instructions for self development were touted as the open sesame to Doc's physical prowess, but keener fans may have noticed their similarity to the brand of isometrics taught by bodybuilder Charles Atlas, another superhuman figure often represented in the pages of the pulps.

Street & Smith was the contractual owner of all of Dent's Doc Savage novels but, surprisingly, they allowed the author ancillary rights to film, radio, and even newspaper comic strip versions. (The reason Dent did not bargain for comic book rights was because such magazines did not exist when Doc was first created.)

Unfortunately, while the *Doc Savage Magazine* equaled and even surpassed the success of *The Shadow*, Doc did not fare as well in other mediums. The Shadow starred in his own Street & Smith comic book for nine years (Doc was sometimes a back-up feature), but Doc's own comic premiered in May of 1940 and ended twenty issues later in 1943.

The Shadow was at least a moderate success in movie serials and grade B features, but poor Doc never hit the flicks at all—at least not at the time.

And of course, The Shadow was one of the most popular radio characters of all; even today, children who cannot possibly have heard the program are able to recite its opening lines like a litany. The radio Doc, on the other hand, appeared briefly in a 1934 syndicated series produced by the West Coast Don Lee Network. Although the scripts were written by Dent himself, the program suffered from a format that restricted each story to a mere fifteen-minute time slot. Although the Doc Savage Magazine carried advertisements for the show, listing scores of stations throughout the United States and Canada which carried it, no surviving transcriptions exist today and few, if any, old-time radio fans remember hearing it.

Doc Savage hit the airwaves again in a twenty-six-week run over station WMCA in New York in 1943. The new version bore little resemblance to the bronze hero of the pulps, even though some of the melodramas bore titles like the kind of thing Lester Dent might have written: "The Pharaoh's Wisdom," "Monster of the Sea," "The Screeching Ghost," "The Miracle Maniac," etc. The first two broadcasts featured Doc's two-fisted assistants Monk and Ham, but by episode three Ham was dropped in favor of a Brooklyn-born secretary named Myrtle. When the radio Doc was in trouble, he donned a hood from which glowed a sacred red ruby, blinding the eyes of his enemies and protecting him from harm. This juvenile shtick was never used in the pulp yarns, but it was integrated into the Street & Smith comic books, where it seemed perfectly at home.

If Doc Savage's gold-plated success was limited to the pulp magazines and subsequent paperback reprints, it was probably for a good reason. The name of the reason was Lester Dent.

As fast as he required them, author Dent's facile mind invented hundreds of gimmicks and bits of business for the Savage saga. In "The Man of Bronze," he introduced Doc's rapid-firing supermachine pistols; they bore resemblance to oversized automatics but featured curled magazines which held sixty rounds of either mercy bullets, incendiaries, tracers, magnesium's, or even armor-piercing slugs.

In the line of hand weapons, Doc's group had everything from recoilless, rapid-firing elephant guns to pocketknives that fired single bullets from their hilts. Doc himself did not favor the wearing of guns because of his theory that they made the bearer dependent on them. Instead, what Doc did become hooked on was an incredible array of gadgets and gimmicks hidden on his person.

In "The Red Skull," he first wore his armor-scaled vest. Its contents included delicate mechanical devices, strange scientific weapons, and glass vials containing "chemical concoctions calculated to accomplish the unusual." In short, almost anything Doc (or Lester Dent) needed to pull him out of a particularly rough spot.

Stripped of his vest, Doc was still a walking arsenal. The hollow heels in his shoes contained everything from tiny radio transmitters to explosives and miniature drills. His belt housed a silken cord with a collapsible grapnel hook at one end. The buttons of his suit were a thermite compound. The suit itself was impregnated with chemical weapons; his undershirt loaded with tear gas.

In addition to fireproof and radiation-proof suits to fit the occasion, he also developed a spray-on over skin that acted as a perfect insulation against heat or cold.

Even denuded he still had his metal skullcap that simulated his bronze hair. A false scar on his back contained still more explosives, as did a pair of hollow capped teeth. Another hollow tooth contained a tiny, coiled saw!

To attempt to get the best of him, wily captors sometimes stripped Doc down to the buff. Once, in "The Submarine Mystery," assailants shampooed his hair to wash out chemicals; they checked out his teeth with instruments. But even bound and gagged Doc remained a holy terror. He could still hypnotize a man with his flake-gold eyes or anesthetize him with the tiny needles hidden beneath his fake fingernails.

Out of the bronze man's lonely Fortress of Solitude poured a harvest of scientific miracles. In "The Golden Peril" and again in "The Motion Menace," Doc treated thugs to the spectacular effects of the world's first atomic disintegrator. In "Mystery Under the Sea," he first tried out the special oxygen pills that, when ingested, rendered it unnecessary to breathe for periods up to half an hour.

In his precious spare moments, he invented the world's first wire recorder. The first telephone answering service. High-speed elevators. Advanced brain surgery techniques. A cure for the common cold. A radar device that could differentiate between metals. An early version of the aqualung. Futuristic airplanes (he even toyed with jet travel). Sophisticated electronic bugging devices. Disposable parachutes. The list could go on and on.

Doc and his aides were communicating via two-way wristwatch television while Dick Tracy was still pounding a beat. Then, too, they often employed an ultraviolet projector and "black light" goggles to work by night or in Stygian quarters. It was a common plot gimmick to leave messages, which could only be revealed using this method. In "The South Pole Terror," Doc's rocket-powered dirigible is even equipped with an ultraviolet searchlight.

Doc was a great believer in lighter-than-air transportation (a faith which is only now being substantiated by aeronautical experts), but his adventurous life created a high mortality rate for his prototype dirigibles. In "The Land of Long Ju Ju," he unveiled a wing-shaped, lighter-than-air craft which was capable of speeds up to and surpassing 500 miles an hour. Unfortunately, the wing met the fate of so many of Doc's advanced gas bags—it didn't survive its maiden launching.

He had better luck with his Cousteau-style yacht, the *Seven Seas*, which saw action in "Fantastic Island," "Land of Fear," and "The Red Terrors." Beneath the seas, his streamlined submarine vehicle Helldiver (complete with collapsible seaplane and infra red TV scanners) was the scourge of aquatic supervillains. The Helldiver was especially designed to work beneath polar ice but, in "The Phantom City," it traveled beneath the Arabian desert to reach a mysterious city of white-haired inhabitants. In "Haunted Ocean," the Helldiver's baby sister, a pocket-sized glass sub, was used to zip Doc from peril.

Although Doc scrupulously avoided publicity, everybody appeared to know about him and his 86th floor headquarters in a certain New York skyscraper. The most exotic of Doc's adventures often began in this tri-suite fortress perched high above the Empire City. From his admirable vantage point, Doc looked down on a sunny, Art Deco version of New York of the thirties—a locale as colorful and as nostalgic as any of the Oriental ports or tropic islands in which his adventures placed him. The Savage manse was guarded by a veritable armory of scientific gadgets, alarms, and traps. In "The Flying Goblin," even a radio-controlled missile attack on HQ is thwarted by a force-field projector which emerges on call from Doc's futuristic lab.

The Hidalgo Trading Company, Doc's Hudson River warehouse, was no trading company at all. It was the gateway to lost valleys and far sunsets. Within its windowless walls were housed all the mechanical magic carpets Doc needed to whisk him to the world's inaccessible places. It contained his turbine-powered sub as well as various armored motorboats and launches. There were a variety of helicopters, Autogiros, and super-speed amphibious airplanes, and even the latest thing in dirigibles. Doc could flit from his skyscraper eyrie to the warehouse via a pneumatic capsule—a route he nicknamed the flea run.

The vast sums of money required for these expensive appurtenances came from a hidden valley in Central America, a lost retreat presided over by the descendants of the ancient Mayan race and was supplied to Doc solely for the purpose of furthering his cause of right. At noon on a prescribed day of the week, Doc had but to broadcast, over powerful radio stations, a few words in a mysterious tongue. Some days later a supply of pure gold would arrive for his use.

It need hardly be mentioned that pulp writers were in the business of supplying dreams that money could buy. For a mere ten cents a month, they gave good value.

Lester Dent's own penchant for adventuring sometimes caused him to miss deadlines. While he was off treasure hunting in the *Albatross,* fellow pulpsters Harold Davis, Ryerson Johnson, William Bogart, Laurence Donovan, and Alan Hathway occasionally filled in. Often the ghostwriters' work was a bare-bones narrative which Dent reworked in his own zippy prose style. To speed things up, Dent also experimented with dictation, using a Dictaphone to record some of Doc's high-speed adventures.

During the forties, a gradual attrition took place in *Doc*

Savage. The hero pulp magazines had been hurt by the coming of the comic books with their colorful compacted stories and their modest demands on young readers' time.

The pulps retrenched. Street & Smith decided to aim at a more mature, more sophisticated audience. As Lester Dent put it,

> *After the flood of super people and phantoms and bat men and such people that Doc started coming out of the cartoonists and writers' inkwells, my stomach kind of turned. I've toned Doc down now to where he is not the slam-bang fire-eater he was. He still discovers strange tribes of people in the heart of the world's deserts, but he doesn't come across nations in the interior of the earth anymore.*

The coming of World War II produced even greater changes. In "The Fiery Menace" (September 1942), Doc traveled to Washington to confer with President Roosevelt and other government officials. He begged to be accepted for military duty and was politely but firmly refused. During the war, most folks looked askance at a healthy male who claimed deferment from armed service. To a patriotic superman like Doc, it must have been a crushing humiliation.

Fortunately, the U.S. government (and Doc's publishers) eventually gave in, allowing him to fight against the Axis as a civilian agent. "The Black, Black Witch" (March 1943) saw Doc preventing the Nazis from acquiring a gas that would enable them to foretell the future. In "The Three Devils," Doc confounded an Axis plan to shut down Canada's wartime pulp paper industry (thus saving his own magazine, one presumes), and in "Time Terror" he kept a super-evolution element from the Japanese. Just to prove he could still hack it, Doc rescued Winston Churchill from the Nazis in 1944, and in 1945 captured Adolph Hitler himself. But something was clearly missing. Some of the heart had gone out of Doc. He was a Bronze Man in a world turning colorless.

The far-out fantasy of the thirty's stories became muted. It was replaced by a hard, brittle quality: the cold light of reality. The Man of Bronze was caught in the middle of a world-shaking battle which was to test the very concept of a superhuman elite. Like a character in a nightmare, he felt his powers slipping away. He became cautious, testy, less idealistic. He began to question his own invulnerability. Poor Doc. It was a wonder he made it through the war at all.

In the postwar period there was little mention of his five aides, and Doc himself became little more than a scientific detective assisting the F.B.I. In January of 1944, the magazine came out in digest size. Under the aegis of a new editor, young Babette Rosmand, the magazine was retitled *Doc Savage, Science Detective* and became a semi slick publication, far removed from its rough-hewn pulp glory. Adding insult to injury, the Doc Savage novels were shoved to the rear of the magazine and a conventional detective novel placed at the front.

The last issue of Doc's magazine was number 181, published summer 1949. With an inspired effort, Dent turned out a final novel, "Up from Earth's Center," which proved to be one of the best and most well-written of all the Doc Savage stories. In that final adventure, Dent strongly suggested—and never retracted—that Doc and his cronies (reunited at last) had met and battled the minions of Satan right up from hell.

After that, what else was left? It was the Götterdämmerung of the pulps.

Following the wholesale demise of the once-ubiquitous pulp magazines, Lester Dent continued to write fiction. The style of his later stories (mostly full-length mystery novels) was assured, mature, polished, realistic. He had always wanted to be regarded as a fine writer but early in the game had found himself trapped on a gold-plated treadmill.

In February of 1959, Dent was stricken by a massive heart attack. He was rushed to the Grim-Smith Hospital in Kirksville, Missouri, where he died on March 11 at the too-young age of 54. Shortly before, he had confided that, in his opinion, the Doc Savage stories would be of little interest anymore. "They would be so out-dated today," he said, "that they would undoubtedly be funny. Hell, when I wrote them, an airplane that could fly two hundred miles an hour was science fiction."

For once, Dent had misjudged Doc's appeal. Unfortunately, he died too soon to witness the emergence of a new generation of fans who would snap up the monthly Savage thrillers with as much dispatch as did their fathers nearly thirty years before.

Doc's reincarnation occurred in 1964 when Bantam Books, under the leadership of Marc Jaffe, a Doc Savage fan in his youth, put out three Doc Savage novels in a brand new softcover format. Wisely, Jaffe prevented Bantam from updating Dent's original plots.

In addition, Jaffe commissioned a top line illustrator, James Bama, to paint new covers for the series in a uniform format similar to the old pulp covers. While differing greatly from the interpretations of Walter Baumhofer, the original Savage cover artist, Bama's paintings were magnificent pieces of commercial illustration which contributed immensely to Doc's second coming.

Even so, longtime pulp fans were shocked by Bama's radical interpretation. They maintained that while the artist had lifted Doc's skull-cap hairline from the pulp descriptions, his portrayal of their hero as a seamed and constantly tattered giant is at odds not only with Dent's descriptions but with the original pulp covers and interior illustrations. (Philip José Farmer wrote that Bama's Doc looked to him like a fifty-five-year-old ex–Mister Universe down on his luck; author and pulp historian Robert Weinberg saw him as a cross between the Jolly Green Giant and a Nazi storm trooper!)

It should be noted that there has always been controversy over the way Doc has been depicted. Back in 1933, the original Doc Savage cover artist was given specific instructions to mold Doc in the image of movie star Clark Gable. Walter Baumhofer, who had little time to read the pulp stories he delineated, ignored the dictate and cast his superb Doc portraits in the handsome image of a model he was then employing. It was left to Paul Orban, a Street & Smith staffer who did the interior illustrations for many years, to bring Doc's image closer to the Gable ideal.

In any case, despite Jim Bama's revisionist interpretation—and more likely because of it—the new books were instant successes. They sold in the millions. It was 1933 all over again.

Other mediums began looking at the superannuated hero as grist for their mills. In 1966, Gold Key Comics timidly assayed a Doc Savage comic book. They brought out their four-color version of "The Thousand Headed Man," complete with a Jim

Bama cover painting. The interior art by Jack Sparling was less than dynamic, however, and the book lasted but one issue.

There was even talk of a movie series in 1966, and once again "The Thousand Headed Man" was chosen as a pilot project. It is possible that the Gold Key comic was meant to be a tie-in with the movie, but the project never got off the ground and Doc's film and comic book possibilities lay dormant for several more years.

In 1973, Stan Lee's Marvel Comics purchased the rights to produce still another graphic picture version. This time the possibilities were more encouraging. Back in the early sixties, Lee had reintroduced the comic book superhero, making household names of such creations as Spider-man and the Fantastic Four. It was intriguing to conjecture what he might accomplish with Doc and his Fantastic Five.

Unfortunately, Marvel's Doc turned out to be a modified costumed hero with a Bama-inspired widow's peak. He limped through a handful of lackluster adaptations that failed to capture either the mood of the original stories or the mystique of the character. DC Comics, the home of Doc-inspired Superman, attempted their own version of a Doc Savage comic but also failed to generate much excitement, possibly because of a mistaken editorial decision to update Doc's adventures.

The Doc Savage revival of the seventies did produce a couple of interesting spin-offs, however. Top science fiction writer Philip José Farmer turned out two book-length Savage pastiches, A Feast Unknown, published by (zounds!) a porno book company called Essex House, and The Mad Goblin, issued by Ace Books. Both novels featured Doc Caliban and his sidekicks Jocko and Porky, and both were interesting examinations of the hero psyche.

Apparently, this was still not enough to purge Doc from Farmer's system, so in 1973 he wrote a monumental biography of his hero: *Doc Savage: His Apocalyptic Life.* The book was conceived in the manner of William Baring-Gould's famous Sherlock Holmes of Baker Street; that is, Farmer postulates that Doc was a flesh-and-blood individual and that Lester Dent served as a mere chronicler—and sometimes exaggerator—of real events. Farmer's engaging literary conceit was a monument to Doc's mesmeric hold on his once youthful readers.

It was probably coincidental that at almost the same time movie producer George Pal announced plans to do a series of Doc Savage feature films. The first film was to be produced by Warner Brothers, and it was to be shot on a multimillion-dollar budget. George Pal was the Hungarian-born puppeteer who parlayed a knack for single-frame animation into a career as one of Hollywood's most successful producers of imaginative cinema. His credits include such science fictional extravaganzas as *War of the Worlds, The Time Machine,* and *Destination Moon.* His participation in a Doc Savage series of films was enough to set any fan's heart aflutter.

In February of 1974, I interviewed Pal by telephone for a newspaper article I had been commissioned to write. He was on the set of *Doc Savage... the Man of Bronze,* overseeing a spate of night shooting. Pal told me that he had become interested in Doc's movie possibilities when he learned of the phenomenal success of the paperback reprints.

"*I bought a few of the books and found them great fun to read,*" he said. "*Almost everybody was buying them—from nostalgic old-timers to a whole new generation of youngsters who still find them exciting. Right from the beginning we knew they'd make a fabulous movie series. They have almost everything, including that marvelous nineteen-thirties background. It took us over a year to clear the rights—we had to buy all one hundred eighty-one books—but it was worth it."*

Alas, Pal's initial Doc Savage film was neither a critical nor financial success. No further movies were produced, even though Philip Farmer had written an excellent screenplay for a follow-up effort.

In the meantime, Doc continued his literary blitzkrieg. All 181 of the original pulp stories had been unearthed, plus another that was editorially suppressed in 1949. In fact, the reprints proved so popular that Bantam Books commissioned Philip Farmer and Will Murray to write new Doc Savage novels in the Lester Dent style. The Murray Docs were based on Lester Dent plot outlines and bore such arresting Dent titles as "Python Isle" and "The Frightened Fish."

As of this writing the Doc Savage novels have sold tens of millions of copies, making ex-telegrapher Lester Dent one of the most popular—although largely unrecognized—authors of our time. Where it will all end no one knows. Whether Clark Savage Jr. will take a place in history beside such fictional immortals as Sherlock Holmes and Tarzan, only time will tell.

Doc and his boys were products of the pulp magazines, those gaudy but ephemeral records of a more innocent time. Like most of the pulp heroes, they emerged during the Great Depression in a time of fear and deprivation—a time of international crisis when ordinary people required a simple escape from the complexities of life. Pulp fictioneers like Lester Dent supplied that escape—in spades. They wrote of a simpler world of dastardly villains and unblemished heroes, a world in which you could tell one from the other; you knew whose side you were on. In today's age of ecological horrors and global terrorism, who can fault readers for once again plunging into that simpler, more innocent time when the worst the fates could muster was The Sargasso Ogre, or The Living Fire Menace or perhaps the red-fingered survivors of an ancient, lost civilization.

With a gent like Doc Savage on your side, that was but the best of all possible worlds.

G-8'S WEIRD WAR

TO THE VERY young, war from a distance can appear to be an exciting adventure. When this writer was a kid growing up in the peculiar milieu of World War II, not learning anything in school was generally considered a badge of manhood, but God help the male youngster who couldn't spot a P-40 from a Zero, or who failed to recognize the square-tipped wing outline of a Messerschmitt 110.

We constructed model planes from balsa wood, used our hands to simulate choreographed aerial dogfights, and pursed our lips in snarling imitations of diving Stukas and chattering Vickers guns. Wise kids collected bubble gum cards with enemy aircraft spotter identification—just in case!—and many of us whiled away countless Saturday afternoons devouring the air-war pulp magazines. Even now, many decades and a state of mind away, who can forget their titles… or fail to thrill to the images they evoked? *Air Trails! Wings! Dare-Devil Aces!*

Who was the greatest aerial hero of them all? If you ask an old-time pulp reader, the chances are he'll give you a name you can't research in any history book. One of the earliest and unquestionably the greatest of all the high-flying pulp heroes was a man who had no name at all. He was known to friends, foes, and readers alike as G-8.

G-8, to the initiate, was also known as the Master Spy. His enemies—who included some of the choicest fiends in the Valhalla of scoundrels—frequently referred to him as "the *verdammt* one," an accolade of frustration which described his effectiveness as both spy and fighter.

"Gott in Himmell," his foes would rage, "Germany would have won the war months ago if it had not been for the *verdammt* one."

Debuting in October of 1933, the *verdammt* one's magazine, *G-8 and His Battle Aces,* ran for an incredible 110 issues, each number featuring a collision-course adventure in the career of the World War I master spy. For over a decade, while one air pulp after another went spiraling down, G-8 winged on, carrying his fight with the Kaiser's minions into the heart of World War II.

G-8 was but one of the many pulp heroes born in the fertile mind of publisher Henry Steeger. By 1933, his Popular Publications' once-popular *Battle Aces* magazine was nose-diving, and the dynamic young businessman realized that it needed some fast thinking to bail it out. Over at Street & Smith, The Shadow and Doc Savage had proved to be instant successes. Popular would counter with their own larger-than-life hero, the Spider. Why not, Steeger reasoned, add a superhero of the air? The publisher discussed the idea with top air writer Robert J. Hogan, and they quickly restyled the mundane *Battle Aces* into *G-8 and His Battle Aces.* The rest, as they say, is history.

While constructing the first G-8 novel, "The Bat Staffel," Steeger and author Hogan decided that a full-length aerial adventure series might bog down without stronger, more bizarre plots. In pulp magazine terms, they conceived the G-8 publication as a hybrid of *Dare-Devil Aces, Amazing Stories,* and *Weird Tales.* To this outré stew Hogan added a hero who, with the aid of disguise, could mask himself in any role. Jaded pulp readers—those hardy souls who enjoyed their yarns considerably larger than life—found the blend irresistible.

It was in the area of the weird and frankly preposterous that Hogan really excelled. Surely no protagonist since the days of the Greek heroes ever faced such a horrendous array of foes both natural and supernatural. Even his titles suggest the horrors he ladled out: "Squadron of Corpses," "The Headless Staffel," "Scourge of the Sky Beast," "Flight from the Grave," "Staffel of Invisible Men," "Claws of the Sky Monster"—well, you get the idea.

Flying Dragons. Legions of defrosted Vikings. Death Rays. Robot soldiers. Invisible Monsters. Tiger-men. Zombies. Hordes of giant, man-carrying bats from the Matto Grosso. Nothing, simply nothing, was too fiendish or too gruesome for the Kaiser's mad scientists. And nothing was so horrific that it daunted the unswerving courage and youthful good natures of G-8 and his two loyal Battle Aces.

One of the oft-voiced criticisms of the G-8 series is that the Battle Aces were little more than Rover Boys at the Front—perennial boy scouts who supplied a bulwark of cheerful normalcy against the horrors of the charnel house and man's ultimate madness. Pulpwood paragons all, it's true that they seemed to face each supernatural challenge with wisecracks and apple-pie aphorisms. Even so, the criticism is probably unfair. A writer for the pulps could not afford to make abstract projections of human motives. His job was to supply vicarious adventure for a largely youthful audience; to do so he was required to invent protagonists with simple and easily identifiable characteristics.

Nippy Weston, the terrier ace, was tow-headed, pint-sized,

and quick as lightning. He practiced magic for a hobby and could laugh in the face of death and superstition—and did so by flying Spad number 13.

Nippy's buddy, Big Bull Martin, was twice the terrier ace's size, with a face like a thundercloud and a jaw that appeared to be built out of solid rock. A former All-American halfback, Bull always figured, despite his power and strength, that he could use all the luck he could get. For that reason, his Spad was adorned with a lucky number 7 on the side.

The third Battle Ace, G-8 himself, is given even less description and nary a name at all. We learn that he is of medium height, athletic build, and has steel gray eyes and sandy hair. We discover his tastes in food and learn that his favorite phonograph record is "Raggin' the Scale," a jazzy tune he uses to stimulate his thoughts. Like many of the great pulp heroes, his outstanding characteristics relate to such traits as courage, devotion to duty, and plain dumb luck.

Battle Aces headquarters was at the airdrome near Le Bourget, just north of Paris. Here, attached to the end hangar that housed their three Spads and an anonymous long, powerful roadster, was the private apartment in which the indomitable trio lived. It was (the magazine informs us) as though these young men at the end hangar had deliberately chosen the point nearest the enemy as their headquarters.

It has been said that disguise was virtually a way of life for the great pulp heroes. The Master Spy was unique among pulp mummers in that he employed his own English manservant, a gent known only as Battle, to apply his numerous disguises. A master of malapropisms and muddled Yankee slang, Battle's uncanny ability with a make-up kit was equaled by his prowess as a cook, although the Battle Aces' tastes placed few demands on culinary imagination. Their sallies against the night and its life-threatening shadows often wound up back at Le Bourget airdrome with one of Battle's breakfasts of buckwheat cakes, sausages, and real maple syrup.

This contrast between the horrors of the dark and the sanguine comforts of home was a recurring image in the G-8 yarns. It is an empathic theme that lies at the root of much vicarious adventure, from Sherlock Holmes to The Lord of the Rings, from Homer's Odyssey right up to and including the pulp-hero pantheon. Hogan understood it well and made the most of it. To make the comforts of home even homier, he found it necessary to make the perils of the unknown even ghastlier.

The author of 1,001 horrific, action-packed encounters, Robert Jasper Hogan was one of the few men to write pulp-hero novels under his own name rather than that of a "house name" supplied by the publisher. The son of a Dutch Reformed minister, Hogan was born in 1897 and raised in Buskirk, New York. A graduate of St. Lawrence University, he served his apprenticeship as a cowpuncher, amateur boxer, piano player, pilot, and airplane salesman, before settling down to a career of writing. Like many fiction writers, Hogan drew upon his own experiences to fabricate the wild plots and outrageous inventions of his pulp yarns. Hogan's friendship with a fellow flyer named Harold "Bull" Nevins, who had done intelligence work in France during the war, served as inspiration for both G-8 and for G-8's fictional sidekick, Bull Martin. The third Battle Ace, and Bull's friendly rival, was named Nippy Weston in honor of one of Nevin's wartime buddies, Nippy Westover, whom Hogan never met.

One of the fabrications that earned reader loyalty was Hogan's idea of basing the G-8 novels on a supposed secret wartime diary maintained by the Master Spy himself. G-8's well-worn notebook is featured several times throughout the series. In "Wings of the Hawks of Death," it is even captured by the enemy. In addition, there was the use of historic characters and real events as background for many of the extravagant plots. Fans were convinced that G-8 (and his secret diary) really existed when they spotted each month's contents page. There it was—"Bombs from the Murder Wolves," as told by G-8 to Robert J. Hogan.

The truth is that every word in the G-8 magazine came from the mind of Bob Hogan. In addition to the monthly novel, Hogan also managed to write the short stories that filled up the balance of each issue. Posing as the Master Spy himself, he wrote the editorial badinage in a column titled "G-8 Speaks", in which readers were introduced to the G-8 Club and coerced to purchase their own copies of each issue. (In his column, G-8 routinely refers to Hogan as "old horse-face.")

Under his own name, Hogan was also responsible for two other major pulp character magazines: *The Secret 6* and *The Mysterious Wu Fang*. Although it failed to catch on, the Secret Six was one of the most imaginative of pulp series, while Wu Fang was an entertaining derivative of Sax Rohmer's famous Fu Manchu novels. For a brief time, this amazing wordsmith was producing lead novels for all three of these books as well as numerous short stories each month. A *Reader's Digest* article of the time claimed that he sold more words than any other living author.

Hogan was churning out a minimum 200,000 words a month

in this period, dictating to two secretaries in his New Jersey home, or typing under a palm tree in a Florida retreat. He worked six days a week from early morning until lunch time, and in the afternoon again if deadlines demanded. In the evenings, he planned the next day's scenes out loud with his wife.

In a letter written to me in 1988, publisher Steeger recalled his writer friend with the following description:

> *Bob was never complicated or burdened with any of the restrictions of the academic world. He invented everything from his own fertile imagination. To look at him you would say this is the last person on earth who could be an author. He had a long, thin face and he was a very thin gangling type of person put together with steel wire rather than glue. He had sort of pale washed-out eyes and thinning hair but was most active physically and, of course, his fertile mind never stopped for a moment dreaming up dramatic situations. He loved nothing better than telling me about new evil doings of his villains and of the great heroics of his heroes.*

G-8's author was under orders never to rewrite or edit copy but to simply get the material in on time. Edythe Seims was the first of his hardworking editors, succeeded by Bill Fay, with Alden Norton taking over in the late thirties. In the magazine's final years, diverse hands took turns smoothing out Hogan's increasingly frenzied prose.

The Secret 6 magazine lasted but four issues and *Wu Fang* a mere seven, which must have been a relief to Bob Hogan, who had enough work on his hands just inventing super villains to harass his Three Musketeers of the air.

Of all of G-8's master antagonists, the ultimate bad guy was Herr Doktor Kreuger. Kreuger was the Kaiser's prize fruitcake—the maddest mad doctor of them all. Compared to him, other mad doctors appeared to be general practitioners. He was called "the little fiend," and he battled G-8 some twenty-seven times across the years, usually producing quite a bloodbath.

As conceived by Hogan, the little fiend is a study in pure evil—a man dedicated to his pursuit of high standards of viciousness. Introduced in the first chapter of the very first G-8 adventure, he immediately disclosed his modest plan to murder every man, woman, and child from the Rhone to Paris by means of giant poison-breathing bats. Foiled in that initial endeavor, he returned the following month with a scheme to enlist captured Yank airmen, their faces turned to a ghastly purple, in leading savage suicide attacks against their own men.

And so it went over the years, with the hell-spawned runt of Hun Land continually frustrated in his simple plans for world destruction. In June of 1943, a full decade after his initial introduction, in a story titled "Scourge of the Sky Monster," he appeared to finally meet his maker. Whether or not the devil accepted him went unrecorded.

Another popular baddie, Stahlmaske, or Steelmask, spilled blood in almost a dozen G-8 novels. An enigmatic genius with Messianic delusions, he created awe and fear even among the German High Command—the Kaiser himself sent informants to check up on what he was doing. A victim of G-8's marksmanship, Stahlmaske hid what was left of his face within a conical, midnight-black steel mask; slits in the heavy metal allowed his eyes to burn through like crimson brands. The twisted but fertile mind of the man in the steel mask invented such devices as exploding pellets, monstrous land carriers, catapults for launching planes, and even one ingenious tank device which solved Germany's incipient food shortage by scooping up Allied soldiers and processing them into canned meat.

Such inventiveness was not limited to the minds of the Bosch. G-8's adversaries ran the gamut of racial stereotypes, including at least two Orientals. Chu Lung, a Chinese, was known as the Oriental Master of Death. He threatened the flying spy eight times in such adventures as "Wings of the Dragon Lord," "Skies of Yellow Death," and "The Sky Serpent Flies Again." Described as a gaunt man with glowing jade-green eyes, Chu Lung boasted an arsenal undreamed of even by Sax Rohmer's infamous doctor. (Would you believe poisonous clouds, mechanical banshee wails, and a gas-powered fire-breathing dragon plane?)

Author Hogan even introduced a Japanese villain to the series—Herr Matzu. While history records that the Japanese entered World War I on the side of the Allies, Herr Matzu preferred the life of a freelancer. Diminutive of body, possessing a soft and diffident voice, he seemed at first to be the antithesis of Rohmer's yellow peril and Hogan's own Chu Lung. In the midst of carnage, he was polite and eager to please—like a small boy playing a deadly game. "I don't hate anyone," he explained. "I like being friendly with everyone, even though I must kill them."

At the climax of his initial encounter with the Master Spy, Herr Matzu is shot and left for dead. Later, however, in an adventure titled "Red Fangs of the Sky Emperor," he returns in an alliance with Doctor Chu Lung. "I was shot in the head," Matzu explains to his unholy chum, "and that delayed my operations."

While the introduction of werewolves and vampires to the Western Front appeared to offend few readers' ecological sensibilities, at least one disgusted fan took umbrage with the idea of a Chinese warlord fighting in the service of the Kaiser.

"It must have been pure accident," the reader wrote, *"that I struck a good story when I read my first G-8 yarn. I thought to myself, 'Here's a swell mag' and I looked forward to the next issue. Well, the next issue came out. So what? It was a lousy story about guys who rose up from the dead and went on fighting and all that silly stuff that everyone knows is impossible. So, I bought the next copy after that. So help me, it was worse. That was a story about that crazy Chinaman you call Chu Lung who was supposed to be helping the Germans. Of all the goofy things I ever read."*

Well, you can't please everyone. But Bob Hogan certainly tried. The long-term success of the G-8 pulp magazine was due in no small part to the numerous fiends who stalked its pages. The bestiary was so large that one can only suggest the diversity. There was the giant Man in Armor, who commanded an army of bloated corpses; the Raven, a beak-faced avian travesty; the Vampire Hag, queen of the winged dead; Herr Doktor Wormer, the Death Master, who planned to blow up the world—quite literally; Herr Feuer, the asbestos-garbed super pyromaniac; and last but not least, there was Grun, the American-born ape man who hated everything lovely and beautiful on earth. The high incidence of stigmata-bearing villains would indicate that either the Kaiser's surgeons were criminally inept or that frantic pulp writers often regurgitated their own ideas.

This writer suspects that several of Hogan's villains and their devices were the inventions of cover artist Fred Blakeslee, working in collaboration with publisher Henry Steeger. One of Popular Publications' greatest strengths was that Steeger made a near-scientific study of readers' tastes and personally supervised the execution of each cover with a master chef's understanding of ingredients. There are numerous occasions in which a cover scene is described graphically in the final pages of a story but sometimes with little conviction. Details are brought painfully into the scene, then disposed of summarily, as if Hogan had achieved his goal of justifying some preposterous cover concept. This theory would explain such macabre villains as Baron von Todschmecker—a walking skeleton with the hilt of a dagger protruding from his gun-blue skull—as well as scores of insane aerial confrontations.

Another unsung hero was interior illustrator John Fleming Gould. Gould's planes were less convincing than Blakeslee's, but his dark-toned sketches excelled in the vivid imagery of awesome aerial combat, shadowy Black Forest castles, and ghastly moonlit monsters. It was these disparate elements that gave the magazine much of its surrealistic appeal.

Author Hogan knew this of course. He took delight in spinning tall tales of fantabulous invention. His only concern—expressed occasionally in the stories and sometimes in the editorial comments—was a fear that readers would think he meant that war was fun. The magazine had sprung up when there was no holocaust in Europe. People thought that the greatest war of all was past, and dead history is always fair game for stories of simple thrills and heroism.

Clearly the yarns were not meant to be taken seriously, for

Bob Hogan was a man who wrote with a twinkle in his typewriter.

In one of the Chu Lung adventures, Nippy taxis up to the 128th airdrome, having dropped the flying spy somewhere over Germany. A concerned Bull Martin challenges him:

> *"Well, come on. Tell me what happened on the flight will you?"*
> *The terrier ace shrugged.*
> *"Oh, I just flew G-8 over," he said. "He hopped out when he got ready and I came back."*
> *"There's something you'll never be, Nip," Bull said, "if you do come out of this war alive."*
> *"What's that?" the terrier ace asked.*
> *"You'll never be a writer," Bull told him. "As far as you're concerned, nothing happens unless about fourteen million people get killed."*

If you listen carefully, you can hear the ghost of Robert J. Hogan—laughing at himself. For the man who wrote the G-8 stories just had to have a sense of humor.

With a story set in mysterious Burma, "Wings of the Death Tiger" (June 1944), the saga of G-8 and his Battle Aces finally ended. Hogan put the pulps behind him forever, making an effortless transition into the slick magazines as well as producing a series of hardcover Westerns. One of his books, *The Stand at Apache River*, was produced as a movie by Universal-International Pictures in 1953. Many of his stories were adapted for television, and several of his books have been translated into foreign languages. Robert J. Hogan died in 1963, with the last G-8 story written nearly twenty years before. Like Sir

Arthur Conan Doyle, he had once hoped to gain recognition as a writer of serious historical novels but had been trapped by the runaway success of his bread-and-butter hero.

Today, Hogan's chief claim to immortality is as sole author of the G-8 stories. While attempts to revive his famous flying spy have had little effect (notably a series of Berkley paperbacks and a 1966 Dell one-shot comic), pulp collectors and readers with long memories remain forever loyal.

If the G-8 yarns were trash—and millions of parents must have regarded them as such—then they were the best of all kinds of trash. They were trash for connoisseurs of trash. Trash for people who understood just how good trash could really be.

Even so, it is not easy for an adult to read G-8 today and still rekindle that precious sense of wonder which the stories once engendered. You must suspend critical faculties. More than that, but better still, you must rediscover that part of you that is forever young and naïve—the lost boy who stirs within the consciousness of any man who has ever known a boy's dreams.

Perhaps, on nights when the wind howls fitfully in the chimney, you remember other such nights. Nights when the boy who dreamed dreams curled up with an apple in one hand and a copy of G-8 in the other. For a glorious hour or two, the sound of Hisso engines fills his mind. Once again, he is with G-8 in the midnight sky, some 10,000 feet over Germany. He is on the wing of Nippy's Spad, his eyes on the luminous dial of his German watch, his body curled to keep from freezing.

The little plane drones over the Vosges mountains. Somewhere down there, amid the stygian darkness, looms the secret laboratory of Herr Doktor Kreuger. The boy's heart pounds, for he knows that within moments he will dive with G-8 into the blackness of the night. End over end he will spin in a series of somersaults until he feels the tug of the shroud cords, hears the parachute making a sound like a bursting paper bag as it snaps open.

Before him are all the exciting, horrifying, suspenseful adventures that a boy could possibly dream.

Bob Hogan understood those dreams. He wrote directly to them.

THE SPIDER'S WEB

HE SCURRIES OUT of the night's black vortex, a stooped horror seemingly spawned from the pits of hell:

> *The skin was sallow, shining where it drew tightly over cheek bones, his mouth a lipless gash, the nose a predatory beak. He wore a wig of lanky black hair. About his twisted, deformed shoulders, a billowing black cape, and beneath the wide brim of a black hat long fangs gleamed in a horrid, sharp-toothed mouth.*

He is the Spider, pulp fiction's most ferocious masked vigilante. Half saint and half headsman, the Spider employed his never cool .45s to scythe the city's streets of some of the most bizarre criminal vermin to erupt from a pulp writer's overheated imagination.

For a solid decade, from May of 1933 to December 1943, the Spider—cryptically billed as the Master of Men—entranced loyal readers who may have found The Shadow too tame for jaded tastes. Even compared to his chief rival in the phantom hero game, the Spider was one creepy character. When The Shadow laughed, it seemed reasonable that he did so to scare the hell out of criminals. But the Spider's weird howl, his shivering peel of maniacal cackles, spoke another language.

Beneath the fright rags and vampiric make-up lurked Richard Wentworth, millionaire philanthropist. He gave thousands of dollars to the poor and relaxed by playing his Stradivarius like a virtuoso, but as the Spider he killed without mercy and used his cigarette lighter to brand the foreheads of murdered thugs and their gloating masters with a vermillion seal of tensed, hairy legs and poison fangs—his weird symbol of swift and ruthless justice.

As pulp historian Will Murray once put it,

> *No stranger hero ever existed in popular literature. The Spider was so weird that his publishers refused to showcase him on their covers as he really was. Instead, he was depicted with cloak and hat, set off by a black domino mask. For a seven-issue stretch in 1940, the editors bowed to reader pressure and the Spider swooped across his own covers, long hair flowing, white fangs gleaming. Then, abruptly, their better sense reasserted itself. Some sights are just too strong for the light of day.*

Like G-8, the Spider was the brainchild of Popular Publications' resourceful young publisher, Henry "Harry" Steeger, a graduate of Princeton University and the University of Berlin. Admittedly, an attempt to cash in on the success of Street & Smith's Shadow character, *The Spider* shared the spotlight with G-8 as the first of Steeger's pulp magazines to bear the name of a character rather than a genre.

In late 1929, when Steeger was in his mid-twenties, he borrowed some money from his stepfather and, with a partner named Harold Goldsmith, started the Popular Publications pulp chain. At first the partners had only four titles—a western, two detectives, and an air war—but by the forties they were running the biggest pulp publishing house in the world.

The youthful partners at the upstart company ran a happy

ship, their offices described as a constant madhouse of larks and bantering. The entire staff was under thirty and they played as hard as they worked. Shirley Steeger, Henry's wife, read the slush pile to pick out stories and ideas, and was responsible for naming the company. It must have been fun—even the story titles mixed sensationalism with wry wit—"You're the Crime in My Coffee," "The Corpse Belongs to Daddy," "This Is the Way We Bake Our Dead." A chance remark, a joke, anything would suggest a new title—and was immediately rushed into print.

As new fads replaced old, new magazines sprang up or disappeared like flamboyant weeds. Steeger instituted a sassy, extravagant style for his popular fiction and developed an instinct for cover art that bordered on genius. Eventually, the Popular Publications colophon identified some of the most exciting fiction magazines ever published: *Black Mask, Adventure, Dime Detective, Famous Fantastic Mysteries, Dare-Devil Aces, Argosy.* The list could go on and on. Over one hundred titles in all. It was Harry Steeger who dreamed up The Spider. He said he got the idea one day when he was playing tennis and noticed a huge spider at the edge of the court. In the earliest pulps and silent movies, the spider had been employed as a frequent symbol for all that was creepy. Harry figured that it would work as the title for a new character magazine designed to compete with *The Shadow*. As usual, his instincts were spot on.

Touted as "a new magazine with a dynamite punch," the initial issue featured a novel titled "The Spider Strikes." The story was supposedly written by the popular Canadian writer R.T.M. Scott, who the publisher billed as "one of the finest mystery-action writers of the present day." I say supposedly

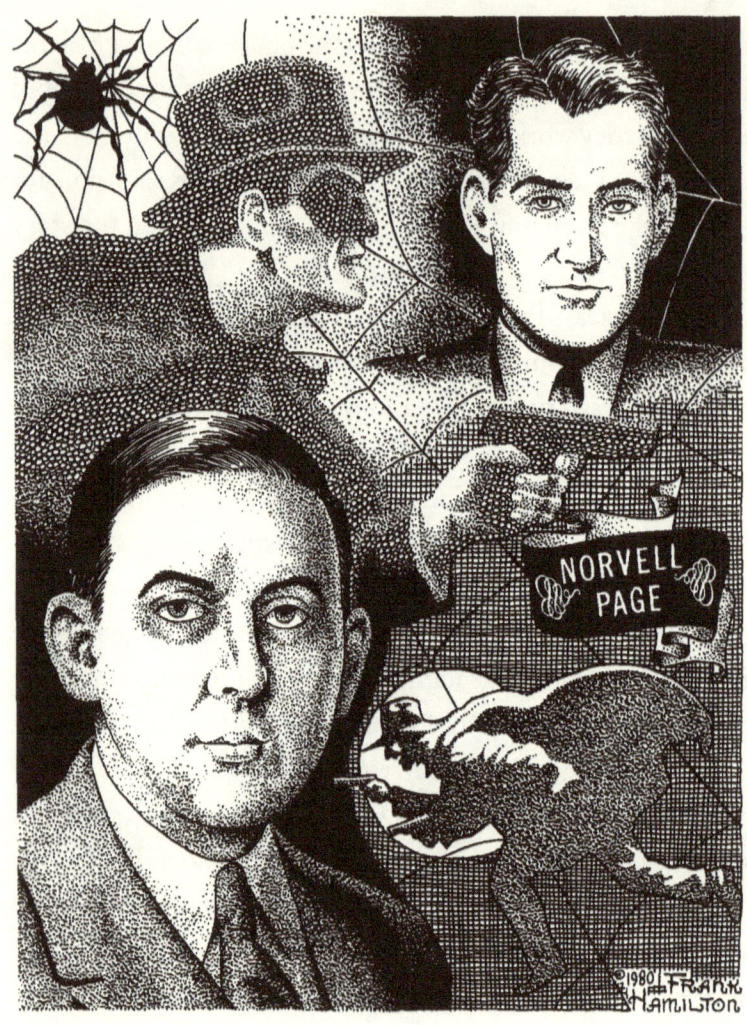

because it appears that Scott's son, R.T.M. Scott II, may have written the first two Spider sagas based on his dad's series of short stories and novels featuring a Secret Service agent named Aurelius Smith. What is known is that young Scott was an associate editor at Popular and that he did write several stories for the mystery pulps. Unfortunately, whatever writing career he may have developed was cut short by service with the 48th

Highlanders of Toronto during World War II. He was killed in action in Holland in 1945.

Scott's two Spider novels were, by pulp-hero standards, fairly routine stuff. They are slickly written but nowhere in them is there a hint of the dreadful night demon who will soon debut as the authentic star of the title. They did serve to introduce wealthy Richard Wentworth, his society paramour Nita van Sloan, and the redoubtable Ram Singh—his fiercely loyal Hindu (later Sikh) manservant. But bigger and better, not to mention wilder, events were in store for Dick Wentworth. Beginning with the December issue, a new writer took over, lurking behind the publisher's distinguished-sounding house name, Grant Stockbridge.

The new writer on the block was Norvell W. Page, an ex-newspaperman turned pulp-story pounder. Over the next ten years, Page would blow up a storm in the magazine, producing some ninety-one Spider novels pulsing with anguish, fury, and blood sacrifice. Under his deft hand, Richard Wentworth, playboy detective, suffered a mutation into the real Spider, a ruthless and terrible cloaked apparition bound by his hero's oath to protect society from the forces of anarchy at whatever personal cost. Other pulp heroes did the same thing, of course. But the Spider did it better.

Norvell Page was one of the pulp field's most reliable professionals, a dynamic purple-proser whose work invariably sported a flair for the dramatic upheld by powerful imagery and content. He worked hard at it, as suggested by his article in the 1935 *Writer's Yearbook*, in which he confessed:

> I never turned out a story in my life that wasn't plain, hard

work. Not that the writing itself isn't enjoyable. I don't have to sweat out words, or worry about action when my characters "come to life."

But somewhere in that story, the work was hard. Getting the idea, working out the outline, revising the copy, trying to get a fast opening that still would carry all the information it should, straining to tell a scene just as I see it in my mind's eye. On my Spider stories I have written as many as six different opening chapters, and spent a full day getting the first two thousand words on paper. I may have written eight, ten, twelve thousand in getting those two, and even then, I don't always like them.

But pulp master Page did get it right, and almost every time. Under his firm hand, the Spider trod boldly in The Shadow's footprints but wielded an even bigger shtick. Page quickly dispensed with Scott's mild plotlines and plunged deliriously into a mad netherworld threatened by master fiends as bent as boomerangs. To state that he brought a level of emotional intensity to the Spider's world of death, torture, and apocalyptic terror is raw understatement. Potboilers those wild old yarns may be but, thanks to Page's scalding prose, the pots bubbled like corked volcanoes.

In Page's premier outing, the Spider waged all-out war with a pulp-style criminal monster, The Black Death, amidst the befouled air of a Manhattan swept by bubonic plague. This approach to the pulp hero formula—the sheer magnitude of the villain's crimes and his utter disregard for human life—was an element that typified the Spider epics of the thirties. Manhattan itself was usually under siege, its major landmarks destroyed by flames, bombs or death rays, tens of thousands—

perhaps millions—of innocent citizens destroyed by disease, drugs, or the ruthless incursions of subhuman hordes. One story alone ("The City Destroyer," January 1935) began with the destruction of the Empire State Building and Grand Central Station, then went on to polish off Brooklyn Bridge and the New York subway system along with miscellaneous real estate and the usual cast of hundreds of thousands of screaming extras.

As Page's plots sped recklessly past the borders of reality, his horrors moved beyond the Big Apple into statewide and even nationwide settings. Snarling Neanderthals pillage the countryside. People burst spontaneously into flame. Hordes of poison vampire bats swarm. Giant robots with fire-squirting fingers stalk. And tigers and hyenas roam the ravaged streets as tens of thousands die from a green gas that strips flesh from bone. In a 1937 epic, "Machine Guns Over the White House," the U.S. government is captured by storm trooper minions of an Eastern occult order. The President himself is impeached on a trumped-up charge of looting the Treasury and, in a cataclysmic finale, fights at the side of the Spider against armed troops and Eastern killers. (FDR was practically an ongoing character in the series, appearing as more than an incidental figure in several of the novels.)

It should all seem ludicrous—if only the author gave you time to think or catch your breath. But his stories race along as if there is a warrant out for their arrest. Perhaps their tail pages are on fire. You can almost smell the cordite as pistols bark, machine-guns stutter, victims topple, blood splashes. The body count is relentless. Events careen from one unimaginably hideous predicament to something even worse. The prose is taut, vivid, muscular, throbbing with blood and resounding with the thunder of overwhelming tragedy. Even the titles leap out furiously: *Prince of the Red Looters. Death's Crimson Juggernaut. The Red Death Reign. The City Destroyer. Legions of Madness.*

It is the Spider's purgatorial.

Dreadful Night shrouds the world's greatest city. *Wings of the Black Death* descend. *The Flame Master* strikes. *The Grey Horde Creeps. The Mayor of Hell* reigns.

"Oh, Spider! They're burning the city! Those people... Oh, Spider!"

So little time until dawn! Alone, injured, perhaps near death, his beloved city in flames or ruins around him, the law, the public, and even his loved ones turned against him, the Spider must fight on. For he is the Master of Men. And for the Master of Men there is no surcease, no rest.

Like most things that excite disapproval, the Spider stories proved to be addictive. He was easily the most popular character produced by Popular Publications, rivaled only by The Shadow and Doc Savage over at Street & Smith. Even his author took to the character with the enthusiasm of his fans. Henry Steeger once confided: "Norvell Page was a very colorful character who enjoyed identifying himself as the Spider. I remember frequently that he would appear in the office in a black cape and a big floppy hat, and on his finger, he wore a Spider ring."

The wearing of Spider garb was not the only connection between author Page and his unusual protagonist. In many ways Richard Wentworth, the Spider, was the most outlandish of the great pulp heroes. And yet, in some ways, he was the most human. Chalk it up to author identification. When Norvell Page assumed the role of Spider scribe, he inherited a cast of characters invented by another author. The roll call, fairly complete, included not only Richard Wentworth and his fiancée Nita, but also featured Wentworth's chauffeur Ronald Jackson, who served under him in the Great War, Wentworth's aged butler Jenkyns, the aforementioned Ram Singh, and Professor Brownlee, who puttered about in his private lab to supply the Spider with such crime-fighting gimcracks as the web, a long silken cord with a break strength of seven hundred pounds. Another major character was long-suffering Police Commissioner Stanley Kirkpatrick, who was at once Wentworth's best friend and the Spider's sworn enemy. Under Page's skilled manipulation, each of these stock characters began to take on flesh—or at least the fictional illusion of real flesh and human warmth.

But it was Richard Wentworth who Page identified with most, not just because he shared his hero's passion for costuming, but because the author found in Wentworth a perfect conduit to express his own deeply held beliefs regarding idealism, faith, and duty—even if those concepts were shrouded in blood-soaked science-fiction nightmares. Under Page, Richard Wentworth emerged as humanity's paladin, a man of patrician tastes whose heart was kind but whose actions were ruthless because of his stern sense of justice and the measureless malignance of his enemies. He was, in a sense, pulpdom's tragic hero. The Spider's monthly triumphs came only through Herculean efforts against impossible odds. And the price he paid was awesome. Readers had met his kind before but never with such heart and feeling. Compared to The Shadow, who seemed to possess no overt emotional life, the Spider was all emotion, often to the detriment of common sense and logic.

As pulp historian Robert Sampson once explained it,

> *The best Spider stories carry an emotional field strong enough to attract nails. They sweep you along, the paragraphs radiating emotion with almost physical intensity, numbing the critical sense. It is basic, simple stuff, overpowering in context. It works wonderfully well. You care for the people. As in other wish-fulfillment worlds, the hero is young, wealthy, adored. Unlike many other heroes, Wentworth is regularly abased, rejected, and scorned. He is alone—staggering, exhausted, gripped by agonies, bleeding from assorted wounds. Forward he reels in solitary struggle—leaving behind a trail of corpses, each neatly shot in the forehead.*

The red badge of the Spider's justice was expressed by those nasty little seals he dispensed so generously. Hundreds of dead bodies, hundreds of burning symbols stamped indelibly on pallid foreheads—human detritus abandoned in the wake of the Spider's Old Testament war against vast conspiracies. Occasionally, even Wentworth had pause to consider. In "Green Globes of Death," we read: "He turned the lighter over curiously in his hand, looking at it with eyes that saw through and beyond it. How many times had that gleaming metal touched the dead foreheads of his victims? A strong shudder shook him."

But it didn't shake him for long. Only a month later, in "The Cholera King," the Spider's guns produced yet another red harvest, each dead thug tattooed with the familiar vermillion trademark. It was the Spider's version of the Puritan's scarlet letter: payment meted out as punishment for sin. So much to do, so many criminals to be punished.

In the Spider's mad universe, freakish enemies with names like The Red Mandarin, The Blind Man, The City Destroyer, and The Death Fiddler are not paranoid nightmares—they are a day-to-day reality. As repetition and the sheer virtuosity of breakneck prose made suspension of disbelief progressively easier, Norvell Page's imagination spawned armies of even more improbable megalomaniacs to add to his hero's over-burdened work schedule: The Flame King, The Sandman, The Skull, The Conqueror, and The Emperor of Vermin, among others. In "Prince of the Red Looters" (August 1934), the Spider even met The Fly. Guess who won?

You had to admire the Spider, though. (How could you not admire a guy who figured that dressing up like a fanged hunchback would terrify hardened criminals?) Through years of rage, sacrifice, and injury, with friends and the forces of law turned against him, madmen forever on the loose, and so little time to practice his violin, he underwent a purgatory of injury and defeat. The dreadful things that befell poor Dick Wentworth and his loyal group are almost too awesome—and certainly too numerous—to describe. Other pulp heroes operated under a bell jar of author security—you just knew they were going to come out of scrapes relatively unharmed. But the Spider suffered—really suffered. And most of the time his author convinced you that Wentworth wasn't going to make it through to next month's issue.

Drugged, paralyzed, disgraced, punctured by bullets through

the chest, stomach, brain and other allegedly vital organs, the Spider fought on to illustrate to loyal readers the benefits of excellence under stress. But the bad guys never got his message. They returned time and time again to make his life a living hell.

In "Legion of the Accursed Light," that eccentric fellow, The Eye of Flame, spread his lethal influence over New York, burning to charred cinders thousands of citizens and innocent commuters who crossed his path. As usual, the fate of America hung in the balance. And the Spider, the only man capable of penetrating to the heart of the enemy's stronghold, was captured and hung by his feet like a trussed chicken from a beam. How to escape? Being the Master of Men, he figured coolly that if he could remove just one of his feet, the anklet holding him would come loose and the chain could be pulled over the beam. It was just the Spider's way.

A Norvell Page capper, though, was the scene illustrated on the cover of "The Spider and the Slaves of Hell" (July 1939). The story featured a mad extortionist who specializes in blowing up landmark buildings. With his Sutton Place headquarters obliterated, his body torn by police bullets and chained to great balls of iron, the Master of Men rescues his beloved Nita by climbing up the sheer face of a building, dragging his metal balls behind him. It's all a matter of will.

Despite Wentworth's vigilance, lovely Nita was herself the subject of uncounted injuries, tortures, and emotional upheavals. In her efforts to aid the Spider in his battle against the ungodly, she was turned into a gibbering drug addict in "Slaves of the Crime Master," threatened with rape by an orangutan in "The Red Death Rain," had some of her brain cells suctioned out by The Scarlet Doctor, and in "Rule of the Monster Men" was transformed into a surgically altered cripple by that crazed practitioner, The Wreck. She was a spunky gal, though, and occasionally, when the Spider was either wounded, crippled, infected with rabies, blinded, dying, or sentenced to death row in Sing Sing, she'd don his old cape and fright mask and off a few bad guys on her own.

One of the things that distinguished the Spider series was that it was a kind of ongoing serial with interrelated events in which the fate of characters changed dramatically. Wentworth's friend Stanley Kirkpatrick was commissioner of police throughout most of the stories, but he ran for governor of New York State in "Reign of the Death Fiddler" and was elected and served until "The Mayor of Hell," eight issues later. He suffered a nervous breakdown in the late thirties, and was felled by a major heart attack. But he was back to his old self in 1941 when he met and fell in love with Lona Deeping, whom he later married.

But not all of Wentworth's pals got off so lightly. Like the Spider himself, they all suffered numerous wounds and near-death experiences. In "Laboratory of the Damned," his beloved Great Dane, Apollo, died of eating poisoned chocolate. His chief aide, Jackson, was bumped off in another story, as was clever old Professor Brownlee. Miraculously, Jackson was later restored to life, explaining that it had only been a bad wound. Perhaps because of his age, Professor Brownlee found it more difficult to shrug off three bullets through his skull; he tended to remain dead.

Not even Wentworth's residences were safe. He had three, perhaps four permanent bases in the stories. Despite secret passages, concealed steel doors, and yards of armor plating, most were either routinely invaded by criminal hordes or occasionally blown to slag. (Everybody seemed to know where the Spider lived, except possibly the police.) Crime fighting took a similar toll on his high-powered automobiles, including his beloved armored Daimler, his Hispano-Suiza convertible, and several Lancia's, which he had hidden away in various places around New York City. In "Hordes of the Red Butcher," Wentworth comments: "I'll have to get a less expensive car. I've destroyed at least a half-dozen of these, and they run into money after a while."

It will appear to gentle readers that homicidal hero Wentworth may have been wound up at least one turn too tight. Frankly, it's difficult to synopsize the Spider stories without presenting them as targets for satire. But clearly, they weren't meant to be taken too seriously. They were disposable entertainments improvised at white-hot heat by a master pro who no doubt entertained himself by stretching nearly everything to near snapping point. Readers back in the "dirty thirties," however, not only found the stories great fun to read (they still are today) but responded enthusiastically to the author's subliminal messages concerning love and trust, loyalty, and duty.

Other pulp heroes went about fighting petty crooks and chiselers, but the Spider specialized. He struggled against the things that Depression-era readers really feared—the death of friends and loved ones, the breakdown of social order, and the destruction of ideals in the face of chaos. The Spider of the pulps had begun life as just another playboy detective. Under Norvell Page's influence, he gradually metamorphosed into something quite different. He became unofficial king of the tenement dwellers. For the dispossessed, he was God's messenger with a gun, a self-sacrificing savior who fought evil that the law did not address. Faced with criminal conspiracies as vast and as frightening as the Great Depression itself, all the police could do was stumble about, banging away at the Spider's departing figure as if he were the cause and not the solution. But only the Spider could triumph, because his heart was pure and his moral judgment unyielding.

The new, improved Spider's colorful mix of action, sensationalism, and quasi-religious moralizing proved to be a formula for success. A Spider club was soon formed, grandiloquently titled The Spider League of Crime Prevention. Thousands of metal Spider rings were sold to enthusiastic readers pledged "to aid the Spider in his ceaseless battle against crime." Members were urged to uphold the law on all occasions, even though that was more than their hero ever did. There was even a Spider radio show (on KMOX St. Louis) and two Columbia Pictures serials, *The Spider's Web* (1938) and *The Spider Returns* (1941), the former earning its gun-blazing reputation as the most cadaverous kiddies' movie ever lensed.

But the Spider's glory was due to more than Norvell Page's scorching typewriter. Thanks to publisher Steeger and editor Rogers Terrill, the magazine was a total environment, from its curiously misshapen title logo to its scarlet spine inset with dripping dagger. Even inside, there were unique editorial touches like creepy little spider sketches and the way the Spider's name was always italicized.

Beneath the crooked yellow logos lurked exquisite cover paintings detailing marvels of maniac action involving undraped females and slobbering wingnuts waving blowtorches and whips or pouring molten metal from bubbling cauldrons. Even the story titles demanded youthful attention: "Master of the Night Demons," "Scourge of the Yellow Fangs," "The City that Dared not Eat."

In the world of the pulp hero, such icons as Doc Savage and The Shadow were defined by the cover portraits of Walter Baumhofer and George Rozen. As for the Spider, few would argue that John Howitt's masterfully lurid tableaus of pandemonium and carnage helped sell copies like ballpark hot dogs. Even so, it seems to me that the Spider's definitive artist was John Fleming Gould, the magazine's pen-and-ink man. Even the publisher must have thought so: cover artists Howitt and the great Rafael De Soto never received a byline, but Gould often did—and right on the contents page.

Gould was a favorite at Popular Publications. His work not only graced such other pulp hero pulps as G-8 and Operator #5, but it was used to launch a staggering number of first issues of other titles. He usually did all the pen-and-inks for any magazine he worked on, from column headings and character portraits down to spot sketches and those tiny, hairy spiders. For the Spider, he slashed out kinetic mini-murals full of the red-hot mayhem described so breathlessly in Norvell Page's apocalyptic melodramas. It seemed at the time—and still does—a perfect fusion of writer and artist. If Page could draw, I am sure he would have done so with Gould's harsh energy.

In "The Citadel of Hell" (March 1934), Page had introduced the real Spider—that sallow, stooped hunchback with the fake canines. A month later, in "Serpent of Destruction," artist Gould pictured Richard Wentworth in his new fear form: a scuttling apparition in black ankle-length cape, grotesquely out of place on a nightclub dance floor. And look! He's stapling some gink's forehead with the point of a venom-tipped cane. What a man, the Spider.

In the years that followed, Richard Wentworth's guns never cooled, and artist Gould was there to illustrate author Page's horrific visions of a world gone mad. "The City Destroyer" (January 1935) kicked off with a spectacular view of the Empire State Building crumbling into pedestrian-jammed streets. "Reign of the Vampire King" (November 1935) featured hordes of vampire bats nipping Broadway theatregoers, bats attacking a night-flying airplane, and a giant bat racing a biplane over a vampire-infested carnival. Wonderful. "Master of the Flaming Horde" (November 1937) began with a panoramic street scene gutted by fire, an eerie horrorscape defined in flames. Explosions and flames were a Gould specialty; some of his best double-pagers nearly leaped off the page with pyrotechnic fury—just like Norvell Page's scorching stories.

But even Page's fury had to wane. From the start, his technique had been to escalate all the elements: bigger threats, more calamitous horrors, more action, wilder plots and villains, and more searing emotional tension. It all built up a glorious head of steam. Unfortunately, once you go over the top, it becomes increasingly difficult to climb higher. Inevitably, old ideas began to be recycled. And then, in the middle of the Living Pharaoh series in late 1937, Page wasn't there at all. A new writer took over. The new man's name was Emile C. Tepperman.

Beginning in 1934, Tepperman had contributed a series of

short stories to the magazine, all featuring his character Ed Race, the Masked Marksman. Late in 1935, he took over the Publisher's Operator #5 series from Frederick C. Davis. He would write some twelve Spider novels in all between 1936 and 1940.

In July of 1937, Norvell Page reemerged with a Spider story titled "The Man Who Ruled in Hell." But the next issue saw yet another writer, Wayne Rogers, begin writing Spiders, more or less alternating with Page, who must have been suffering from author fatigue. Rogers was a conscript from the publisher's so-called weird menace pulps-magazines that featured tales of grue and horror based on the tradition of the legendary Grand Guignol theatre of Paris. His Spider novels usually reflected those sensational elements, culminating in his notorious "The City that Dared not Eat," with its cover illustration of a cleaver-wielding butcher and human corpses hanging on meat hooks.

The new Spider scribes tried hard—their stories were shrill and furious—but neither would nor could reach the emotional heights climbed by author Page. They tried to copy the Page mystique without understanding it. In their skilled but uninspired hands, Richard Wentworth slipped in and out of character. Sometimes he seemed more like The Shadow and sometimes even the Phantom Detective. The real Spider waited in the wings for the second coming of his creator.

Norvell Page, presumably rested and recharged, returned to glory in 1939. He would continue to write most of the Spiders until the magazine's demise four years later. In the August 1941 issue, it was announced that a fire at the author's hunting lodge had destroyed his entire collection of Spider magazines. This was a genuine loss to Page, who often spoke of Wentworth and his loyal circle as if they were his own close friends. Perhaps inspired by his loss, subsequent novels contained increasing flickers of the author's philosophy and faith, woven like silken threads through crude tapestries of destruction. It is in this period that Page engaged his readers with overt discussion of Wentworth's extraordinary inner strength and nobility of purpose. In a footnote in "Slaves of the Ring," he stated unequivocally, "Selfless strength is what men attribute to gods."

January of 1942 saw publication of the 100th Spider novel, "Death and the Spider." It was an event of some celebration in the magazine's editorial pages. For this special issue, Page concocted a stew of mysticism and menace that was strange even by his own iconoclastic standards. In it, an ancient Tibetan Lama prophecies that when Death walks the earth in the form of a man, the Spider will die. And Death does walk the earth in the classic form of a cowled skeleton with a bloody scythe. Death is, of course, impervious to the Spider's bullets, and Wentworth is only able to save himself by reciting the Twenty-third Psalm like an incantation. (Meanwhile, in Tibet, 10,000 holy men pray for him.) And the Spider, to save the President of the United States from Death, endures a mortal chest wound. He dies. Dies dead. Or seems to die. Or perhaps only his physical being dies.

With the Master of Men, such things were always tricky judgment calls. But then:

> *He drove his lagging body upward from the snow. He seemed to be detached from his body. He was up there in the air above*

his head somewhere, looking down. He felt sorry for his body, but it had to obey him. It had to live.

The dead man got up and walked. He pushed himself up with arms like broken sticks, he got up on legs that were limp and bent, his body sagged and his chin rested on his chest.

A man turned and saw him, and his white set face. He stepped aside. Wentworth's body sagged, but his head was up. His jaw line was carved from granite, and his eyes were chips of fire. He walked, and paid no heed to the mob, and it opened before him like the Red Sea.

Inside, Death has hypnotized the President into heart failure. In lurches the Master of Men, his body a bloody mess but his mighty will strong enough to defeat even Death himself. When the President recovers, the church bells of Christmas ring out, and the great man is able to deliver his scheduled speech in that familiar, resounding voice: *"People of America, we have nothing to fear save fear itself."*

It is all very exciting. But strange. It is pure Spider. And pure Norvell Page.

There would be nineteen more Spiders—all but one written by Page—but never again would they reach the delirious heights of that 100th issue.

And then, abruptly, it was over.

The Spider magazine was terminated during the Christmas season of 1943, a year that was to take a heavy toll on familiar heroes. In fact, the war years were boom years for the pulps. But paper was limited, so less popular titles had to make way to supply increased print runs for better-selling books. The fact that such "character" magazines as *The Spider* and *G-8 and His*

Battles Aces were axed within the same period would indicate that infallible heroes were finding less favor with increasingly sophisticated readers. Many of the Spider's youthful fans were now in uniform, and they were embroiled in battling real-life villains on foreign shores. The new bad guys dressed in neither hoods or masks and didn't bother to pose behind secret identities.

The last Spider novel, "When Satan Came to Town," was ghosted by Prentice Winchell, a writer also known as Stewart Stirling. It was a poor story and must have been a letdown for those who remembered the great days of the Spider's former glory. Suitably, the final lines belonged to Nita: "I could do with a night's sleep."

As for that typewriter titan Norvell Page, he had already deserted the sinking pulp ship for government work in Washington, where he wrote for the Office of War Information and, later, for the Atomic Energy Commission's Information Division. His death from a heart attack in 1961 at the age of fifty-seven was recorded in the New York Times. He was credited with "writing more than 100 detective novels." No mention was made of the real nature of those novels.

So, the question remains, what kind of a man was responsible for churning out those totally outrageous Spider stories? Acquaintances remember him as a nice guy who took delight in dressing in the fright garb of his famous hero and who probably took equal delight in scaring the hell out of impressionable readers.

But the other Norvell Page, the amateur philosopher who dared inject unmistakable messages regarding the meaning of love and duty, trust, honor, and the consequences of responsibility, into bleeding pulp-hero melodrama, seems to have emerged, like his character, on paper.

In a series of sensitive, revealing letters addressed to a young fan, the author of the Spider sagas once wrote,

> *Consult your conscience and you will know what is good. Consult your God and you will conquer. I make no forecast of bliss undisturbed or of ease or luxury. If you have developed strength, it is because you will need it. God wastes nothing, not the smallest tear.*
>
> *If you love battle, you will win. If you are good, you will triumph.*

It was the Spider's code. And the Spider was Norvell Page.

PRE-WAR PARANOIA: OPERATOR #5

On the twenty-second day of the invasion of the United States by the Purple Emperor, a crowd of stunned, hopeless men and women gathered in Union Square in New York City to hear a proclamation of the conqueror.

The gray-shirted, steel-helmeted, stony-faced guards of the Central Empire used their sabers indiscriminately to keep the crowd in order. In the center of the square, a wide platform had been erected and upon it was a gruesome block, with a groove in the top, upon which a man might rest his head before it was chopped from his body by the executioner.

Suddenly, a stir ran through the sullen thousands in the square as a squat, broad-shouldered man stepped up on the platform in the center. He was naked from the waist up, and his chest was entirely covered with hair. His trousers were spattered with blood, and there were flecks of blood on his shoes. Black hair, matted and uncombed fell over a low forehead to his eyes. He carried a huge broadsword on his shoulder, and when he stopped beside the block, it took both hands to rest the cumbersome weapon on the floor.

A low growl arose from the throng at the sight of him. Voices murmured:

"The Executioner! God, when will they stop?"

The above scene, which began the June 1936 issue of *Opera-*

tor #5 magazine, was but the beginning of a group of thirteen apocalyptic novels known as the Purple Invasion series. By pulp magazine standards, the Purple Invasion was daringly innovative. In the past, other paper heroes had grappled with avaricious dictators but never with such horrendous consequences.

In a series of cataclysmic cliffhangers, the Purple Invasion chronicled an assault upon America by the hordes of dictator Rudolph I of Bulkaria, the Purple Emperor. The complete saga ran well over 750,000 words. Each novel detailed immense battles in America's second War of Independence. Numerous major characters were introduced, fought for several issues, then were disposed of summarily. At the end, America was left in ruins, with Canada and Mexico under the subjugation of vandal rule. Small wonder that the Purple Invasion has been called the War and Peace of the pulp magazines.

While *Operator #5* is best remembered for the Purple saga, in fact the magazine ran for some forty-eight issues from April 1934, with a novel called "The Masked Invasion," until December of 1939, with "The Army From Underground." It treated an isolationist United States to not one but scores of paranoid daymares without parallel in the history of literature.

Unlike his contemporaries, Doc Savage and The Shadow, Operator #5 is long forgotten, replaced in the hearts of readers by hordes of pallid, latter-day imitators. But back in the thrill-hungry thirties, his adventures were devoured by hundreds of thousands of youths and adults. To his fans he was a combination of James Bond, Tarzan, John Wayne, and Superman all rolled into one. Furthermore, in the early thirties the secret service agent was almost a fresh concept in genre fiction. There were a few well-known undercover sleuths, notably George Bronson-Howard's Norroy in *Norroy, Diplomatic Agent* (1907), *Slaves of the Lamp* (1917), and *The Black Book* (1920), Melville D. Post's *Walker of the Secret Service* (1924), and R.T.M. Scott's Aurelius Smith in *Secret Service Smith* (1923). But there was nothing like the deluge of secret agent novels engendered by today's political machinations.

Secret Service Operator #5 was James Christopher, a young man of incredible attributes. One is tempted to call Operator #5 the James Bond of the thirties but, compared to Jimmy Christopher, Bond is a piker, a Johnny-come-lately whose adventures pall into bland obsequies.

To be frank, Jimmy Christopher was a Superman.

Like most of the pulpwood heroes, Jimmy was a larger-than-life figure absolutely dedicated to the eradication of America's enemies. He bested Bond in almost every field save one—that of sexual gymnastics. While Jimmy Christopher had a girlfriend—Diane Elliot by name—there was little or no hanky panky between them. If there was some dalliance, it happened not between the sheets but simply between issues. The probability of Operator #5 even finding time for such shenanigans seems statistically unlikely. Instead, Jimmy's days and nights were taken up with the most incredible series of adventures ever to pour from the high-speed typewriter of a pulp thriller writer. The titles alone were enough to prickle hairs on a reader's scalp: "Invasion of the Crimson Death-Cult," "The Coming of the Mongol Hordes," "Corpse Cavalry of the Yellow Vulture."

Savage hordes from mythical lands like Balkaria, actual enemy powers like Germany and Japan, aliens from other worlds, and even creatures burrowing up from under the earth plunged America's Secret Service Ace into one overheated paranoid fantasy after another. As a surreal social mirror of the collective phobias of its time, the magazine remains unparalleled in the history of popular culture.

Even so, Operator #5's position in the pulp pantheon seems open to controversy. Some fans place him on the very top of the heap, up there with the Spider and Doc Savage. Others find his adventures to be naive and jingoistic, particularly when compared to the fashionably modern cynicism of today's post–cold war espionage thrillers. Clearly the stories belong to an earlier age, when such words as patriotism and sacrifice were not regarded as tools in the vocabulary of political fanatics. They were addressed to the youth of the thirties, young men as wholesome as apple pie and as American as Gary Cooper.

In an early novel, "Master of Broken Men," the Vice President of the United States is introduced to Operator #5. The description of Jimmy is typical:

> He was in his early twenties; his face was clean-cut and strong. His bright blue eyes flashed with the alertness of youth, his forehead was high, his chin firmly determined. He possessed a poise that added stature to his years and obviously he was American through and through.
>
> The young man removed from his pocket a flat silver case. His thumbnail pressed upon a corner of it, and a shining leaf of metal sprung up. The Vice President gazed curiously at the right hand of the young man as the case was proffered toward him.
>
> On the back of that hand shone a peculiar scar—a black and white marking shaped strangely like a spread-winged American

eagle. Its wings seemed to flex, as though straining to take flight, as the young man's fingers moved.

Inside the silver case reposed a credential. The Vice President's faded eyes brightened as he read:

THE WHITE HOUSE

Washington

To Whom It May Concern

The identity of the bearer of this letter must be kept absolutely confidential. He is Operator #5 of the United States Intelligence Service.

The signature affixed to the document was that of the President of the United States.

Quickly Operator #5, otherwise known as James Christopher snapped the case shut and returned it to his pocket. "I am at your service, sir," he said.

If the scene appears corny now, not to worry. Operator #5 was written in the grand manner of pulp tradition. The invention was unflagging, the action frenetic. Even today, the stories hold up remarkably well from the standpoint of pure, hell-raising thud and blunder.

The scene in which Jimmy is introduced to the Vice President occurs at the very beginning of "Master of Broken Men." It takes place in Washington at the annual ball of the Daughters of the American Revolution, a scene of pomp and splendor as the general staff and the highest heads of state regale themselves with music and laughter. Yet, within paragraphs of Jimmy's meeting with the Vice President, incredible horror explodes:

As if at a signal, the doors of the ballroom entrance swing open. Ten, twenty fearful apparitions appear.

They stride inside, naked bodies glistening, faces turning slowly right and left, their arms raised, hands gripping broad-bladed knives—a score of savage tribesmen—in the midst of the most fashionable event of the social season.

Behind them the doors stood open. Startled hundreds saw a path marked by violent death. Still bodies lay in the corridor. Others sprawled on the steps rising from the street. Each bore the fearful marks of blows struck by the bright-bladed knives in the hands of the intruders.

They had literally slashed their way into the hall and now, weapons held poised to hack again, they began a slow advance.

Operator #5 stood in a cleared space, alone. Darkness clouded his blue eyes as he watched the living menace spreading. Moving with queer, dancing steps, they formed a ragged circle, their grotesque faces outward. Two of them peered straight at Jimmy Christopher, brandishing their knives, their black eyes glinting like beads.

Operator #5's hand clicked loose the buckle of his belt. He whipped it away, and it sprang out straight. It was a narrow sheath of leather; he flicked it off the thin, bright blade of a rapier. It flexed in the light, slender, supple, a needlepointed line of steel.

This scene was typical of openers in the hero pulps. The writer usually set up a bizarre, arresting situation, embroiled the hero in immediate action and then kept the poor devil riding a rollercoaster plot for some eighty or ninety relentless pages. There was no time-out for commercials and little time for the reader to catch his breath. It was storytelling in the grand manner—larger than life, chock full of audacious, delicious hokum.

To cope with assorted fiends and monsters, Jimmy's belt rapier was but one of the weapons he carried in his wardrobe arsenal. Others included his famous death's-head ring which bore the numeral five and contained a powerful explosion in the hollow top. There was a small gold ornament, a reproduction of a skull with ruby eyes, which Jimmy usually had clipped to his watch chain; inside the skull there was a silver ball containing diphenylchlorarsine, a death-dealing liquid that would change into gas upon contact with air. Jimmy was strong on belts. In addition to the belt rapier, he sometimes wore a three-strand leather job, the strands of which could be unloosed and opened into one continuous length of leather rope some nine feet long.

The Secret Service Ace needed these and all the other weapons he could muster to combat such scourges as "The Melting Death," "The Red Invaders," and "The War Dogs of the Green Destroyer." As in all the hero pulp magazines, the contents page for each issue gave a fair sampling of what the hero had in store for him. In "Attack of the Blizzard Men" the synopsis read:

> *It was a sultry day in August when the ghastly cold first came. Snow began to fall; ice formed, and in a brief hour, New York City was paralyzed. A new and deadly weapon had been directed at America by a ruthless, international syndicate, for, under the cover of the sub-zero weather, barbarous, armored warriors swarmed into the United States, turning our country into a helpless colony to be exploited savagely. In quick succession, other*

cities—Washington, Los Angeles, Chicago, New Orleans—fell before the assault of the astute enemy and the marrow-chilling cold. Could Operator #5 of the disabled Secret Service—Jimmy Christopher to his friends—save our land from shameful slavery?

Well, you had to pay your ten cents to find out. Certainly, with monthly problems like that a fellow needed all the friends he could get. Jimmy was blessed with several close aides; foremost among them was Diane Elliot (spelled Elliott in later stories). Diane was a special writer for the Amalgamated Press news service but became a full-fledged intelligence agent during the Purple Invasion crisis.

As Jimmy's girl, Diane led a life of harrowing adventures. Many of the *Operator #5* cover paintings bear likenesses of Diane: strapped to the muzzle of a cannon; about to be hurled from a giant catapult; facing firing squads; tied to dynamite kegs; and once—shades of silent movie heroine Pearl White—bound to railroad tracks, the thundering locomotive mere yards away.

Young Tim Donovan was Operator #5's unofficial assistant. They had met one drenching night on the lower East Side when Tim, a bootblack huddling in a dark doorway, had saved Operator #5 from death by a bullet from a criminal's gun. Jimmy had virtually adopted the plucky youngster, accepting him into his family circle and into his numerous adventures. Young Tim appeared in each of the Operator #5 novels, the only sustaining character to do so. He was even allowed to mature during the series and eventually entered the intelligence service himself.

A leading character in the series was the man who was

commander-in-chief of the United States Intelligence Service, a man known even to his most trusted agents only as Z-7. Dressed entirely in gray, with black hair and black, glittering eyes, he is described as an older man of stocky build and grim visage. There is a bond of affection between Z-7 and Operator #5, a bond which is sorely tested in the novels. Later in the series, Jimmy replaces Z-7 as head of intelligence.

Another character who figured in many of the stories was the President of the United States. Although never mentioned by name, there are reasons to assume that he was intended to be Franklin D. Roosevelt. The identification with FDR becomes strange indeed when, in the August 1936 issue, the chief executive places a gun to his temple and pulls the trigger rather than agree to an ultimatum from the Purple Emperor. This was just one of the reasons why the Operator #5 novels must be regarded as science fiction. They were set in a curious parallel world—a world sharing a common history with our own yet diverging at right angles somewhere in the thirties.

Jimmy's twin sister, Nan, was an important figure in the novels as was his father, ex-Secret Service Operator Q-6. Despite a bullet lodged near his heart that constantly threatened his life, John Christopher managed to assist his son on several cases.

The elder Christopher was, in fact, one of the most durable invalids in fiction. In the first Purple Empire story, "Death's Ragged Army," he is one of the initial victims of the emperor's deadly green gas. Later, in "The Suicide Battalion," Jimmy discovers his father alive, dressed as an old, bearded peasant in an Alpine inn. After being discovered by his son, Q-6 explains that he had been captured, kept as a slave behind enemy lines, and finally brought to Europe. It is one of the most miraculous recoveries in the history of the pulps, particularly for a man who has been dead for some fifteen novels.

Later, in the penultimate Operator #5 adventure, the old man is again laid low—along with the new President, the cabinet and the congress—when the Japanese drop an atom bomb on Washington. But in the very next issue he is alive and hale enough to lead a mass counter migration from west to east through hordes of Oriental forces. Obviously, Jimmy's own invulnerability was hereditary in nature.

As America's Secret Service Ace, Jimmy himself played many parts. Among the aliases he often assumed were Huntley Walsh, Morton Clagg, George Wakley, Anthony Andrews, and particularly Carleton Victor, noted portrait photographer. It was in his guise as Carleton Victor that Operator #5 employed a manservant by the name of Crowe. The estimable Crowe, gentleman's gentleman extraordinaire, did not dream that Carleton Victor, photo-portraitist of worldwide reputation, was a convenient cover for Jimmy Christopher. Like the famous personages who considered it a privilege to sit before Victor's camera, the manservant considered his master a great artist.

The sharp-nosed, stiff-shouldered Crowe was, in fact, one of the few "in" jokes in pulp-hero history; his colossal cool was a running gag that consciously or unconsciously satirized the sensational nature of the pulp series. Though Crowe was sometimes baffled by his master's eccentricities, he permitted himself no curiosity whatsoever. The four walls of Victor's penthouse were the boundaries of Crowe's entire world. Outside, the nation reeled; havoc and ruin stalked the streets;

dead men marched; Mongol hordes raided; America's proudest cities were reduced to ashes or frozen with giant neutron projectors. But Crowe was oblivious to it all. He was the one "normal" person in a universe overtaken by madness.

Crowe was dropped from later issues, as were other characters and shticks from the early numbers. In fact, unlike most other hero pulp novels, the Operator #5 books can be divided into two distinct series. The first, running for some twenty issues, was in the mold of prevailing bizarre fantasy pulps. The second, beginning in early 1936, concentrated more heavily on militaristic exploits. Even the style of writing changed at this point, leaving even a casual reader to conclude that there were at least two writers—perhaps more—who worked under the resounding pen name of Curtis Steele.

The first of these men was the late Frederick C. Davis, author of the famous Moon Man series in *Ten Detective Aces*. To help pay his way through college in the twenties Davis wrote and sold a story a week to the then-burgeoning pulps. By the thirties he had developed a daily regimen of writing from nine o'clock in the morning to four in the afternoon, six days a week. His daily output was thirty completed double-spaced pages, or 125,000 words a month. He wrote over a million words a year for nearly a decade before World War II.

It was Davis who originated the Operator #5 series and developed most of the characters and situations. I asked Mr. Davis (in a letter dated December 1972) why he abandoned his famous character after some twenty novels. He replied:

> *There were several reasons. One, suitable ideas were becoming increasingly hard to dream up. Two, I was sadly under-*

paid—$500 per story, about half my word rate with other pulp publishers and with other magazines of the same publisher. Three, I was feeling the strain of my heavy workload. While writing Operator #5 I was also turning out more than an equal number of words for other markets—among those, the long-running Moon Man series, a novelette every month.

I never read any of the Operator #5 stories after I stopped writing them, which accounts for my ignorance of the Purple Invasion. (I never read any of the Doc Savage or Shadow stories either.) I had had a surfeit of him and I was busily putting my nonworking time into the pleasure of dating a lovely girl whom I later married and who still later presented me with a son whose name is neither Jimmy nor Christopher.

Following Davis' exit, the series was taken over by Emile C. Tepperman, that prolific pulpster who was to perform similar duties for the Spider and The Avenger, in addition to continuing work on numerous series characters of his own invention.

Tepperman was the sole author of the epic Purple Invasion stories. It would take an article in itself to synopsize the events of that momentous conflict. Even the highlights can only be skimmed: the conquests of the Purple Emperor over Europe and most of Asia; his invasion of America and the establishment of his headquarters amid the ruins of New York City; the deadly green gas; Diane's rescue as she is about to be hung from the Liberty Bell on the fourth of July; the attack on the gold train; the battle against the Purple Naval Fleet; Operator #5's destruction of the Panama Canal; the cholera bacteria loosed on Utah and Washington; the suicide march into Phoenix; the bombardment of San Francisco; the suicide charge of the Canadian Lancers (sic); the destruction of the Maximilian Dam and the Pittsburgh steel mills; Jimmy's destruction of the giant blimp; the capture of Chicago by Mongol troops; the Emperor's pact with the Yellow Warlord; Operator #5's battle to the death with Urslup; the second battle of Valley Forge; the siege that brought the Black Plague; and, finally, the fall of the Purple Empire and the rebuilding of America.

A common ruse used throughout the Operator #5 stories was the attempt to lend verisimilitude with the use of footnotes. Some of these footnotes make for fascinating reading, particularly in the early stories of Fred Davis, when they consist of actual news items from journals of the era. The footnotes alone constitute a popular history of the political machinations of the thirties. Later, in Tepperman's Purple Invasion series the footnotes become part of the fiction; references are made to such pseudo-historical documents as "Harrison Stiever's Monumental History of the Purple Wars."

The editorial opinions in the magazine were no less fascinating, both in the unsigned editorial columns and in a monthly feature titled, The Secret Sentinel. In the June 1936 issue, The Secret Sentinel column ruminated:

> *In spite of the fact that Italy is the only great nation today with an army of veterans, Mussolini did not, and does not want, and cannot afford war.*
>
> *Another dictator also attempted a bluff. Nazi Germany is today developed along military lines to a point where some observers claim she is far more powerful than the empire of the Kaisers.*
>
> *Yet, ringed around as she is by hostile neighbors she cannot risk war. But the successful bluff of Benito Mussolini encouraged the*

unimaginative mind of the Nazi leader to try the same thing. He moved his troops into the Rhineland and barked at his neighbors.

But Hitler has not the personality of Mussolini. And he has done nothing to stimulate love or admiration. And he has no imagination. He did not understand that by his unconsidered move he was only playing into the hands of Mussolini.

So much for political acuity.

The *Operator #5* magazine was another offspring of Henry Steeger's Popular Publications, a giant of the pulp adventure field. The editor was Rogers Terrill, who served on the equally crazed Spider magazine. Jerome Rozen (of Shadow fame) painted the cover for the first issue but most other covers—and there were some beauties—were executed by John Howitt. Amos Sewell and Rudolph Belarski were responsible for interior illustrations in the first issue. John Fleming Gould, the "inside man" responsible for vivid delineations of the Spider and G-8, carried on beginning with issue two and running through until December of 1936. Ralph Carson illustrated the remaining issues, excepting that of January 1938 when Harry Fisk helped.

The magazine ran monthly from April 1934 through April 1936, when it became bi-monthly. At the end of 1936, it resumed monthly publication but quickly dropped back to bimonthly, reflecting an obvious weakness in sales.

By the time Jimmy mopped up the remnants of the Purple Invaders, the year was 1938. Earlier villains had masqueraded under Graustarkian labels, but in the battles still to be waged there was little need for euphemistic nationalities. The enemies were clearly named: Germany, Japan, Italy.

It was at this point that a third and final writer, Wayne Rogers, took over the series, still writing under the familiar Curtis Steele byline. In Rogers' "The Suicide Battalion," the three bandit nations stage an assault from "friendly but helpless Canada," a country now prostrate under tyrant rule. Only the Ferrara Line—a long string of entrenchments which stretch from the Great Lakes to Vancouver—stand between the U.S. and total annihilation.

Jimmy organizes a band of 200 suicidally loyal volunteers. Together they wage an underground war that takes them to the German dictator's own headquarters.

"Now it is our day," the dictator gloats to a captured Operator #5. "The day of the deprived nations who were forgotten when their greedy neighbors carved out colonial empires for themselves. Now it is our turn to take colonies—west of the Mississippi has been allotted to Japan, east of the Mississippi and below the Great Lakes to Italy, and Canada will be the German portion. Colonies worth having, those will be."

As usual, Jimmy faces numerous personal Gethsemanes, but in the final minutes he turns the enemies against one another, makes peace with the Italians and pursues the fleeing Germans into Canada.

Just one month later, though, in "The Day of the Damned," Mexico proves an adequate base for invasion by heavily armored Japanese forces.

"In the hot hills of Old Mexico," the synopsis reads, "Operator #5 launched his great counter-espionage campaign against a

plotting Asiatic horde which threatened to loose the entire barbarous Mexican guerilla Southwest upon America, in an attack that also combined modern Japanese mechanized warfare and dread tropical disease. Then, in the final, decisive minutes, America seemed to turn back the very pages of history as she made her last stand for freedom at the Alamo!"

And so it went. Month after month, a nervous nation was subjected to one bizarre onslaught after another. In one episode, "Invasion from the Sky," the enemy appeared to be chimeras from some other world, landing amid cities in immense spaceships—a yarn undoubtedly inspired by Orson Welles' Martian panic broadcast.

Fantastic weaponry abounded in the stories, some of it predating actual World War II devices. The most advanced terror tools were employed by a foe known as The Yellow Vulture—Japanese warlord Moto Taronago. The Yellow Vulture stories were among the most imaginative of Jimmy's adventures. The series might have eclipsed the Purple Invasion saga had it not ended abruptly after only four episodes due to the demise of the magazine itself.

The final story, "The Army from Underground" (November 1939), contained an especially prophetic scene—a description of the effects of the first atom bomb dropped on a civilian population—with victors and victims eerily transposed:

Soon they reached the edge of the recognizable ruins and were picking their way through a desolation that resembled the debris-littered trail of a devastating tornado. Wreckage encompassed them on every side. Tall buildings had been flattened, stout steel girders twisted and snapped, concrete shattered and crumbled.

Streets had ceased to exist, except as barely distinguishable canyons through the mounds of litter. And nowhere was there a living human being... only mangled, half-burned corpses to indicate that this stricken wilderness had once been a great city.

For more than a mile they trudged through that ghastly shamble, into a district where the leveled buildings were not so completely obliterated, where the streets were less choked with wreckage—and where the tortured moans of imprisoned sufferers came to them from out of the darkness. Here they encountered the first survivors—a hastily organized patrol seeking trapped victims.

"Everything is destroyed," one dazed worker told them as he tore away tumbled wreckage to reach a screaming woman pinned beneath the debris. "Philadelphia is wiped out... everything but the suburbs. It's all gone—disappeared. Houses, cellars, bombproof shelters—all blown to nothing."

His incredible words were all too true. Operator #5 found them corroborated even before the grey light of dawn revealed the tremendous crater that was the huge empty grave of the Quaker City.

Philadelphia had been utterly obliterated, wiped from the face of the earth—with a loss of life that probably would reach a million!

"They never had a chance," he said bitterly as he stared out over that terrible waste. "This is the ghastliest mass murder the world has ever seen—the most heinous crime ever committed against an innocent and defenseless people!"

In almost every story, Jimmy's beloved nation suffered a purgatory of conflict and defeat. Victory came only when all seemed darkest. But even victory was often Pyrrhic. At the end of "The Army from Underground," with Philadelphia, Washington, Knoxville, and Baltimore demolished, with giant slaughter machines burrowing out of the ground and carving bloody furrows through the countryside, Jimmy receives further news:

> *"There is no more Canada," Quillen's whisper cut like a cold wind. "The Japanese have wiped it out... destroyed the remaining cities... annihilated the population. The Dominion is a great wilderness... and the Japanese are using it at this very minute as a base from which to sweep down into New England... coming down to destroy arms... ammunitions..."*
>
> *His dying voice faded, was gone.*
>
> *In that moment Operator #5's triumph turned to bitterness. He had won back territory and snatched a great population out of the hands of the Japanese, yet certain destruction and merciless annihilation now faced them all... Instead of into safety, he had led the millions of Pacific coast emigrees into a death trap worse than the one from which they had fled... A death trap out of which he somehow must deliver them and build again a new and great America!*

That November 1939 issue was destined to become the biggest cliff-hanger of them all. Another novel, "Hell's Last Battalion," was announced but never saw publication. Jimmy Christopher's battles were over.

America's real war was soon to begin.

TWENTY YEARS OF MURDER

1933. IT WAS a dynamic year not only for Depression-weary America, but for America's favorite form of lowbrow entertainment, the pulp fiction magazine.

In March, Franklin Delano Roosevelt became the thirty-second President of the United States and soon instituted his famous "fireside chats." As if to celebrate the New Deal, new pulps sprang up like public works programs: *Magic Carpet, Nick Carter, Black Book Detective, Ten Detective Aces, The Lone Eagle,* and dozens more.

Nor was FDR alone among superheroes that propitious year. Four of the most durable of all pulp characters were introduced: the Spider, G-8, Doc Savage, and the Phantom Detective.

Of all the major pulp heroes, the Phantom best reflected the thirties passion for yet another form of escapist literature: the classic detective story.

In hard covers, such sophisticated sleuths as Lord Peter Wimsey, Ellery Queen, Hercule Poirot and Philo Vance sold books by the millions. It was this type of detective novel—the story of ratiocination—which attracted the attention of most critics and literary pundits of the era. But, in America in the thirties, for every reader of S.S. Van Dine there were dozens of readers of *Dime Detective* and *Black Mask* magazines. The pulps alone had introduced a new kind of detective who was in some ways a city version of the Wild West hero. Unlike the police, the hard-boiled detective was bound by no rules other than his own. He was armed and dangerous, and he walked down mean streets simmering with the potential for ready violence.

If the Phantom (he was not called the Phantom Detective in the novels—that was the magazine title) deserves any place in the history of mystery fiction it is because he was a calculated attempt to blend the indestructible action detective of the pulps with the cerebral problem solver of the Sherlock Holmes school. It was not always a comfortable amalgam, but the attempt paid off handsomely in two decades of successful publication.

In all those twenty years, the Phantom had but one policy from which he never deviated. He would not take on a case unless he felt that it had elements unusual enough or sinister enough to warrant his efforts. But when such a case did present itself (usually about once a month), he struck like a hawk in the dark underworld of crime.

According to the magazine's own carefully concocted legend, the Phantom was Richard Curtis Van Loan, one of the wealthiest playboys in the country, a man who was believed to live only for the pleasure he could get from life. As the Phantom, Van Loan was called into action by a crimson light blinking on the apex of the towering *Clarion* building.

The Phantom was the only pulp hero to be sponsored by a newspaper—or to be more precise, by a newspaper publisher, kindly old Frank Havens of the *Clarion*. An early issue of the magazine explained their relationship:

> *Young Van Loan's father had been a lifelong friend of Havens, and it was after the elder Van Loan's death that Frank Havens*

had been responsible for the existence of the Phantom. The idea had first been born when Havens had suggested that Dick Van Loan, bored with life and restless, try his hand at solving a mysterious crime which had stumped the police of the nation. And so successful had he been that the young heir to the tremendous Van Loan fortune had gone on and on perfecting himself in that which had become his lifework until now the name of the Phantom led all the rest in the annals of crime detection, a name known and admired by the police of every nation.

One of the unusual aspects of the playboy's secret war on crime is that it was conducted in a dispassionate style. Van Loan did not fight crime out of some personal rage. He fought it because it was wrong and because crime fighting was an anodyne to boredom.

The Phantom had no supernormal powers but, like most of the great pulp heroes, possessed an awesome range of abilities. Wide-shouldered and powerful, Van Loan could stay on his feet for ninety-six hours at a stretch. He was adept at nearly all sports, an expert with the fencing foils, at jujitsu, la savate, and his marksmanship with guns of all kinds was uncanny. In addition, he was a skilled pilot, a master of ventriloquism and hypnotism, and could speak a dozen languages fluently.

If there was one thing Dick excelled at, however, it was the art of disguise. Van was the finest make-up man outside of the Actor's Union. He had to be, because death was the certain penalty for a single botched job.

While the sleuth of a thousand faces often wore a small, black cloth mask (as depicted in Rudolph Belarski's cover paintings), mostly he preferred to adopt the guise of another living being.

Like a shadow passing the sun, a layer of skin cream would blot out his own familiar features and then, with the aid of crayons and shadow pencils, he could assume any other identity. He always carried a compact portable make-up kit on him, and another more elaborate one in his special souped-up car.

Headquarters for the Phantom was Van Loan's own Park Avenue penthouse apartment. It was serviced by a private elevator and was curiously devoid of servants or valets out of respect for the Phantom's lone wolf lifestyle.

Within the hushed luxury of his apartment, Van needed only to press a button concealed on the back of his Louis Quinze bed, and a section of the wall would unfold to reveal his inner work room. Here the Phantom kept a small but complete scientific laboratory, a wardrobe containing some of his various disguises, a make-up table, and a staggering arsenal that included small pistols tiny enough to fit into the palm of the hand, large-bore Lugers, Colt Peacemakers, derringers, nickel-plated S&W's, and blue-steel automatics with easy-action triggers made especially to the Phantom's order.

An even more impressive lab and armory were set up in an old warehouse along the waterfront. All that the people in the neighborhood knew about the building was that it belonged to a Dr. Paul Bendix, a bearded, querulous old scientist who had the reputation of being a recluse. Only newspaper man Frank Havens was aware that Dr. Bendix was but one more version of his friend the Phantom.

The Phantom Detective magazine was the property of a publisher named Ned L. Pines. Fresh out of college, Pines entered the pulp publishing field in 1931. Throughout the years, his firm remained one of the big three of the pulp world (trailing only Popular Publications and Street & Smith). For some reason Pines' company was variously identified as Standard Magazines, Beacon Magazines, and Better Publications, although they were known in the trade as "The Thrilling Group"—partly because of a logo running on the covers and partly because of editor Leo Margulies' penchant for magazine titles with the world "thrilling" prominently displayed: *Thrilling Mystery, Thrilling Adventures, Thrilling Wonder Stories, Thrilling Ranch Stories,* etc.

One reason the Thrilling magazines have often been underrated by pulp fans and collectors is that they were less flamboyant than many of their rivals. But if the Phantom lacked the pure sensationalism of Operator #5 or the bizarre melodrama of the Spider, you couldn't tell it by titles dreamed up for his stories: "The Corpse Parade," "Master of the World," "Cities for Ransom," "The Talking Dead," "The Criminal Caesar," and so on.

The covers portray casual homicide, either real or threatened; above it, the masked face of the Phantom looms symbolically like—well, like a phantom.

Inside, the slaughter continues. A man is turned into a human torch by a booby-trapped cigar. Wealthy men are found chained to moving vehicles—each with one arm missing. Kidnapped victims cry out from buried coffins. Bodies plummet from an empty sky. Rampaging lions turn Manhattan into a concrete jungle.

They called them the "bloody pulps," and not without reason. There were 170 issues of *The Phantom Detective* magazine, thousands of pages. And throughout them all the action is violent, unremitting. The need for pace dictates the narrative;

whenever the plot flags, another body bites the dust—or plummets from a seemingly innocent sky.

It is all hackwork, of course, but hackwork developed to an art by old pros who constantly demonstrate their instinctive timing and their well-developed flair for the preposterous and the melodramatic. The world of the Phantom is that heightened universe of the pulp hero where violent physical action is the dominating law of man and nature.

Despite the Phantom's claim to be the "World's Greatest Detective," his is a milieu alien to such cerebral detectives as Sherlock Holmes or Philo Vance. Holmes proved that thought is action; he did not need to leave his flat to solve a case. Indeed, Holmes' closest American counterpart, Nero Wolfe, makes a point of seldom venturing forth from his old brownstone on West Thirty-fifth Street. The Phantom Detective stories were written for a hero-oriented audience. Phantom readers did not demand that they be given a chance to solve a detective riddle on their own; instead, they were content to enjoy the Phantom overcoming an intellectual problem—just as they were content to watch their indestructible hero overcome such physical obstacles as getting knifed or being tossed off a cliff.

To be sure, there was always the obligatory denouement scene in which the Phantom strutted his mental stuff before a room full of red herrings—at least one of whom would be unmasked as the villain of the piece. These scenes were in the tradition of the classic mystery and sometimes ran for three or more pages. Perhaps this is why the Phantom's publishers saw fit to call him the "World's Greatest Detective," and who was there to argue?

But, for a mental marvel, Van spent a lot of his time getting out of physical scrapes. In fact, if anything distinguished the Phantom plots, it was the number of capture and escape scenes featured. Many of the escapes were reminiscent of cliff-hanger endings in the then-popular Saturday afternoon movie serials. Even the chapter headings, "Tommy-Gun Rampage," "Pawn of Death," "The Well of Murder," suggested greater fealty to chapter plays than to the intellectual puzzler.

The Phantom would have made a good movie-serial character, but no one seems to have thought of it. Curiously, he elicited very little interest outside of the pulps. His publishing company did own its own chain of comic books, and for a few years his adventures appeared in strip form in Thrilling Comics. But in the comics, he was a mere back-of-the-book figure—a masked dandy in top hat and tux—who held limited appeal for young fans of Captain America and Superman.

Until recently no one seemed certain just how the Phantom came to be created or who dreamed him up. Years earlier, a writer named Herman Landon had written some books featuring a character called the Gray Phantom, also a disguise whiz. It's unlikely that the Gray Phantom was the Phantom Detective's literary ancestor, though, because the character was rather uninspiring except to lovers of oddball names (his civilian sobriquet was Cuthbert Vanardy).

The real inspiration for the Phantom was undoubtedly the same as that of the Spider. They were both calculated to cash in on the great success of Street & Smith's *Shadow* magazine. Not only did the Phantom cognomen sound as mysterious as that of The Shadow, even the author's name rang bells. Robert Wallace was a fictitious byline chosen by editor Leo Margulies because he felt unsophisticated readers might link it to Edgar

Wallace, a popular writer of the day whose name symbolized mystery and detection.

The truth was that G. Wayman Jones (supposed author of the first eleven titles) and Robert Wallace (credited with the balance) were not the exclusive pseudonyms of any one individual. They were so-called house names that cloaked the work of a stable of writers operating under first the Jones and then the Wallace identity.

Editorial director Leo Margulies claimed that he and a writer named D'Arcy Lyndon Champion created the Phantom Detective in 1932. Certainly, many of the early Phantoms appear to have been the work of Champion, who also wrote under the name Jack D'Arcy. (As D.L. Champion, he was one of the mainstays of *Black Mask* in the forties.)

The problem with Champion was that while he was a fine writer and a witty fellow, he had a reputation for giving editors angina attacks concerning deadlines—a cardinal sin in the hero pulp game. Other writers were called in to keep the Phantom on course. Chief among these was the dependable, awesomely prolific Norman A. Daniels.

According to his own records, Daniels began writing the Phantom with novel #20, "Merchant of Murder" (October 1934). For another two years, he wrote better than half of the monthly novels, contributing some thirty-six Phantoms in all, including the final one, "Murder's Agent," published in summer of 1953.

Of his part in guiding the Phantom, Daniels confided to this writer:

> *It might be interesting to you if I tell you that the publisher*

Frank Havens really had a live counterpart. His name was Marcus Goldsmith. He had some kind of financial interest in Ned Pines' outfit, though I believe that it was only in regard to the Phantom. I also believe that he thought of himself as Frank Havens. In his opinion, the Phantom was the best crime magazine in existence. Mr. Goldsmith was extremely wealthy and one of the finest gentlemen I ever had the privilege of knowing.

He discussed each synopsis with me in detail, sometimes in his Manhattan apartment, a luxury residence if I ever saw one. We got along fine. Other writers who worked with him, hated him. He would nitpick and was not easy to please. However, he certainly enjoyed his role in the Phantom and he could dream up some mighty hard revisions which I learned how to simplify.

He would invariably pick a section in the middle of the book which he didn't like and give me his idea of how it should be done. So I used to write the book in its entirety, just as I felt it should be, give him the manuscript with an inserted middle part weak and absurd.

He would pick that part to pieces and instruct me how to improve it. I'd simply remove the inserted part, replace the pages already written. He was always completely satisfied. How the other writers handled him, I don't know, but I assume they met with the same reception I did.

Unlike such rivals as the Spider, and Operator #5—whose adventures were controlled by one or two writers with a little help from their friends—the Phantom was a wide-open market for freelancers. Ghosting the Phantom was practically a cottage industry. The roll call of ghosts included Laurence Donovan, W.T. Ballard, George A. MacDonald, Edwin Burkholder, C.S.

Montayne, Stewart Sterling, Whit Ellsworth, Charles Green, Ryerson Johnson, and even science fiction specialists Henry Kuttner and Ray Cummings. It became a standing joke that every writer had polished off at least one Phantom.

Pulp hero books like *The Phantom Detective* were frankly mass-production goods written to formulas as rigid as gun metal. To the average reader, there was little to separate one author's contribution from another, although a single writer would occasionally recycle identifying phrases and descriptions. Thus, in a 1938 adventure, "Yellow Shadows of Death," one writer wrote "The little Chinese, a crimson devil's stitch across his chest, was hurled a dozen feet by the terrific impact of that spray of lead." A full five years later in "Murder Money," he wrote "He had practically been decapitated by bullets, and there was also a crimson devil's stitch of machine-gun lead across his chest."

Despite multiple authorship, the Phantom Detective format was reasonably consistent over the years. Such recurring characters as Frank Havens, Muriel Havens, Steve Huston, Inspector Gregg, and others, remained inflexible personalities because each writer drew them from the same template.

Frank Havens' petite daughter, Muriel, supplied romantic interest in the stories. Unfortunately for her, the Phantom's true mistress was Adventure.

Pity poor Muriel on a date with her amorphous boyfriend. As recorded in a scene from "City of Dreadful Night," she had to keep her eyes open just to recognize him—and, once spotted, her lover was less than solicitous.

> *Muriel leaned back and watched the entrance to this smart*

restaurant. Through that door would come a man who was an utter stranger to her. She had no idea what he would look like. He might be stocky and give the illusion that he wasn't very tall, or he might be lanky and rangy. He might look like a prosperous professional man, a down-in-the-mouth failure, an indolent cafe-hopping playboy, or a shifty-eyed gangster. She wouldn't know it was the Phantom until he sat down beside her and smiled, and she looked into his eyes.

She hardly noticed an ordinary-looking man who did enter unobtrusively. It would have been difficult for anyone to tell whether or not he belonged to this place, though he had a certain assurance about him. He stopped for a moment on the low balcony at the entrance, and his eyes quickly scanned the room and everyone in it.

Then he made his way down the steps to the main floor, between tables, and came straight to Muriel's booth. His right hand slowly moved up as if to massage his jaw. Instead, he gently tugged at his left ear lobe, and that was the signal by which Muriel knew him.

"Phantom!" she said softly. "It's so nice to work with you again."

He grinned at her as he sat down. "You might not think it's so nice by the time this is finished, Muriel. We're bucking a tough proposition. Let's order first, then I'll brief you on all the details!"

So much for romance.

Not even Muriel was cognizant of the Phantom's identity, at least not until one of the last adventures, "The Silent Killer," from winter 1952.

Another of the regulars in the Phantom saga was Steve Huston, one of the *Clarion's* star reporters. Steve was a brisk, redhaired, freckled-faced young fellow for whom publisher

> # DEATH BELLS RING OUT ON NEW YEAR'S EVE
>
> *in*
>
> ## THE BROADWAY MURDERS
>
> *A Long Complete Novel of Manhattan Mystery*
>
> ### By ROBERT WALLACE
>
> Featuring THE PHANTOM in Rapid-Fire Action
> In Next Month's Issue of THE PHANTOM DETECTIVE

Frank Havens had an almost parental affection. Steve was of inestimable help to Van on any number of cases and, in the adventure "Stones of Satan," revealed his intense admiration for the Phantom when he blurted to a disguised Van, "As often as I've worked with you, I can't get over the thrill I always feel when meeting you. I'd rather be on a case with you than own the *Clarion!*"

In that same adventure, the Man of a Thousand Faces repaid the compliment by disguising himself as Steve. It was a scene typical of the way in which pulp writers tried to suggest the Phantom's magical way with make-up.

> *His first step was to remove his current disguise—the swarthy complexion, the pellets which flattened his nose, the hard rubber gadget over his lower gum which lent a pugnacious cast to his*

under-jaw, the thick shading of the eyebrows. Richard Van Loan's handsome face was now reflected in the mirror.

And then, magically, that face again began to change. Something which looked like powdered rust, diluted with a tablespoon of water and rubbed into his hair, in a matter of seconds made a redhead out of Van. He used some of it on his eyebrows, too, and combed his hair the way Huston did. An orange paste from a tiny jar gave his face Huston's pinkish complexion. And a fine-pointed brush, dipped into a vial containing some fluid, dotted heavy, brownish freckles over his nose and cheekbone.

Next out of the make-up kit came a pair of what looked like tiny clamps. They were rubber-tipped and cleverly made to lock at any angle. He adjusted them to a certain width and thrust them into his nostrils. They were invisible, and what a moment ago had been a straight nose now was the exact replica of Huston's. The final move was to wedge a little rubber gadget under his upper lip to give it a protruding effect.

There were other recurring minor characters. A streetwise boy named Chip Dorlan was allowed to mature in the series, eventually entering military service. Most of the other characters remained static. There was a Police Inspector Iverness in the early stories, replaced by Captain Brady by 1936, and eventually by Inspector Gregg, who remained a fixture until the end. Inspector Gregg was typically Headquarters from the brim of his felt hat down to his square-toed brogans. When it came to the Phantom, however, Gregg displayed open cooperation.

The World's Greatest Detective was unique among masked avengers in that he operated with the full sanction of the law.

The Spider, the Whisperer, and dozens of other pulp vigilantes were condemned murderers wanted as much by the police as by the Underworld; in their pragmatic and possibly psychotic minds what worked was not Law but Justice.

The Phantom was a teacher's pet by contrast. He had only to display his secret emblem—a tiny, jewel-studded platinum domino mask—and the minions of the law fell over themselves in open relief. They knew, as did every one else, that the publisher of the *Clarion* was the Phantom's only contact, and when things got tough, they hoped that Havens would send along a call for their mysterious ally.

Like The Shadow, the Spider and even Doc Savage, the Phantom's home base was Manhattan. The Big Four of the Big Apple may have met at some time—perhaps in Lamont Cranston's elegant Cobalt Club—but if they did there was no record taken. Most of them worked for rival publishers who probably weren't too eager to publicize the event.

Also, each hero's Manhattan was a uniquely different city. The Doc Savage novels record it as a bustling, sun-washed Art Deco Shangri-La, home of the world's tallest building where Doc moors his dirigible and maintains his fabulous scientific headquarters.

The Spider's turf is a city under siege, a nightmarish metropolis of yawning chasms filled with the crackle of flames and the screams of dying citizens. It is a vibrant, bleeding set piece for unlimited science-fictional terrors.

The Shadow's urban world is a surrealistic night town reminiscent of the Expressionist German cinema of Fritz Lang.

The Phantom, fittingly, operated in a rather characterless Manhattan—a city interchangeable with most others, in the way that the Phantom himself was the interchangeable avenger-hero: a black mask, a top hat, a disguise kit for all emergencies.

Sometimes his writers rose to the occasion, as in "The Broadway Murders," in which the opening paragraphs shrilled:

> *A million lights! Broadway! The heart of Manhattan!*
> *New Year's Eve! Ear-splitting sound and fury! The old year marching out to a cacophony of blaring horns, racketing noisemakers, and the screeching, roaring joyousness of thousands of throats. Throats of thousands given to unfettered merriment and mirth as they voiced humanity's ever-reborn hope for the new year, due to arrive in four short hours. Thousands who surged and swirled in the aimless, purposeless tide of packed bodies flooding the width of Broadway in the space above the gray, old wedge of the Times Building, with its flashing, brilliant band of ceaselessly moving words in new parade.*
> *Words conveying the news of the world to those who paused long enough in the mad carnival to lift their eyes. Ever-moving words of silver light that could exhilarate or play upon the fear-chilled sense of throngs avid for sensation, or quick to sense through the glittering words the pulse of a moving world.*

With all those exclamation points and hyped-up description, you might know that something unusual was going to happen.

Within moments the sensation-seeking crowd is treated to spectacle beyond expectation: the burning of two living men before their eyes—two fiery bodies hanging from a Broadway sign. A pretty girl cries out and falls to her knees. The body of one of the burning figures strikes her in its plunge. Minutes later, three charred corpses are ghastly heaps under the still moving, still brilliant sign of the Sunny Seas Cruise Line.

Welcome to the Phantom's Manhattan. There isn't a mugger in sight.

Many of the magazine's openings were real grabbers. Pulp scribes called it the narrative hook—that first scene, paragraph or even sentence which hooked the newsstand browser into a commitment involving his hard-earned dime:

> *Hundreds saw the death plane before it dived.*
> *—The Curio Murders*

> *Nothing about the quiet residential street on the outskirts of Fairmount indicated that death lingered there. Yet murder waited on that summer day.*
> *—Murder Under the Big Top*

> *Night, black and rain-swept, shrouded the Kirty Institute for the insane. Gusts of howling wind attacked the ugly gray buildings like seas pounding some bleak, rocky coast. There was the same impression of desolation, of a savagely forbidding place that humans shunned.*
>
> *A small car lurched to a stop in front of the guardhouse at the gate. Two men got out, collars upturned, hats pulled low. They dodged toward the booth—and paused involuntarily, lingering despite the drenching rain. There was a brief lull in the wind, and from within the buildings somewhere, they heard a voice lift in song.*
> *—The Melody Murders*

> *It was a huge house, a venerable house. And it was articulate with the eerie creaking voice that comes with architectural age. It spoke now, and the single man who heard was pale with terror. Ghosts trod the carpeted stairway. The weird, crackling sounds peculiar to old wood, old brick, old mortar sighed audibly through the emptiness.*
>
> *Roger Arkwright paced the study and listened. He was alone.*
>
> *He was the only living thing in all these scores of high-ceilinged rooms. His heart thudded against his breast, and his nerves were darting quicksilver...*
>
> *A bell tolled in the empty house.*
>
> —*Death Glow*

The editorials in *The Phantom Detective* magazine were usually written by the Phantom himself in a chummy hero-to-reader fashion. Usually, they touted the following month's Phantom novel in much the same manner as a movie trailer. The Phantom would write:

> *Bob Wallace has taken the story of the menace to the Mattling shipping interests and its relationship to the American overseas export trade and has woven it into an intriguing and challenging detective story in "Masterpiece of Murder," the Phantom Detective novel appearing in the next issue of The Phantom Detective magazine. I, personally, got a great kick out of working on the case, and I know that when "Masterpiece of Murder" comes your way that you'll get just as much satisfaction in reading about the incident that led up to the uncovering of the whole nest of criminal vipers in the plot.*

Sometimes the Phantom was less modest.

> *Murder Acres is a story that is as dramatic as human emotions can ever be, as forceful as the evil powers involved can make it, and as superb as the triumph of justice can become for us all! You'll like the story.*

For most of the Phantom's career his magazine carried a membership offer in a Phantom club called Friends of the Phantom. There were no dues or fees, although a special bronzed replica of the Phantom's badge could be obtained for fifteen cents (for the traditional "postage and handling"). Membership in the club and the special badge came with a dire warning: "It must be clearly understood that membership in the Friends of the Phantom gives you no special privileges or police powers whatsoever."

The Phantom often seemed perturbed about this problem.

> *"A question that comes up frequently in connection with Friends of the Phantom," he wrote, "is whether or not membership confers special police powers. Naturally joining our group does not give you any special rights or privileges regarding your local or federal law-enforcement agencies. There is no connection between our organization and any of these law-enforcement bodies. Our chief purpose is to express, tangibly and collectively, the feelings of the right-thinking, law-abiding readers who follow the Phantom Detective."*

The right-thinking readers were even invited to mail in their comments on the magazine. Their letters were either addressed to "Bob" (for author Robert Wallace) or simply "Dear Phantom." Nearly all were self revealing:

Dear Phantom:

I love to read your magazine. It has some interesting stories in it. I do a lot of reading because I live in a small town and there isn't much to do here in the way of entertainment. I'm eighteen years of age and a junior in high school.

Dear Phantom:

I sure get a big kick out of reading your story, "The Chinese Puzzle," in the January 1947 issue. I happened to be serving in the Army in the South Pacific, and before coming back to the States this year I got into China. I found out a good deal about some of the intrigue that was going on there, and your story sure stirred up some colorful memories. More power to you.

Dear Phantom:

I am a friend and admirer of the Phantom, and have been for some time. Richard Curtis Van Loan is a real person to me, and I glory in his every triumph. Sometimes, however, when the 'enemy' gets him, my heart is in my mouth, but I should know I can count on him every time getting out of all kinds of danger... Van Loan never ceases to be a gentleman, even if he has to twist the neck of a gunman at times. He does it so that my heart swells with pride. I can see him dusting off the soil accrued from the crook, probably saying 'This hurts you worse than it does me.' It is odd, that it never makes me feel anything but happy when he bests a criminal, but when Van Loan gets hurt, I die.

— *(signed) Just a Bad Old Gal, I guess.*

Dear Bob:

Your stories are all good except that I don't like your main character.

Your plots are interesting, but not the Phantom.

"Occasionally," the Phantom replied testily, "letters that come in are a bit difficult to interpret, but they do provide food for thought."

The Phantom Detective magazine ran from February 1933 to summer 1953. It was one of the last surviving pulps.

In the early issues, the stories were suitably melodramatic with bizarre murders perpetrated by such spook villains as The Fang, The Beast-King, The Satan, and even (gulp) The Green God. These Depression-era issues betrayed the poor man's fixation with the wealthy; not only was Van Loan fabulously rich, but most of the victims were bank presidents, heads of large companies, and famous politicians. ("Pity the poor rich man" was a basic theme.)

As the magazine moved into the war years, the masked villains were phased out, and such earlier set pieces as waterfront warehouses and blood-flecked back rooms began to be described in the hard, unblinking style of the *Black Mask* school. The atmosphere became sleazier, denser; the criminals diminished in size toward realistic dimensions.

There were some good yarns written in this middle period, but by the end of the forties even the new format had calcified. The magazine went quarterly in 1949 (a certain sign of diminished vigor), and it sleepwalked through another four years to its final story, "Murder's Agent." Like most fictitious heroes, the Phantom never announced his retirement, he just faded away.

The pulp-hero magazines were a short-lived phenomenon;

they lasted but twenty-two years in all. The Phantom blasted and slashed his way through twenty of those flamboyant years. It was an honorable record.

Each issue of his magazine would do a wrap-up scene in which the Phantom faded into the shadows, always promising to return. Any one of these farewells would serve as a fitting tribute to the character:

> *But as the Phantom turned from them all, to fade inconspicuously from sight of the excited, chattering group, he was weary—weary of death, and with the realization that there were other men in the world like the Green Mask and his cohorts who fattened on murder. Perhaps, someday, thanks to the efforts of the Phantom and the men who aspired to be like him, the criminal population would be decreased appreciably.*
>
> *Even now the world was cleaner, freer, because one such group no longer breathed the world's air. But it would be a long, hard battle still, and no one realized that more fully than the Phantom, world-famed nemesis of the underworld.*
>
> *He would keep on, however, always on call when there was need for him and his uncanny powers. But now he was tired—tired. The life seemed to have sagged in his over-wearied body. As he slipped away from ancient Half Mansion to make his way to the nearest railroad station, he pondered his next step. Should he refresh himself with a plunge into New York social life, or would a cruise best suit his needs?*
>
> *But whatever it would be, he knew it could not be for long. Some day—perhaps soon—a red light would flash atop the Clarion Building, and the Phantom would come eagerly to answer that call, to do battle again with some dire force of evil.*

It was the detective story version of riding off into the sunset.
The Phantom never failed.
And he never really died.

BLACK BATS AND GREEN GHOSTS

IN THEIR ROISTERING heyday, pulp heroes were almost a dime a dozen. Only a handful achieved genuine fame, returning issue after issue for many years. The rest fell victim to the ruthless odds of showbiz: for each success, a hundred failures.

In the late thirties and early forties, Ned L. Pines, publisher of *The Phantom Detective* magazine, decided to push his luck by introducing a quintet of Phantom-type heroes—the Black Bat, the Ghost, the Purple Scar, the Crimson Mask, and the generically named Masked Detective. Of these, only the Black Bat triumphed. The others are mostly forgotten now but deserve appreciation as one small part of the colorful pulp hero mosaic.

If the Black Bat's position in the pulp hero hierarchy is not of the first magnitude, it is perhaps because he had to be content with filling the front pages of *Black Book Detective* and lurking as a background figure on the magazine's covers. Despite this handicap and a late start, the masked and cowled Bat was the only mystery man hero to rival the Phantom's admirable run from the thirties into the final dissolution of the pulps in the fifties. While he is seldom mentioned in the company of such icons as Doc Savage or the Spider, he did offer his fans a long series of well-crafted stories, most of them produced by the estimable Norman Daniels.

Born in Brooklyn, Connecticut in 1905, Daniels was one of

the most prolific of all pulp-hero writers. He sold his first story in 1931 and remained a highly successful freelance writer until his retirement many decades later. He and his wife Dorothy were a fiction factory; he turned out the stories and Dorothy typed and edited. Later, she became an author on her own. By their own admission, there were months when they turned out a Black Bat novel, a Phantom Detective, a Crimson Mask, and maybe even a Candid Camera Kid as well. They also produced many of the Dan Fowler novels in *G-Men Detective*.

> *"As I recall,"* Daniels wrote, *"I originated the series characters of the Masked Detective, Candid Camera Kid, the Crimson Mask and, though I can't call them to mind at this writing, many others. But of them all, the Black Bat was my favorite, mainly because the characters seemed so real to me.*
>
> *"Many years ago, Leo Margulies asked me to come up with a series to be in competition with The Shadow. I concocted the set-up that, without change, became the Black Bat. Originally, I called him The Tiger. It seemed a natural since the hero's face was scarred from an opening sequence in the first book. The scars on his face resembled the markings on a tiger. However, as it was going into Black Book Detective, Leo decided to change the title for the character to conform with the magazine and so, to blend with Black Book, he renamed it Black Bat. I suspect that was what they were after anyway."*

Daniels' Black Bat was yet another refutation of the trite observation that "bad guys wear black." In fact, the good-guy hero outfitted himself in black from head to toe—black shoes, black gloves, black shirt, black mask and cowl, and a ribbed black cape almost identical to that legendary creation of the comic books, Batman. Interestingly, the Black Bat and Batman made their initial appearances at almost the same time. Batman was introduced in *Detective Comics* #27 in May 1939, and the first Black Bat novel, "Brand of the Black Bat" appeared in *Black Book Detective* a mere two months later. After a brief flurry of litigious wrangling by the two publishers, cooler heads prevailed when they realized that the synchronous appearance of the nocturnal bat guys was too close to be anything but coincidence. In fact, Daniels had submitted his first Black Bat novel in December of 1938, several months before Bruce Wayne donned his own trick suit to become a crime-fighting rodent.

In the long pulp tradition dating back to Zorro and beyond, the Black Bat was a wealthy young bachelor who fought criminals while disguised as a masked phantom. He was ex-district attorney Tony Quinn, who would have been handsome except for the deep, disfiguring scars burned into the flesh around his eyes, the result of acid thrown at him by criminals. To the world at large, Tony Quinn was "as blind as a bat," but readers of his magazine were informed that a secret, miraculous operation had not only restored his vision but had also given him super sight, with the ability to see in the dark. Then, too, during his blindness, other senses had developed. His touch was acute, his hearing almost uncanny.

Tony used his newfound powers to bring justice to criminals that the law could not touch. He pretended to be blind so that he could moonlight as the Black Bat—the cowl obscuring his telltale facial scars. As a lawyer, Tony Quinn worked patiently within the justice system but, in his persona as the night-prowling Black Bat, he frequently hurried things along.

> *"We'll use whatever means we think best in our fight against crime,"* Tony vowed. *"We'll fight them with their own weapons—with treachery, intimidation, theft. We'll worry them until they are as jittery as a one-legged man on a tightrope. We'll work with the police or against them if need be. We'll make our own laws and we'll enact our own judgments."*

Daniels' early Black Bat novels were less-vivid reflections of the vigilante themes blazed by Norvell Page in his Spider epics. In titles such as "The Faceless Satan," "The Black Bat's Dragon Trail," "Murder Among the Dying," and "City of Hidden Death," the Bat squared off with super fiends and Nazi spies intent on widespread schemes for conquest. And, like the Spider, his .45-caliber automatics thundered out messages of death to the ungodly, accompanied by his personal signature—a tiny black bat in flight—stuck on rapidly cooling foreheads. Superstitious criminals believed him unkillable and, because of his membranous cape, they thought he could fly.

Quinn shared his secret identity with a trio of helpers: ex-con man Silk Kirby, pugilist Butch O'Leary, and Carol Baldwin, the mysterious lady whose generosity had restored Tony's sight. It was Carol's donation of the eyes of her murdered police officer father that had enabled the super-sighted Black Bat to be born. Tony only dropped his pose as a blind man when he operated as the Black Bat or when he was in his laboratory, hidden behind a door in his large home on a spacious estate within the city limits. An underground passageway led from the laboratory to a secret exit from his estate, and a dilapidated, souped-up coupe parked on a nearby side street served as his own personal batmobile.

Like the Spider, the Black Bat was branded a criminal by the authorities and thus faced the threat of capture or death at the hands of the police as well as by his numerous criminal foes. His persistent nemesis was a cigar-chomping police lieutenant named McGrath, who not only set out to prove that Quinn was the Black Bat but constantly set up wily traps to prove that the young lawyer's supposed blindness was a sham. He would slam doors in the man's face, throw lit cigars at him, or offer his hand in a friendly manner, all to trick Tony into an instant of forgetfulness. For his part, Tony appeared to enjoy the game. I suppose it kept him on his toes.

In a 1944 story titled "Markets of Treason," McGrath's bag of tricks hit a new low—even for him. He presented Tony with the gift of a seeing eye dog named Gwendolyn. Secretly, McGrath had trained the normally docile pet to attack any man wearing a cloak. When Quinn next donned his familiar bat costume, Gwendolyn launched a murderous attack on her new master. The incident so unnerved Tony that he discarded the cape that had been his near undoing. The story was probably an editorial dictate emblematic of a new look for the Black Bat and of a new, more realistic trend in the single-character hero magazines as well. In the forties, as war gripped the nation, readers turned indifferently from the wild old plots involving master fiends and costumed heroes. By the end of the war, the realistic crime story was firmly entrenched. Soon there would be no more hero pulps at all.

"I wrote all of the Black Bat series over a period of eleven years," Daniels once confided. "I was paid exactly what [Walter] Gibson was paid and raised when he was raised. The final Black

Bat was taken over by a new group (pulps were rapidly fading then). They wanted to load the story with sex and I wasn't about to comply.

"They loaded it, I understand, and it was the final book."

Norman Daniels' commitment to the Black Bat resulted in a long-running series for his publisher. Despite a late start, the character lasted more than thirteen years, topped only by the Phantom at twenty years, The Shadow at eighteen years, and Doc Savage at sixteen years. Even the Spider did not last as long, although he saw more adventures. Alas, the publisher's four other Thrilling tryouts were to prove less successful.

The titular hero of the *Masked Detective* magazine (written by Daniels as "C.K.M. Scanlon") was something of a dull fellow by comparison to the author's own Black Bat. Perhaps this was because he had so few characteristics of his own and not even an interesting name or costume to alleviate the problem.

To be fair, the Masked Detective novels were all fast-paced stories with the same brand of cliff-hanger captures and escapes that helped make the Phantom so successful. Several of his adventures, often violent, reflected the dynamism of his wartime milieu: "The Fifth Column Murders" and "The League of the Iron Cross." In "The Canal Zone Murders," the Mask was even sworn in as an official F.B.I Agent, although nothing was made of this in future installments.

Like the Phantom, the Masked Detective was a master of disguise and ventriloquism and was a trained boxer to boot. Despite cover artists' delineations, he seldom resorted to weapons. His one real secret weapon was his proficiency in the ungentlemanly art of la savate, the French type of fighting with

Norman Daniels

the feet. His specially built shoes, with square, hard toes, could deliver bone-crushing kicks to crooks and killers. He spent long hours practicing on a life-sized dummy that—unlike the crooks—kept bouncing back for more.

The gumshoe with the killer feet was really Rex Parker, a crime reporter for the *New York Comet*. The public and criminals alike recognized newshawk Parker as the one man who was able to reach the Masked Detective in times of trouble. Why they didn't also suspect him of being the mysterious crime fighter was never explained. Perhaps he just wasn't impressive enough—the stories usually described him as being lazy and easygoing.

Unimpressive or not, Parker did have a girlfriend—a fellow reporter named Winnie Bligh, cozily referred to as Cap'n Bligh by the occasionally insufferable Rex. Winnie was also lacking in original attributes; her main talent seemed to be that of inviting frequent kidnapping by crooks.

While most of the Mask's adventures were routine detective yarns, he occasionally bumped into villains worthy of more flamboyant rivals. "The Poison Puzzle" introduced a white-hooded master menace, and "Crimes of Stilicho" featured a mysterious art vandal who fancied himself the modern version of a fifth century marauding general. One novel described a scene of purest pulp invention—the sight of a corpse apparently standing on its head in the East River. "Whose were the murderous hands which held the doomed man's ankles and dipped him into the dark water as a man might dip a roll into his morning coffee?" the magazine asked. "Whose brain directed those hands?" Fans had to read on to find out.

Unfortunately, it was the Masked Detective himself who failed to capture readers' overburdened attention, probably because his publisher had conceived him as little more than a utility-grade hero in a cheap domino mask. Even the covers reflected this problem; most were previously used paintings retouched by adding a mask to some central figure like an afterthought. Sometimes they didn't bother. "Death Island" was a title that referred to the island of Moaxacelo in the Gulf of Mexico, yet the issue's cover inexplicably featured an Oriental menace and a gun-blazing hero sans mask. The cover on the spring 1942 issue features a masked character, but he's wearing a welder's hood, not the Masked Detective's slash of eye-covering silk. With such half-hearted endorsement, it was no surprise that after a mere dozen issues the Masked Detective received his early retirement. Fortunately for him, he still had his dummy to kick around.

Unlike the Masked Detective, who at least commanded his own magazine, the Crimson Mask and Purple Scar appeared as features in the publisher's existing titles.

Like the Masked Detective, the Crimson Mask was yet another proletarian version of the Phantom. In real life, or at least what passed for real life in the detective pulps, he was known as "Doc" Clarke, a young pharmacist who was the son of a cop killed in the line of duty. The flash of a small red bulb beneath the counter of Doc's old-fashioned pharmacy was his signal to stop dispensing pills and start dispensing justice as a masked vigilante. It wasn't a bad premise, but it wasn't original either, and few of the Crimson Mask adventures (all of them written by the indefatigable Norman Daniels under the pen name Frank Johnson) ever attempted to rise above routine status.

Of course, the Crimson Mask was not designed to set the pulp world on fire. He was launched in *Detective Novels* in 1939 when the publisher attempted to boost circulation with the addition of series characters. Another character, Jerry Wade, the Candid Camera Kid, appeared first in a series of snappy novelettes featuring a young redheaded news photographer. When the Crimson Mask was brought in to help, the two series ran as a double feature in each issue. Later they began to alternate.

Impressively, the Candid Camera Kid series was also written by Norman Daniels, using the pen name John L. Benton. This was at the same time as the one-man fiction factory was churning out the Black Bat novels along with much other material. If readers did not respond to the Masked Detective or the Crimson Mask, it was not a reflection of Daniels' proven ability to entertain but simply a rejection of mundane masked detectives at a time when such certified loonies as The Shadow and the Spider were still cutting their ferociously melodramatic swath through crime.

Yet another of the publisher's masked crime fighters suffered the misfortune to appear as an infrequent character in an ongoing magazine. *Exciting Detective* was host to the Purple Scar, a lesser known but intriguing gent who appeared briefly in a series of full-length novels in 1941 and 1942. One might be tempted to say that the Purple Scar was unusual because he was not written by Norman Daniels, but that would be unfair to a hero with distinct, although somewhat unrealized, possibilities.

Like most of Standard's also-ran series, the Purple Scar novels barely rise above the level of routine detective thrillers. What makes this aborted series noteworthy is the utterly bizarre nature of the character's masked identity.

In civilian life, the Purple Scar is Doctor Miles Murdock, described by author John S. Endicott as "the most brilliant young plastic surgeon of his time." Six feet tall and handsome as a movie star, young Murdoch decided to fight crime as a masked avenger when his brother, a member of the city's police force, was murdered by gangsters. Because most of his publisher's mystery men chose to fight crime while wearing skimpy domino masks of red or black, Murdoch must have decided he had to be different—really different. That was where his skill as a plastic surgeon came in handy.

Miles Murdoch had stood in the morgue and had viewed the acid-destroyed face of his murdered brother, turned a ghastly purple by its days of soaking in river water. From this personal horror, he had conceived the nemesis of evil known as the Purple Scar. From police photographs taken of his brother's bloated, scarred face, Murdoch had made a grim mask of purple-dyed gum elastic. It was a perfect reproduction, copied skillfully even down to the smallest detail: a ghastly network of torn, acid-destroyed tissues, features almost totally eaten away, eyes only empty shriveled sockets, mouth a twisted slash. A face so horrible to look at that even the least sensitive recoiled at the sight of it. It was the face of a corpse!

> *"I'll use the mask when I want it known the Purple Scar is on the trail," Murdoch decided. "It's a name the underworld will find easy to remember. I choose purple because I want to imitate my brother's features. Flesh that's been eaten by acid and submerged in water turns a dark purple. Purple becomes black at night, which will make my face invisible instead of a betraying pale glow in the darkness."*

Unfortunately, the Purple Scar novels were less imaginative than their protagonist's wild disguise. Abetted by the usual coterie of helpers, a nurse-fiancée, a friendly police captain, and a reformed second story man, the dreaded Purple Scar confined his cases to such routine problems as stolen gold and poisoned meat shipments—hardly the stuff of great pulp melodrama. One can only guess what bizarre possibilities a Norvell Page might have wrung from a hero who stalks the night wearing an imitation of his own brother's dead face.

Of the Thrilling Group's less successful tryouts, The Ghost is perhaps the most noteworthy, partly because he also terrified crooks with a frightful countenance and partly because he belonged to that interesting subgenre known as the "magician detective."

From the days of folklore involving witches and warlocks and other practitioners of the Black Arts, a vague sense of the sinister has always permeated the air around magicians. The affinity between magic and mystery proved irresistible to thriller writers of the thirties and forties. Various magician types skulked through pulp paper pages. They ranged from genuine sorcerers and necromancers like Doctor Satan and Doctor Death to such hocus-pocus hawkshaws as Norgil the Magician and Don Diavolo, the Scarlet Wizard. (The creators of Norgil and Diavolo, mystery greats Walter Gibson and Clayton Rawson, were in fact real-life prestidigitators.)

It is interesting, although not surprising, that two pulp heroes known as "the Ghost" should have shared a similar magical background. In my book *The Super Feds* (Starmont House, 1988), I wrote of the Ghost series that ran in fourteen issues of Popular Publications' *Ace G-Man Stories*. That shade was known in civilian life as Brian O'Reilly, a former stage magician who used his tricks of sleight-of-hand and ventriloquism in a freelance vendetta against the F.B.I.'s most vicious foes.

The G-Man Ghost first appeared in a yarn titled "The Ghost Wears a Badge" by Wyatt Blassingame in the September 1939

Ace G-Man. A mere four months later, Thrilling Publications brought out *The Ghost Super-Detective*. The new magazine also featured the exploits of a mystery man outlaw who, in civilian life, was a former stage magician who used his showbiz background to confound criminals and the police alike.

Such creative synchronicity was not unusual in the copycat world of pulp publishing. Once you have a Shadow, and then a Phantom, can a Ghost be far behind? But there are laws governing such things, coincidence or not. And occasionally a phone call from one publisher to a friendly rival would solve copyright problems short of litigation. This may be the reason that *The Ghost* magazine became *The Green Ghost Detective* with its fourth issue.

Unfortunately, the Ghost/Green Ghost was another failed attempt at a major pulp hero by the Thrilling Group, even though they gave the character a good sendoff with his own magazine and a series of eye-catching covers. He lasted but seven issues in his own title and then was relegated to a further six novelettes in the publisher's *Thrilling Mystery*, a popular dumping ground for failed heroes. Even so, he deserves a special place in the pulp hero old boy's club, if only for his imaginative entrances:

> *Through the open door of the den eddied a thin column of grayish mist, barely visible in the uncertain light. An unearthly laugh sounded from the darkness just beyond the door.*
>
> *"Who's there?" Turrin's voice was taut.*
>
> *The mist expanded until it seemed to clog the darkened doorway with swirling gray. A pinpoint of greenish light seemed to be the nucleus of the misty cloud as it moved slowly into the room.*

The green light brightened, caught the highlights of a ghastly death's head that seemed floating without bodily support.

"Don't you know, gentlemen?"

The voice came from the skull-teeth of the green-tinted death's head.

"The Ghost," Werges whispered. "The Green Ghost. I've heard of him."

Small wonder. The face of the Ghost was a bloodless white (or a sickening green, depending on which issue you read). Teeth the color of old ivory popped naked from fleshless gums, nostrils gaped, dead eyes threatened. When occasion demanded, the head came right off, floated across rooms, or was hurled at suitably impressed thugs. Not an easy thing to forget.

The Ghost's alter-ego was a little less impressive, but only when compared to a head-throwing dead man. The first of the novels is titled "Calling the Ghost" (January 1940), and in it we are introduced to George Chance, magician-detective. Surprisingly, Chance introduces himself. Unlike other hero-pulp journals, all transcribed by omnipresent authors from "case books" or secret diaries, the Ghost's adventures are credited as autobiography, recounted in a chummy manner by Our Hero himself. While some of the hard-boiled detective hacks had already worked the first-person narrative into near parody by 1940, it was still a novel form in pulp-hero terms.

"I was born in the show business," the Ghost confided to his readers. "My father was an animal trainer and my mother a trapeze performer in a circus... I learned much of the secrets of

makeup from a clown named Ricki. To the grave-eyed man with the long black sideburns who traveled with the show under the name of Don Avigne, I am indebted for knowledge that has made the knife one of the deadliest of weapons in my hands. Then there was Professor Gabby, who taught me principles of ventriloquism which are today responsible for the hundreds of voices of the Ghost. But most important of all, while I was hanging around the circus, I won the confidence of Marko, the Magician... Magic was the ladder that helped me climb from the circus to vaudeville and from there to my own revues."

What further prompted George Chance, a showbiz success, to dress up as a spook and run around New York risking his life and reputation fighting criminal maniacs is never explained. In the world of the pulp hero, it was just the thing to do.

As the Ghost, Chance surrounded himself with loyal assistants, from a lady friend named Merry White to a middle-aged, cigar-smoking midget called Tiny Tim. His real ace-in-the-hole was a man named Glen Saunders. Chance and Saunders were identical doubles. By assuming the part of George Chance while the real George Chance, suitably disguised, was out playing cops and robbers with his magic, Saunders supplied the Ghost with a perfect alibi to confound criminals and the police alike.

Like Norgil and Don Diavolo, the Ghost uses illusion as a nucleus of misdirection. To make the magic stick, he togs himself in fright clothes and a horror face to scare hell out of superstitious criminals. Even the police are impressed.

Chance worked his Jekyll-and-Hyde act with the full knowledge of New York Police Commissioner Edward Standish.

Unlike many pulp top cops, Standish not only approved of his friend's nocturnal vigilantism but even kept in touch with the Ghost via the private wire from his apartment. In addition, Standish allowed Chance to haunt police headquarters while disguised as Detective-Sergeant Hammill or consulting physician Dr. Stacey. Even police department medical examiner, Dr. Robert Dumarest, is a sardonic commentator on George Chance's double life. "You left a nice gentlemanly profession like magic to play in a slaughterhouse," he clucks.

To play in crime's slaughterhouse, handsome young George Chance routinely transforms himself into a ghastly apparition.

> *To create the character of the Ghost, I take small wire ovals and put them into my nose, tilting the tip and elongating the nostrils. For the somewhat ghastly effect proper to a ghost-character, I darken the inside of each nostril… Brown eye shadow goes on to darken my eye pits. Pallor comes out of a powder box. I highlight my naturally prominent cheek bones. Over my own teeth I place shells the color of old ivory. After that, I have only to affect a fixed vacuity of expression and my face becomes something very much like a skull.*

The shock effect of the Ghost's fright face was supplemented with a rollicking graveyard giggle and a suit full of secret pockets containing magical paraphernalia. As backup, his suit jacket concealed a double-edged throwing knife and a razor blade (handy for slicing bonds when tossed into a pool of hungry piranha). He also packed a flat automatic even though he admitted to being a rotten pistol shot.

But even originality has its drawbacks. While George

Chance's leisurely first-person narrative gained the advantage of verisimilitude, it deprived readers of the knockabout pace and melodramatic violence that permeates the typical pulp hero novel. When sales figures proved less thrilling than the publisher's colophon, Editorial Director Leo Margulies was quick to act. With its fifth issue, *The Ghost Detective* (now re-named *The Green Ghost Detective*) dropped the George Chance byline and gave credit to the series' real author. Along with the new credit was a return to the more comfortable third-person narrative.

Despite his pseudonymous-sounding byline, G.T. Fleming-Roberts was the real name of a top notch pulpster who, as early as 1935, ghosted many of the better Secret Agent X novels and who, in 1949, created the final pulp hero, Captain Zero. Because characterization was a Fleming-Roberts specialty, his heroes were stigmatized by perversely human fallibilities: the Ghost carried a gun but couldn't shoot worth beans, and Captain Zero was just a little squirt, bland of personality and uncoordinated under stress. Some kind of hero, huh? But magic persisted. He turned invisible every night at the stroke of midnight.

Fleming-Roberts' Green Ghost was essentially the old Ghost with the addition of a chemical vapor and a green light in his tie pin to turn his already ghastly head even more bilious. Unfortunately, plastic surgery wasn't enough to save the magazine. There were only two more issues, seven in all, then the character was retired to *Thrilling Mystery*, where he appeared in a further six short stories, all written by Fleming-Roberts. The demise of the Ghost/Green Ghost was unfortunate because, except for Daniels' Black Bat, he was the most promising of Thrilling Publications' tryout titles.

If Ned Pines' Thrilling heroes of the forties failed to duplicate the impact of such rivals as the Spider and The Shadow, it really wasn't their fault. They were conceived as low-budget efforts from the beginning. Compared to such major pulp heroes as G-8 or Doc Savage, they were what B-movies were to A-movies—entertaining but routine. And, like those old B-movies, they are enjoyable today as nostalgic whiffs of the past—pleasant reminders of those gloriously innocent years when a newspaperman or a pharmacist could don a little face mask and sally forth to rid the streets of crime.

G-MEN

"Don't shoot, G-men, don't shoot!"

THOSE WERE THE historic words that George 'Machine-Gun' Kelly uttered in 1933 when a group of F.B.I. agents and local law enforcement officers surrounded his house in Memphis.

Kelly's abbreviation of 'government men' soon passed into the argot of the underworld. It would have greater impact two years later when Warner Brothers decided to put their dynamic bad boy gangster star James Cagney on the right side of the law for a change. The movie was titled "G-Men." It was an overnight sensation.

To no one's surprise, the feisty pulp magazines of the day were quick to tool up for this new genre in the making. To the list of cowboys, detectives, pirates and space jockeys would be added a new and exhilarating type of vicarious alter-ego—the gun-blazing G-man.

As early as September of 1935 the venerable *Black Mask*, home of the hard-boiled detective, introduced the first of seven Dwight V. Babcock stories about G-man Chuck Thompson. Significantly, the second of the series, "Death Goes Free," was heralded on the cover as "A Crashing 'G' Man Story."

Small wonder that in October of that year Ned Pines' Standard Publications rushed out a magazine dealing entirely with this new breed of pulp action hero. *G-Men,* the first and most successful of the Bureau-inspired pulps, lasted for some eighteen years and 112 issues. Each issue featured a short novel—as sanguinary as its movie namesake—concerning the adventures of rough-hewn special agent Dan Fowler (AKA "The Ace of the F.B.I.," "Scourge of the Underworld," and "The World's Greatest Manhunter.") Aided by his fellow agent, Larry Kendal, Dan was to be the prototype for dozens of pulp-style G-men. Before the tide was stemmed some would bear as much resemblance to strait-laced government agents as kangaroos to rabbits.

True to his G-man origin Dan Fowler's first case involved two out-of-the headlines incidents involving a kidnapped child and a gang of Mid West bank robbers. Within a few months Dan moved on to bigger game—pulp-style murderous masterminds who threatened society itself. His monthly adventures ran the gamut from tong wars and gold thefts to hijackings and Axis spies and saboteurs.

Major George Fielding Elliot originated the series and wrote many of the early stories under the publisher's 'house name' of C.K.M. Scanlon. The March 1940 issue saw a title change to *G-Men Detective*, at which time numerous series authors were allowed to use their own names, among them the irrepressibly prolific Norman Daniels.

J. Edgar Hoover himself was an ongoing character in the Dan Fowler adventures, though referred to only as The Chief. To make the connection secure the magazine frequently printed chummy lectures regarding the state of crime in America supposedly written by Hoover himself. For ten cents loyal readers could even join the magazine's G-Men Club.

In March of 1936 rival publisher Popular Publications introduced its own G-man magazine in its familiar house style, dated May–June 1936. From the beginning readers of *Ace G-Man Stories* could be assured that this would be one F.B.I journal not to be troubled by ambitions of realism or respectability. It was the brainchild of publisher Harry Steeger; whatever faults critics might find with Steeger's boisterous pulp line, blandness was a charge they seldom levelled.

Ace G-Man covers were some of the best in the business, bursting to the edges with gun-blasting action. Early paintings featured a lone G-man—most often a tall blonde man with blue suit and red tie. Later, a triumvirate of heroes took over: three embattled figures arrested in compositions of raw power.

Despite pictorial allure and the talents of such top authors as Norvell Page, Paul Ernst, and Hugh B. Cave, *Ace G-Man Stories* initially lacked continuing action series characters. But pulp magazines were living, flexible organisms, as responsive to public apathy as they were to approval. To stoke up reader excitement the May 1939 issue of *Ace G-Man Stories* introduced a mid-life image change. The cover of that landmark issue did nothing to alert readers. Indeed, the lead novel that was to institute the change, "Mr. Zero and the F.B.I. Suicide Squad" by Emile C. Tepperman was not mentioned on the cover, nor was a second innovative novelette, "Captain of the Corpse Crew," by Harry Lee Fellinge.

What made these two yarns distinctive was that they introduced a series of eccentric characters who would begin to infiltrate and eventually dominate the magazine. Faced with flagging interest (and sales) the publishers had decided to pin gold-eagled G-man shields on those popular figures of projective fantasy, the pulp mystery men. It was those derring-do series heroes, wildly preposterous and luridly violent, who would propel *Ace G-Man Stories* into the pulp pantheon of fondly remembered titles.

Strapped by the dictates of a short story played up as a "short novel," the new breed of G-men protagonists live in an intense world of violent events in which atmosphere is truncated and characterizations revealed as a series of recognizable traits. Their stories race along as if there is a warrant out for their arrest. Pistols bark, machine-guns chatter, victims topple, blood splashes. The body count is relentless. There is no room for compassion, no time to reflect. You can almost smell the cordite as the fate of the Republic is resolved in 20 to 30 breathless pages.

The promised Tepperman 'novel' (25 pages including illustration, publisher's blurb and an ad promising bowel relief) introduced the crime crusades of "The F.B.I. Suicide Squad"—special agents Kerrigan, Murdoch and Klaw. Described grandly as the mightiest trio of man-hunters in modern times, and the greatest adventure triumvirate since Dumas' immortal Three Musketeers, the Suicide Squad must have made an impact on jaded readers because the boys were to be featured in prime spot in all but one of the remaining 22 issues. They would be joined by other distinctly unorthodox government employees: GX—the Phantom Fed, The Voice, The Ghost, The Black Celts, and The Trouble Twins.

In the pallid world that the rest of us are doomed to inhabit, the exploits of any one of these Bureau-sponsored spooks would guarantee a halt to further F.B.I. appropriations. Fantasy being fantasy, each of the bizarre fictional agents worked directly under the uncritical aegis of J. Edgar Hoover himself.

In fact, it is Hoover, only slightly disguised as "The Chief," "The Boss," and "The Director," who is the unifying constant throughout the new breed of stories. He is the chief hero in a magazine overrun by heroes.

Like their father-figure mentor, the Suicide Squad agents were not destined to be darlings of the liberal press. One mark against them was that they routinely took fewer prisoners than the Japanese at Iwo Jima.

"SUICIDE SQUAD DOES IT AGAIN," the headlines shrilled in an early adventure. "FIVE KILLED, SEVEN WOUNDED BY KERRIGAN, MURDOCH AND KLAW IN SPECTACULAR BATTLE."

> *'Last night, the three notorious desperadoes of the F.B.I. staged an attack upon a peaceable place of business, without benefit of search warrant. The fact that all their victims were criminals with long records does not excuse the conduct of these notorious gunmen. This paper has often wondered why these professional killers have not long ago been summarily dismissed from the Federal Bureau of Investigation. No doubt, their brilliant previous accomplishments have influenced the Director to keep them on the rolls. But the time has come...."*

The fact was that the Director was extremely reluctant to assign the Squad to any job unless compelled to by circumstances.

As legend has it, Kerrigan had once punched a senator's son in the nose. Murdoch had shot a croupier to death in a gun duel in a crooked gambling house—where he should not have been. And Steve Klaw had told a Senate investigating committee to go to hell when he was questioned about a gunfight in which he had killed three bandits.

Other agents guilty of such offences would have been pounding pavement in short order. But the three hellions had records which few could equal, so they were kept on as part of the Suicide Squad—a secret group of men who have no regular duties, but who wait for the one inevitable assignment from which there will be no return. As the magazine direfully suggested: "Six months ago there had been five of them. Two months ago, there were four. Now there were only three—Kerrigan and Murdoch and Klaw."

The personalities of the three were easily sketched: Kerrigan's full name: John F. Kerrigan. He was husky and powerful, with shoulders like a stevedore's and a pair of hands that could rip a telephone book apart. His voice is described as big and booming. Dan Murdoch was the best looking of the three—dark and lithe, with slender hips and the long legs of an athlete. Stephen Klaw was so innocent looking that he could be taken for a kid just out of college. Among the three there was no leader. But whenever any one of them saw fit to issue an order to the others, they knew that there was a crisis which demanded instant obedience and acted accordingly.

Despite, and possibly because of the relative short word lengths imposed on the Suicide Squad stories, many of them contain as much action and complexity as in more inflated hero pulp novels. In their second adventure, "The Suicide Squad Reports for Death," the indomitable trio faced a criminous mastermind named Augustus Jarger. Known as The General, the Alcatraz graduate commanded a stupendous sleaze-pool of crime that he liked to call the Army of Death.

As The General explained it to some less-than-willing draftees, "I already have fifty cities in line. Your twelve cities are the last of the larger ones. With you twelve as part of the Army of Death, we will have an organization greater than anything in the world. We will have a gross annual income of four billion dollars. We will be able to smash everything in our path—including the Federal Bureau of Investigation. We will be able to elect mayors and governors and congressmen. Who knows—maybe even the President!"

Tough talk. Carried along by his own pomposity, The General even posted a reward of fifty thousand dollars each on the bodies of Kerrigan, Murdoch and Klaw.

As was usual with such criminal megalomaniacs, Jarger failed to account for the reckless fury of the three agents who courted death bi-monthly. Within the space of some thirty machine-gun prose pages, The General's army crumbled, and his schemes vanished when six slugs from Steven Klaw's .45 smashed his chest with the force of a battering ram.

Kerrigan, Murdoch and Klaw were the brain children of Emile C. Tepperman, on of the most prolific of pulp authors. In a letter column in the August 1939 *Writer's Digest*, Tepperman boasted "I have written several million words of pulp, including a flock of book-lengths for two or three houses. Even now I can state with sincerity that nothing I write is 'hack stuff,' or the product of a stereotyped system or formula."

Less subjective analysts might argue that Tepperman was one of the masters of pulp formula. It is a well-honed talent that endeared him to editors as one of the "take-over" specialists. When Frederick C. Davis stopped writing the popular Operator #5 novels, Tepperman picked up the reins without a break.

During the same period, when Norvell Page grew weary of his ferociously inventive stint as the Spider's sole confidante, Tepperman again moved in—taking over from Page in the middle of an ongoing quartet of novels, the Living Pharaoh series.

In one of Tepperman's ghosted Spider novels, ("The Spider and the Pain Master," January 1940), the Spider picked up a copy of *Ace G-Man Stories* from a local newsstand and began reading it—no doubt perusing that month's lead novel, "Coffins for the Suicide Squad."

If Tepperman's Suicide Squad appeared to be the greatest thing since sliced bread (no idle cliché in the thirties and forties), that was merely the intention of the publishers. To give their fans their money's worth, a slew of other gun-toting buckaroos was quickly introduced.

G-X, the Phantom Fed, was the protagonist in the aforementioned "Captain of the Corpse Crew." G-X was an interesting (no, let's say outrageous) addition to the G-man canon.

In appearance G-X was an ordinary-looking young man with "a fighting Irish pan." What made him unique as a Federal Agent was that he bummed around the country as a hobo known as Hobo Jerry, his sole companion a ferret-faced, predatory little criminal known as Sydney Gimp. As the magazine had it, the Phantom Fed's hazardous existence—ghosting among crooks and killers from the inside of hobo jungles—had given him an understanding of the problems of the down-and-outers who were so often prey to the ruthless.

Unlike Hoover's real-life agents, who spent endless hours on routine reports and who were required to phone their offices at three-hour intervals while on duty, G-X seemed never to doff his hobo duds or take a bath, much less report to top management. In his peregrinations he left his symbol everywhere, a circle pierced by an arrow, with the initials "G-X" scrawled inside. As the magazine suggested, the sign was a warning to strike a chill to the hearts of criminals who travelled via "side-door Pullman" when the heat was on them; it was emblazoned on box cars and water tanks on every railroad right-of-way from Maine to Mexico.

Another odd fellow was Brian O'Reilly, the Ghost, who appeared first in a story titled "The Ghost Wears a Badge," by Wyatt Blassingame. The Ghost was a former stage magician who, as an undercover agent, was forced to kill a member of a foreign power. F.B.I. records show O'Reilly as officially dead but, as the Ghost, he continues to receive secret assignments from The Chief in person in the big man's office in the Department of Justice building.

Like so many mystery men, the Ghost is technically an outlaw, hunted and hated by policemen and crooks alike. As a means of escape, he uses his magician's tricks of sleight-of-hand and ventriloquism. Each new story finds him in the middle of a deadly mission because "a Ghost has no vacation, no time for romance." Typically, the end of a Ghost adventure sees him limping off into the cold pre-dawn street, alert for policemen.

What editorial laxity allowed still another outlaw hero in the same magazine to be named Dennis O'Ryley is an unsolved mystery. For those who care about such things, Dennis O'Ryley was the secret identity of the Voice, not to be confused with Brian O'Reilly, the Ghost.

The voice was a one-man Sixth Column, spreading doubt

and confusion among foreign agents. Described as a "rugged Irish bogtrotter," and "a big man with blue eyes that burned with the cold, hard light of a diamond, O'Ryley (as opposed to O'Reilly) had been transferred from anti-espionage to other fields after his exploits had made him the hero of America. As the magazine explained it, "publicity and the work of the F.B.I. cannot mix." In the best style of pulp mystery men, the supposedly crippled O'Ryley stalks the night as the Voice, exiting his home through a trap door in the kitchen, which leads to a hidden exit through the garage.

The masked Voice brought his message to trouble-making spies by breaking into network radio programs at gun point, naming names and exposing plots before they were consummated. As pulp historian Robert Sampson once noted, the Voice seems never to have interrupted a single commercial. It's the American way.

Then there was Special Agent Phil Towne, whose adventures were chronicled by the durable William R. Cox. Compared to the Ghost, the Voice, and a hobo agent who paints warning signs on water towers, Phil was a touchstone of normalcy in a magazine overrun with weirdness. "Slope-shouldered, indolent, nondescript beyond belief," Phil loved attending the fights as often as possible. He didn't possess any unusual powers or gimmicks, and he wasn't even Irish.

Phil Towne was hard-bitten in the *Black Mask* style. Although he packed a .357 Magnum—guaranteed to have more wallop than a .45—his was the art of being an inconspicuous character, light framed, without bulging muscles. In "Feed the Feds with Hot Lead" he is pictured as a drab figure in a neat blue suit, tan shoes, and a gray hat tilted back on sparse brown hair.

For an ordinary guy, Phil's adventures were no less spectacular than that of his mystery men counterparts. In a series of well-written, entertaining stories he was usually up to his slope shoulders in gangs of spies, gangsters, and criminal nogoodnicks of all stripes.

Ace G-Man series heroes of shorter duration included B.B. Fowler's Liam O'Connor, an Irishman (naturally) and Dave Evans, a Welshman, known as the Black Celts, "ace trouble-shooters of the F.B.I." The boys were a battling buddy team, fighting each other in the few moments when they weren't knocking the bejabbers out of spies.

A more distinctive team-up appeared in the magazine's penultimate issue. Day Keene's "Herr Yama from Yokohama" introduced Lee Sin of New York's Chinatown (a nice break from Irishmen) and his fellow G-man, Brad Hatfield. Sin and Hatfield were known in the Bureau as The Trouble Twins, but as the story confided, the big boss called them his corpse makers. The Trouble Twins' rapid-paced Chinatown adventure boded well for a successful series run but it turned out to be a solo effort due to the magazine's imminent demise.

Perhaps it was no coincidence that the super Feds of *Ace G-Man* began their exploits in 1939, the year that war broke out in Europe. From the beginning they were to spend most of their days embroiled with saboteurs and foreign agents. Even in their initial adventures *Ace G-Man* heroes did not mind calling a Swastika a Swastika and a Nazi a Nazi. To give you an idea, some of the pre-Pearl Harbor titles were "Stukas Over Texas," "School for Nazis," and "The Suicide Squad and the Murder Bund."

In June of 1940 President Roosevelt bestowed espionage and

counterespionage in the Western Hemisphere on The Federal Bureau of Investigation, transforming the nation's top cops into its chief spy smashers. For the heroes of *Ace G-Man Stories* it was a summons to all-out conflict.

In the front line of G-men patriots were Kerrigan and Murdoch and Klaw—the fighting Suicide Squad. In the pulp hero tradition, they took on whole legions of home front foes. In "The Suicide Squad Meets the Rising Sun," they use a beautiful Axis spy to find and destroy a Nipponese Expeditionary Force of nine thousand—hidden within the State of Maryland!

"The Suicide Squad's Private War" (December 1941) found the F.B.I. hellions fighting the Little Gray Man, a top Axis agent operating out of a secret enemy airbase on Staten Island. *"Unaided, they had to fight off the desperate attack of the swarming hordes of Nazis—and live long enough to allow a squadron of Navy bombers to blast them forever from the rolls of the F.B.I."*

In "So Sorry, Mr. Hirohito," (August 1942) Steven Klaw travels to neutral Chile to aid an American shipbuilder who has developed a new process for building ships five times faster than usual. Klaw is a sitting target in the Axis-packed city of Valpraiso, so it's not long before agents Kerrigan and Murdoch join their pal in a bloody impossible-odds war against hordes of Japanese armed troops.

In April of 1943 the Squad again went south of the border to combat Nazi schemes in Mexico. It was to be their ultimate foray against the Axis. They, and their fellow super feds, were eliminated not only by the enemy but by home front dictates from Washington. The reasons given for their magazine's demise were twofold: that of paper purchasing demands of the Army and constraints put on the transportation of wood pulp paper from Canada.

There were at least five editors in the eight-year history of *Ace G-Man Stories,* perhaps more. (Editors at Popular Publications tended to play musical chairs, particularly in the frantic forties.) According to that reliable source, *Writer's Digest,"* Henry Sperry was the original editor. Sperry died in early 1939 and was replaced by Moran Tudury. By the end of the same year Tudury himself was out, replaced by Willard Crosby. It was in the Tudury/Crosby period when the Suicide Squad and other series characters hijacked the book. It is difficult to say which editor was responsible for the startling transition, although Crosby was also the editor of *Strange Detective Mysteries,* a magazine more in keeping with *Ace G-Man's* new breed of oddball agents.

In addition to its monthly fiction quotient of a short "novel," three "novelettes" and two or three short stories, *Ace G-Men Stories* also featured departments and articles. "Turn on the Heat," an editorial column expressing anti-criminal outrage, ran until the end of 1941. One series of articles, "Qualifications and Training for the F.B.I.," was touted as material provided by the Big Guy himself, J. Edgar Hoover, presumably as a direct service for readers of the magazine. Another feature, "Wanted by the F.B.I.," provided a crime history, fingerprints, photo and description of wanted criminals that loyal readers could attempt to spot. Editor Tudury bragged that once an arrest was made by Bureau officers, telegraphic notification was wired by Mr. Hoover himself to the magazine's offices.

But it was the series heroes that gave *Ace G-Man* its spicy flavor. From 1939 on they waged their savage assault on domestic gangsters and foreign agents, leaving the pulpwood pages splattered with pulpwood bodies. They moved in a deliciously lethal world of speeding cars, waterfront warehouses, bus stations, pool rooms, wartime boom towns, seedy rooming houses, nightclubs, cheap hotels and blood-flecked streets. It was all simplistic, formula stuff, but finely honed by experts—an action-lovers paradise.

And then, abruptly, it was over.

Ace G-Man Stories was terminated in April of 1943, a year that was to take a heavy toll on familiar titles. In fact, the war years were boom years for the pulps. But paper was limited so less popular titles had to make way to supply increased print runs for better-selling books. The fact that such "character" magazines as *The Spider*, *G-8 and His Battle Aces* and *Ace G-Man Stories* were all axed within the same period would indicate that infallible heroes were finding less favor with an increasingly sophisticated readership.

There was to be but one other Bureau-inspired pulp, *F.B.I. Detective Stories*, first issue dated February 1949. Issued in the last gasp days of the pulps, it was but a regressive shadow of the glory days. Gone were the larger-than-life heroes, and the masthead saw fit to carry a disclaimer: "No affiliation with the Federal Bureau of Investigation."

In truth, *F.B.I. Detective Stories* was probably an embarrassment to J. Edgar Hoover who, by the fifties, was intent on changing the cultural image of his agents from gun-toting G-Men into God-fearing nice guys like the one portrayed by James Stewart in the reverential 1959 movie *The F.B.I. Story*.

It was this revisionist, squeaky-clean image that was at odds with alarms voiced at the scope and secrecy of the F.BI.'s vast intelligence empire, which included allegations of Bureau wiretapping, foreign embassy burglaries, and the intimidation of defense witnesses. In addition, there were personal criticisms of the aging Director himself that would have been unthinkable in the days of *Ace G-Man Stories*. Fans of the Suicide Squad or the Phantom Fed would not have blanched at a little eavesdropping or the roughing up of a hostile witness or two, all in the name of justice. Hell, they would have thought it normal. But you didn't expect this kind of thing from, by gosh, Jimmy Stewart.

On May 2, 1972, John Edgar Hoover, once idolized in the long-forgotten pulps as "The Boss," "The Chief," and "The Director," died in his sleep at the age of 77. Congress voted that his flag-draped body lay in state in the Capitol Rotunda. President Nixon eulogized him as "a peace officer without peer."

But the myth of the Super Fed had been interred many years before. It lives on in the brittle pages of those magazines we call the pulps: repositories of antique daydreams wherein steel-nerved heroes continue to lead lives of breathless adventure in a vivid alternate universe. It is a place where words like patriotism, honor and courage remain forever in fashion.

CALLING CAPTAIN FUTURE

James Carthew went to the window and stepped out onto the little balcony. He looked up at the full moon that sailed in queenly splendor high above the soaring towers of nighted New York.

There was a look of desperation in the President's aging, haunted face as he gazed up at the shining white face of the lonely satellite.

Far out beyond New York's towers, the moon was declining from the zenith. They could see the distant rocket-flash of liners taking off from the spaceport for far Venus or Saturn or Pluto.

"Why doesn't Captain Future come?" North Bonnel burst out, unable to keep silent longer. "That ship of his can get from the moon to the Earth in a few hours—he should be here by now."

James Carthew's gray head lifted.

"He will be here. He's never yet failed to answer our call."

"As a matter of fact, I'm here now, sir" said a deep, laughing voice.

It came from the balcony outside the window. A big, red-headed young man had miraculously appeared there, as though by magic.

"Curt Newton—Captain Future!" cried the President eagerly.

RIGHT. CAPTAIN FUTURE it was. The smartest, most handsome, most daring good guy on all the nine planets. A strapping redhaired scientific adventurer, Captain Future was the past's future crime fighter, an implacable nemesis of all oppressors and exploiters of the System's planetary races.

Whenever a menace threatened to conquer, enslave, or destroy hapless mankind, President Carthew had but to send out a distress call to Cap's secret base beneath Tycho crater on the moon (a kind of extended bat-signal), and Captain Future would zoom out, proton pistol in hand, to do battle with the wicked.

The good Captain was the titular star of his own magazine (the only space opera character to be so honored), which ran from early 1940 to 1944, as well as a series of further adventures in *Startling Stories,* which ran sporadically from 1945 to 1951.

There is little question that *Captain Future* is the one magazine that apologists for pulp science fiction would prefer to have forgotten. Both the magazine and its title were unabashedly juvenile in tone—considered a joke or even an insult by many science fiction fans of the day who foresaw great possibilities in the nascent genre.

When the first issue of *Captain Future* burst forth, the so-called Golden Age of science fiction—that memorable and to some almost legendary period—was just beginning. John Campbell was on his editorial throne at *Astounding Science Fiction,* and he was developing new and exciting writers who would extend the horizons of the field. Many of the Campbell protégés—Robert Heinlein, Theodore Sturgeon, Isaac Asimov, A.E. van Vogt—were soon to give it status as a mature and even thoughtful literature. By comparison, the advent of Captain Future must have seemed an ill-timed embarrassment.

Why then is Captain Future still remembered fondly? The answer has to be in the storytelling magic of the writer hired to produce the series. His name was Edmond Hamilton.

Edmond Hamilton was born in Youngston, Ohio, in 1904 and was raised on a nearby farm. When he was young, the term "science fiction" did not exist—it had yet to be invented—but the precocious country boy devoured the scientific romances of H.G. Wells and Jules Verne and later snapped up copies of adventure pulps like *All-Story* and *Argosy* when they ran serials featuring lost races and pioneer interplanetary romances.

As Hamilton recalled it in an essay published in 1934:

> *I have been a strong science fiction fan since 1916, when I started in with the old Argosy tales of Burroughs, Julian Hawthorne and others. I had a newspaper route about that time and when Merritt's long-awaited sequel to "The Moon Pool" came out, I carried papers one night each week with the All-Story Magazine held three inches before my eyes, avoiding automobiles and streetcars by the grace of God and heaving every paper on the wrong porch.*

At an early age, he determined to become a professional writer and devote his own life to entertaining people, as he had been entertained, with yarns of derring-do on far planets and wondrous worlds. At the time of that momentous decision, he had no idea that science fiction was about to become a category in its own right or that it would eventually encompass scores of magazines specializing in that brand of fiction.

When Edmond Hamilton's first pulp yarn appeared in the August 1926 issue of *Weird Tales*, science fiction magazines were just five months old (*Amazing Stories*, April 1926, was the genesis). Hamilton's initial venture into science fiction, bearing the simplistic title, "Across Space," was published only a month later. Within a short time, he was routinely selling stories that took men out beyond the planets to the stars, then to other galaxies, and finally outside the known universe altogether.

Hamilton was almost the perfect pulpster. Working in the fabulist tradition of storytelling, his wildly imaginative, action-packed space operas just about jumped off the page with writer-to-reader urgency. He once recalled how, in putting the finishing touches to an epic space battle, he became so excited that he punched his typewriter so hard that the machine "walked" over the surface of his old flat-topped desk—with the writer following it, banging away at it as he finished his climactic scene.

Such stuff wasn't great literature, nor was it meant to be. But his readers caught the excitement, and the Edmond Hamilton byline sold tons of magazines.

As a full-time pulpster, Hamilton wrote under the pseudonyms Hugh Davidson, Robert Castle, and Robert Wentworth, as well as the house names Brett Sterling and Will Garth. He also worked other fiction categories—mystery, detective, and even the supernatural—but he thought of himself and was thought of as a science fiction writer.

Hamilton was a founding father of the science fiction pulps. His "Interstellar Patrol" stories (1928–1930) constituted the first space opera series, predating E.E. "Doc" Smith's more famous Lensman series by several years. The author of such archetypal yarns as "The Universe Wreckers," "Crashing Suns," and "Locked Worlds," his virile brand of far-out adventure stories soon earned him the sobriquet "World-Saver," or alternatively, "World-Wrecker," Hamilton due to his penchant for smashing worlds around like glass marbles.

There were few bounds to the young author's soaring imagination. In "Thundering Worlds" (*Weird Tales*, March 1934) he wrote a yarn in which the planet Mercury is weaponized as a cosmic bowling ball to bombard threatening alien planets. Immersed in Hamilton's fictional universe, anxious readers never knew which world might bite the big one.

If characterization was virtually nonexistent in Ed's early stories, he more than made up for it with his prodigal inventiveness, rocketing narrative drive, and deep-felt instinct for the heroic. He wrote about "the great booming suns of outer space," and readers didn't stop to ponder whether suns could boom or not. It sounded just right.

As his career progressed, the old super-science melodramas were occasionally supplemented by more thoughtful stories in which depth of characterization and emotional drives became prominent. Hamilton proved he could write as sophisticated a story as the best of them, and some of his short stories remain small masterpieces.

But we seldom get to choose our own epitaph. In 1940, when science fiction was just beginning to take itself seriously as a mature literary form, Edmond Hamilton was assigned the job of writing a series of book-length novels for a brand-new magazine, *Captain Future*. The new title was designed to carry the breathless adventures of a futuristic Doc Savage–type superhero, aimed mainly at teenagers.

Legend has it that Hamilton was given the assignment for the series while attending the First World Science Fiction Convention in New York City, July 2, 1939. Leo Margulies, that feisty little editorial director of Standard Magazines, was also at the convention and had been impressed by the enthusiasm of the early science fiction fans. Margulies announced on the spot that he planned to create a new pulp-hero magazine aimed at younger readers to win them over to the new brand of future fiction. He reasoned that this innovation would do for science fiction what The Shadow had done for mystery and what Doc Savage had done for adventure.

The fact was that the Captain Future magazine had been planned some months before, and the World's first-ever science fiction convention had been deemed an appropriate place to announce the new title's imminent arrival.

Originally, the new magazine was to be called *Mr. Future... Wizard of Science.* Hamilton was supplied a story and character outline by the publishers. In the publisher's scenario, Curt Newton was not a man of heroic proportions but a biological mutant with a small body and big head, born of radioactive emanations, like some freak in a fifty's exploitation movie.

His three companions were to be as follows: an old man who was little more than a living memory bank, a telepathically controlled robot who served as a metallic doppelganger for Mr. Future, and a crystalline warrior from Ganymede, who was to be a living jewel set in Future's ring. Hamilton found the outline and the characters unworkable. He was forced to go to New York and argue with Margulies and editor Mort Weisinger for days until the proposed setup was changed to his liking. Eventually, the character—now called Captain Future—emerged in a form acceptable to Hamilton, his new bosses, and their suitably impressed young readers.

In the freshly devised legend, Captain Future was really Curtis Newton, the son of a brilliant biologist who had established a secret base on the moon to escape an unscrupulous enemy. When the elder Newton was murdered by his old foe, young Curt Newton was raised by his father's three nonhuman aides—the strangest trio of sidekicks in the annals of pulp literature.

Known as the Futuremen, Captain Future's three companions are as follows: The Brain—Simon Wright, who at one time had been Earth's greatest biologist. Faced with mortal death, the elderly Wright had proposed to Curt's father that his brain be transferred into a special serum-case in which it could live and think and work. Imprisoned forever within the transparent, indestructible case, The Brain's optic nerves were attached to artificial lens-eyes, while other nerves operated such appurtenances as microphone-ears, and the resonator by which he spoke. (At first The Brain could not move about by himself—one of the other Futuremen had to carry the serum-case by its attached handle—but Hamilton found this too hampering a restriction and eventually equipped his bizarre Futureman with tractor beams to supply locomotive powers.)

Otho, the android—not human but a living man of synthetic flesh created in the moon laboratory by The Brain and Captain Future's father. Otho's hairless, streamlined body was many times stronger and more flexible than that of normal humans, enabling him to run faster, jump higher, and move more quickly in an emergency than almost any other creature. By softening and resetting his synthetic skin Otho could disguise himself as almost anyone—or anything—in the system.

Grag, the robot—another creation of Curt's father. He towered over seven feet in height, a massive, manlike figure of gleaming inert metal. The robot was not designed to be merely an automaton but to have an intelligence and individuality of his own. The only thing not built into Grag was a sense of humor, as humans know it. The giant, naive robot would like nothing better than to be considered human. One of the running gags in the Captain Future novels is an ongoing battle between Grag and Otho (à la Monk and Ham in the Doc Savage series) as to which is the more "human" of Captain Future's nonhuman pals.

Perhaps the Futuremen's only true human link was that of Curt Newton himself, the child they helped raise to manhood, a perfect specimen of mental and physical human superiority.

Not all of Curt's friends were nonhuman. Romance entered the series in the person of Joan Randall, a young secret service agent of the Planet Police. She first met Captain Future in the Space Emperor mystery and then again when she was kidnapped by Doctor Zaro's legion of Doom. Joan and grizzled Marshall Ezra Gurney, another friend of Curt's, were listed on special detached service with the Planet Police to hold themselves in readiness to aid Captain Future and his band when the occasion required.

Almost as important as the cast of living characters was the Futuremen's cyclotron-powered spaceship, the *Comet*—the flying laboratory of Captain Future and his roistering space soldiers. The *Comet* was designed like an elongated teardrop, a piece of Art Deco streamlining that would have no value in the resistance-free depths of deep space. It looked pretty, however, and must have impressed the natives of remote worlds as it zipped along their space trails.

The first issue of *Captain Future* appeared on the stands in late 1939, inexplicably cover-dated winter 1940. The heroic cover painting featured Cap Future and his two mobile sidekicks, Grag and Otho. The captain was decked out in a red spacesuit and bubble helmet, his proton blaster firing what appeared to be expanding Lifesaver mints, while Otho was pictured with TV antennas jutting from each of his dead, white shoulders. (Simon Wright was to appear on only two of the series' covers, indicating a bias regarding the visual appeal of raw brains in see-through boxes.)

Hamilton called the first novel "The Horror on Jupiter," but that title was changed to "Captain Future and the Space Emperor" to capitalize on the Captain Future name.

Space Emperor was not an auspicious debut. It and a half-dozen stories to follow read like first draft efforts (which they were), rushed out to meet deadlines. Five of the first seven stories were to feature the same basic plot, in which Captain Future—an amalgam of Doc Savage and the publisher's own Phantom Detective in a futuristic setting—must catch and unmask a criminal in disguise who threatens Earth's solar system. None of the stories took place outside that system—a snug group of nine cozy planets with breathable atmospheres and native races of human descent. At this point the author was clearly working to restrictive and unadventurous guidelines.

"To tell the truth," Hamilton admitted, "so little was paid me for the early ones that they were all written first draft right out of the typewriter. After the first six, they paid me more, and I then did two drafts, and they improved a lot."

To say that they improved was an understatement. In the first issue, an anxious editorial had solicited advice:

> *Shall the scope of Captain Future's quests be limited to our Universe? Or shall his experiences plunge him into the fourth*

> *dimension—into the past, remote eons of time—or into the far-distant vistas of eternity a million years from today?*

Reader response must have been positive because the editors finally allowed Hamilton to drop the scientific-detective constraint. From that point on, not even the sky was the limit in Captain Future's Universe. "World Saver" Hamilton had been unfettered.

In "The Lost World of Time," crime takes a holiday as Cap and his buddies traveled a hundred million years back in time to an Earth where carboniferous plains are lit by flaring volcanoes and the silver glow of twin moons. To save the native inhabitants of Katain—the tenth planet which exploded eons ago, forming the asteroids between Mercury and Jupiter—the Futuremen leaped another three billion years backward still, only to find themselves stranded in an unthinkable time before the planets of our solar system existed.

The following novel, "Quest Beyond the Stars," took the red-haired sojourner out of our solar system altogether. To save the dying planet of Mercury, the Futuremen traversed strange zones of space in which all ordinary scientific laws are overturned. They flashed past alien suns, great meteor swarms, somber dark stars, and then skirted the flaming coasts of gigantic nebulae of glowing gases. No piker when it came to travel, Hamilton brought his adventurers clear to the heart of the galactic core in search of the mysterious Birthplace of Matter.

In "The Comet Kings," Captain Future pursued disappearing spaceships into the gaseous heart of Halley's Comet. He encountered a world of electrical splendor and terror, a race of glowing beings, and invaders from a four-dimensional region outside the universe. And that was just for starters.

"Planets in Peril" found Curt Newton cast in a stellar role as the savior of a dying island universe, where the very stars are flickering out. He had to battle the Cold Ones—living products of a disastrous chain of biological events that took place on the frozen planet of a long-dead star.

And so it went, with each new issue presenting breathless variations on a cosmic feast as World Saver Hamilton upped the fictional ante to become Universe Saver. Then an upheaval occurred when Hamilton's name was dropped from the series.

> "I wrote all the Captain Future novels until Pearl Harbor in December 1941," Hamilton explained. "As I was then a bachelor and figured I would soon be in the army, I notified Leo that I wouldn't be able to write any more, so he got two other writers and changed the authorship of the magazine to the pseudonym, Brett Sterling. But, in 1942, the army ruled they would not accept men over thirty-eight years old, so, on the verge of being inducted, I was ruled out and went back to writing Cap. Future again. Some of my stories then appeared under the Brett Sterling byline, and others under my own name."

Seventeen issues of *Captain Future* were issued between 1940 and 1944. Fifteen of the novels were written by Hamilton and two by William Morrison (pen name of Brooklyn author Joseph Samachson). The Morrison stories, "Worlds to Come" and "Days of Creation," were more than acceptable entries in the series, capitalizing on the potential of Hamilton's freakish heroes.

"Star of Dread," a Brett Sterling byline penned by Hamilton, continued to pursue Curt Newton's new destiny as dedicated cosmic archaeologist. This was the story in which the author went deeper into his consistently developing past history of the solar system. On the distant planet Deneb, it is learned that our human race came originally from another galaxy many millions of years ago. Before they came, two nonhuman races held sway in the galaxy—the protozoan Linids, whom our ancestors conquered long ago, and the mysterious Kangas, the mighty lords of darkness who sailed the star ways and sucked power from the suns a billion years ago. It seems that all of mankind has descended from the Denebians, who terraformed and settled many of the other planets as well.

In William Morrison's "Days of Creation," it was revealed that Captain Future's beloved solar system was bulging at the seams with population density. To solve matters, the ingenious super scientist proposed to do nothing less than create a brand-new world between the orbits of Earth and Mars—the artificial planet Futuria. Create it he did. And Futuria became a decent enough answer to the housing shortage—if you had nothing against carnivorous plants and Jovian flame breathers as neighbors.

"Worlds to Come," Morrison's second and final CF yarn, featured a return trip to the Saggitarian System, the scene of Cap's previous epic voyage in search of the Birthplace of Matter. This time our adventurers were locked in mortal combat with the deadly Sverds. The Sverds? Ah yes, the Sverds. Ten-foot-high, green-gray, dog-headed creatures who were half-in and half-out of another dimension. Upon the outcome of the cataclysmic battle hinged not just a single star system but possibly the entire universe.

Despite apologists and critics, nearly all the Captain Future novels were entertaining stories filled with color, excitement, and fantastic adventure. Like all the hero pulps, the magazine had but one aim: to give the reader an hour or two of simple, infectious escape from life's hardships. The extent to which it succeeded was reflected in a fan letter in the winter 1944 readers column:

Dear (editor):

If the paper shortage becomes so acute that you must cease publication of some of your magazines for the duration, may I suggest that you hang on to CAPTAIN FUTURE until the very last?

I do the work of four or five people every day. I have an invalid father and an ailing mother to care for and it's up to me to look after everything besides performing heavy manual labor every day six days a week on my railroad job. I'm so tired and exhausted that I almost collapse. So, occasionally, when I have an hour or so to spare, I treat myself to the super treat of treats—CAPTAIN FUTURE! That gives me the lift necessary to carry on. But without CAPTAIN FUTURE, my life would be dreary, gloomy and lonely indeed.

Despite editorial assurance that Captain Future was one of the lustiest of the science fictioneers, the lonely railroader must have been bitterly disappointed when no other issue of the magazine was ever issued. It had, indeed, been cancelled due to wartime paper shortage.

One consolation was that three additional Captain Future novels had already been written; these were published in *Startling Stories*, one of the publisher's companion magazines.

The first of them, Hamilton's "Red Sun of Danger," sported a memorable cover painting of Grag the robot entwined in battle with a winged, fire-breathing night dragon.

The final Captain Future novel, "The Solar Invasion," was ghosted by Manly Wade Wellman, a highly regarded American regional writer and fantasist. Unfortunately, science fiction was not Wellman's long suit, and his lack of enthusiasm for Captain Future's milieu resulted in an uninspired adventure for the rugged redhaired space hero.

While "The Solar Invasion" marked the end of the book-length novels, the character staged something of a comeback in 1950 with a series of seven novelettes (pulp euphemism for "long short stories"), all written by Hamilton. In this third phase, the mood changed from juvenile adventure to stories emphasizing atmosphere and characterization.

While even the longer novels were seldom as stereotyped as they have been depicted, the later Captain Future novelettes are excellent fiction by any standards. They are beautifully written stories, revealing an unexpected sense of melancholy as the aging writer examined the brevity—and frailty—of human life set against the vastness of space and brooding eons of time.

Edmond Hamilton's final Captain Future story, "Birthplace of Creation," appeared in the May 1951 issue of *Startling Stories*. In it, a more sober Curtis Newton again traveled beyond Sagittarius to the fount of the universe, the birthplace of material creation. There, in teeming star jungles ablaze with the glow of drowned and captured suns, he wrestled with—and ultimately renounced—the opportunity of godhood. As a pulp hero's swan song, it was an ending that couldn't be topped.

While the Captain Future novels were aimed at a younger

audience than most science fiction magazines, Hamilton's fecund imagination and zest for storytelling insured that they were great fun to read. Who can say how many young readers were influenced by them and went on to shape the very future they dreamed about? There are no statistics on such things.

A few years before his death in 1977, Ed Hamilton and his wife Leigh Brackett (one of the great science fiction writers herself) were invited to sit in the reporters press box at Cape Kennedy, and they watched Apollo 12 take off for the moon. Ed later wrote about his reactions to the launch:

> So, as I watched Apollo 12 rise in flame and thunder, if anyone at that moment had asked me, "Was it worthwhile to spend forty-four years writing science fiction?" I would have unhesitatingly answered "Yes." For I feel we had a part... a very tiny part... in this. We did not plan or build or launch this craft. We only dreamed about it. But perhaps the dreams helped a little to create a climate in which it could be planned and launched and built...
>
> Without a single exception all of my oldest friends, and some of them go back forty years, are science fictionists. Many others who were friends are now gone. And as the rocket soared up into the clouds, I found myself thinking of them all... looking back to the days when we were all looking forward, when we met in tiny groups and tried to peer into the future, discussed it, argued about it, and attempted awkwardly to put it into fiction. And it did not seem to me, with the thunder still echoing in my ears, that what we did or tried to do was completely unworthy.

Who is to say where imagination ends and reality begins?

Calling Captain Future / 187

CLOUDLAND CAVALIERS

Flying alone! A hundred miles, north, south, east, west. Thirty thousand square miles of unbroken cloud-plains! No traveler in the desert, no pioneer to the Poles had ever seen such an expanse of sand or snow. Only the lonely threshers of the sky, hidden from the earth, had gazed on it. Only we who went up into the high places under the shadow of wings!
— Cecil Lewis

ONE OF THE great obsessions of the Depression years was with the romance of flying. Things were rough down on the ground, but they couldn't be rosier up there in the endless vista of the skies—or so it seemed when you were stuck hopelessly on the ground.

To weary job seekers and downtrodden laborers, flying must have appeared a near miraculous escape from earthbound burdens, its practitioners akin to the gods as they rode the winds with white scarves fluttering in the slipstream. The trouble was that it cost a small fortune to own one of those crates. And you had to devote long hours achieving mechanical skill to fly them.

As usual, the pulps came up with a vicarious fix. Each month, armchair aviators could take off from their corner newsstands with a choice of dozens of high-flying magazines, each promising delirious visions of winged glory. Although there were never as many air titles as detective, western, or even love stories, aviation fans remained a dedicated group of pulp consumers.

The magazine laying claim to being first off the ground was Fiction House's *Air Stories,* whose cover proclaimed itself the "First Air Story Magazine." On the other hand, Dell Publications' *War Birds* called itself the "Oldest Air War Magazine." Both were published within a short time of each other in 1927. A third magazine, *Wings,* zoomed out soon after, ultimately achieving some kind of record by being the last aviation magazine to fold nearly thirty years later.

Most of the early stories were about air fighting in World War I, "the war to end all wars." The magazine logos reflected that fixation: *Flying Aces, Battle Birds, Dare-Devil Aces, War Aces, Sky Fighters,* and so on. Each was packed with romanticized epics featuring dashing Allied airmen and ruthless German foes locked in mortal combat above the clouds. Even the story titles soared: "Thundering Wings," "Sky Grave for the Gallant," "Brothers of Aces," "Sky Rider's Reckoning."

Since most pulps were essentially hero oriented, it was inevitable that the aviation titles would come up with some recurring fictional characters. Although never as plentiful as detective mystery men, aerial series characters did prove popular. The most famous of these were G-8 and His Battle Aces. There were dozens of other daring young men in their flying machines. A few commanded their own magazine titles. Others were used to help boost the popularity of conventional aviation magazines.

And what names they had, those cavaliers in oval goggles! Speed Rossiter. Loop Murry. Coffin Kirk. Jinx Jones. Ace Dallas. Luke Lance. Buzz Travers. Ding Darley. There was even a flying jester named Phineas "Carbunkle" Pinkham, who didn't land planes—he crashed them.

Writer Arch Whitehouse, himself a Royal Flying Corps veteran with sixteen air victories, unleashed Larry Ledbeater and Todd Bancroft against the Japs. He wrote of Tug Hardwick and Beansie Baker in *Flying Aces*. Adventurous aircraft salesman Crash Carringer (reassuring name for a pilot!) appeared in the same magazine. Whitehouse also wrote several stories about the Coffin Crew, pilots Armitage, Townsend, Ryan and Tate. Erle Stanley Gardner dreamed up a hyperactive flying detective named Speed Dash. And Doc Savage's Lester Dent wrote of Hair Noon, a Coast Guard pilot.

Most of the wind-bronzed highflyers were preposterously brave and handsome, with only their odd names to distinguish them. But a few stood out from the crowd.

A WWI series by Donald E. Keyhoe concerned the bizarre adventures of Philip Strange, "the phantom ace of G.2." Strange's exploits appeared in *Flying Aces,* a tripartite pulp which routinely mixed tales of Spads and Spandaus with factual articles and detailed model building instructions.

Although Strange pre-dated G-8 and shared similar characteristics, he never achieved G-8's popularity. Known as the Brain Devil because of his ESP and other near-occult mental powers, Strange was an ex–child prodigy who had performed feats of magic, ventriloquism, and hypnotism in showbiz. Like G-8, the Brain Devil was also an ace flyer and intelligence agent who used the art of disguise to confound the machinations of the Kaiser's evil scientists.

Philip Strange was the creation of Major Donald E. Keyhoe, who had flown in active service with the Marine Corps and had been an aide to Charles Lindbergh after his famous Paris flight.

In later years, he was to gain some fame and notoriety as the author who first brought UFOs to the attention of the public, with five best-selling "fact" books including *The Flying Saucer Conspiracy* and *The Flying Saucers are Real*. Critics of his UFO books often pointed out that he had once written masses of "far out" pulp fiction.

In the mid-thirties, Keyhoe sensed that youthful readers might be growing tired of beating the Boche. He developed a more contemporary barnstormer in Richard Knight, who was blind as a bat by day but eagle-eyed after dark. Not tied to the Western Front, Knight clocked considerably more miles than the WWI mental marvel, including flights to the Far East.

Flying Aces boasted other heroes of the crimson skies. Arch Whitehouse was responsible for Buzz Benson, an aviation reporter and undercover man for the Secret Service. The Benson plots usually involved peril to the U.S. Fleet in the Pacific, with Buzz zooming in to wreak havoc on bands of international crooks and not-too-disguised Oriental aggressors.

Another Whitehouse character, the Griffon, was Kerry Keen, young millionaire layabout by day and flying avenger by night. Whenever stratospheric evil threatened, Keen would don a scarlet silk-and-rubber mask and zoom out in his supercharged plane, the *Black Bullet,* from an underground hangar on his Long Island estate. (Years later, radio's Green Hornet would use the same shtick in an earthbound format.)

Flying series heroes became so popular at one point that prolific author Harold F. Cruickshank managed to maintain the monthly exploits of three different characters—Sky Wolf, Sky Devil, and Red Eagle—in consecutive issues of three different Popular Publications' titles.

One of the more unusual characters (by reason of sex) in the macho air pulps was Barbe Pivet, an aviatrix who appeared in a series written by Herman Petersen in *Air Stories* and later in *Wings*. A typical Pivet story, "Flaming Gas" (*Wings*, August 1928), had Barbe winging solo to the rescue and downing the villain's plane while her boyfriend watched helplessly on the ground.

And speaking of villains—Steve Fisher invented Mr. Death, a physically crippled Hun murder master who had "a face like powdered chalk." Death squared off with Yank flyer Jed "Babyface" Garrett in a series of eight wild flights in *Dare-Devil Aces*. These ran from March to November 1936 and terminated with Mr. Death and his black Fokker still terrorizing the Western Front.

Arthur J. Burks, Marine pilot and prolific pulpster, wrote of Jim Swain, an aerial Robin Hood in war-ravaged China. Robert Burtt picked up the aerial mercenaries theme with his stories of Battling Grogan and his Dragon Squadron of China. And Frederick F. Nebel turned out a series in *Air Stories* concerning tramp flyers Gales and Mike McGill, who roistered through the mysterious skies of the Orient in the early thirties. In a companion magazine, *Wings*, Joel Rogers pulled the chocks with that amazing gentleman Captain Death, top king of the sky sleuths.

The instant success of Popular Publications' *G-8* magazine led several publishers to attempt single-character air-hero titles. As might be expected, Street & Smith's entry in the air race downplayed the flamboyant excesses of their rival's zombie-fighting Master Spy.

Bill Barnes, Air Adventurer began in early 1934 with a novel titled "Hawks of the Golden Crater." Compared to the likes of Coffin Kirk and Crash Carringer, Bill possessed the blandest of pulp-hero monikers. Barnes was meant to suggest "barnstormer"—in honor of those frolicsome gypsy flyers who found exhilarating freedom while courting aerial death. He even had a plane named the *Stormer*.

The initial Barnes novels were written by ex–cavalry officer Major Malcolm Wheeler-Nicholson and most of the others by writers Charles Spain Verral and Harold P. Montanye—all under the house name of George L. Eaton. The main plotline dealt with young flyer/designer Bill Barnes achieving fame and fortune as a daring air racer. With his prize money, he assembled a gang of loyal aides and started his own ultramodern airfield on Long Island.

One of the charms of the Bill Barnes stories is that he was a recognizably human character living in a recognizably real world. Many of his problems were financial (a change from millionaire crime fighters), with Bill constantly running short of operating funds and desperately trying to hold things together.

In his first adventure, Bill flew his self-designed plane, a stubby little fighter called the *Bumblebee*. It featured rocket-assisted takeoff, folding wings, and folding rotors for vertical takeoff and landing. In his third issue, he introduced the *Porpoise*, a submerging seaplane-submarine. As each of his super planes was shot down or bombed in its hangar by various flying fiends, Bill was forced back to the old drawing board to come up with new ones. *The Scarlet Stormer* was a favorite for several years, but it was eventually stolen and replaced by the newer, faster *Silver Lancer*. When even the *Lancer* became a cropper (destroyed by a thermal bomb), it too was replaced by the newer, more modern *Charger*.

Even Bill's pals were fallible—the kind of people you might really know. Sandy Sanders was a teenager who could fly like a fool but was just a kid like any other. Others in the cast included Shorty Hassfurther, a stocky little World War I ace; Bev Bates, a Bostonian; Scotty MacCloskey, Bill's master mechanic; and Tony Lamport, his ground radio operator. Occasionally an aide was injured and remained out of action for a while. At least three of his friends were killed outright, including close pal, Texan Cy Hawkins, who was bumped off in a 1938 adventure.

Obviously, Bill Barnes had to be on his guard; he lived in the dangerously fragile world we all inhabit. At the end of many of his exploits, he sometimes realized that he had worked his heart out, risked his life and those of his associates—and all for nothing. Yet, like all pulp heroes, he recognized adventure as an attitude toward discomfort. If he and his pals came out of a story with their lives, his blue eyes would brighten as he headed for home and the prospect of another perilous venture.

One of the mainstays of the *Bill Barnes* magazine was artist Frank Tinsley, brother of The Shadow ghostwriter Theodore Tinsley. It's safe to say that the *Bill Barnes* pulp is collected today as much for Frank Tinsley's covers and interior illustrations as it is for the stories themselves. Tinsley dreamed up Bill's slightly futuristic airships and even helped plot the stories. His intricate, painstaking drawings of the *Bumblebee*, the *Stormer*, and the *Lancer* were complete down to every rivet and bolt—so much so that few readers ever stopped to consider that Bill's advanced-design planes were just imaginative fabrications. Even the Barnes Long Island airfield was portrayed in exact, unsparing detail in both the stories and in Tinsley's delightful interior sketches.

Unfortunately, after some twenty full-length novels, Bill Barnes suffered the ignominy of seeing his pulp refashioned into *Bill Barnes Air Trails,* a large-size semi slick. Bill's own adventures were reduced in scope to accommodate articles and model-building departments. Poor Bill. Eventually he was squeezed out of his own magazine altogether, winding up as a back-of-the-book character in *Doc Savage Magazine.* Writer Verral and artist Tinsley stuck with Bill through his tribulations, but by the mid-forties, his glory days were clearly over.

One flying hero who commanded his own book without fear of eviction was John Masters, the Lone Eagle. Named in honor of Charles Lindbergh, the Lone Eagle first spread his wings in September of 1933—a month before the debut of *G-8 and his Battle Aces.* Although doomed to fly forever in G-8's prop wash, he was the only air hero to last almost as long as the durable Master Spy—ten years and some seventy-six novel-length adventures.

Billed as the "World's Greatest Sky Fighter," the Lone Eagle was a legend of the Great War, a lone-wolf ace of Yank Intelligence who appeared in the skies where the fighting was the toughest and under whose watchful eyes no Hun treachery could be perpetrated. But the man himself, John Masters, could not collect any of the glory that was his due.

The moment he stepped out of his mottled Spad, he ceased to be the Lone Eagle. Like a cloak, he flung off that romantic personality and became merely John Masters, a man whose drab uniform bore neither insignia nor rank and whose papers showed him to be a newspaper correspondent from Chicago.

To justify Masters' heroic nickname, his writers made him a sharp-eyed hermit of the skies. He flew alone, fought alone, a freelance dealer in death and destruction armed with apparently limitless ammunition. His only friends and confidantes were Colonel Tremaine, the paternal, grizzled chief of Yank Air Intelligence, and a fiery little French general, Viaud. There was no romance in his life, and only one woman of note—the seductive but deadly German undercover agent known as R-47.

Perhaps it was the Eagle's austere life that made him less exciting than G-8. Perhaps it was just the nature of his magazine to be less flamboyant and thus less attractive to jaded pulp readers. The *Lone Eagle* covers were technically good, but they featured routine air-war paintings at a time when routine air-war magazines were glutting the market. By comparison, the *G-8* covers glued your eyes to bizarre compositions juxtaposing snarling Spads and Fokkers with skeleton men and giant vampire bats.

Although John Masters faced a few recurring villains (some masked suicide pilots known as the Lemmings, the dread organization of Boche spies called the Ring of the Nachrichtendienst, and the always provocative R-47), essentially the Lone Eagle stories were well-written, no-nonsense air-war adventures.

What made the Eagle unique among pulp flyers was that he fought in two World Wars. In February 1940, with "The Nazi Menace," he aged twenty years in one month as he jumped from the heart of World War I into the new conflict.

The character's updated legend had it that Masters had stood on the passenger deck of the Athenia and witnessed it shot from under him by a ruthless U-boat commander. He had been on his way home from Europe with the full intention of remaining a neutral. But the sight of innocent women and children struggling in the freezing waters of the Atlantic had turned him back with the determination that he would not head west again until Adolf Hitler had been destroyed.

Once again, John Masters had thrown in with the Allies, on condition that he carry no rank and wear no uniform except when necessary. No mention is made of the age of the still virile Lone Eagle, but this time he is equipped with more youthful confidantes: Pierre Viaud, the son of old General Viaud, Chief of French Intelligence in WWI, and Henri Laval. Henri had been a Boy Scout back in those hectic days and is now a pilot in the French Air Service.

Even R-47, the Eagle's old nemesis, returns in the form of the German spy's own daughter. The new R-47 is beautiful, sinister, and vicious—and she wears her mother's old perfume.

But something is missing in the new Lone Eagle—a sense of innocent adventure perhaps. War is never fun. It can only appear so when distanced by time and memory. In the early and mid thirties, it was easy to romanticize WWI flying spies, their planes slicing boldly through the clear winds high above the verminous trenches. By 1940, the reality of a new horror in Europe produced a more sober, oftentimes brooding, fighting ace. Perhaps he was contemplating the fate of his magazine.

Hindsight indicates that Masters' abrupt switch from one war to another was a result of declining reader interest. The magazine's publication frequency had dropped from monthly to bimonthly as early as 1937. It switched to quarterly in 1942. Even the name of the magazine was changed to *The American Eagle* and finally pluralized to *American Eagles,* as poor old John Masters was pushed to the back of his own book for a final, ignominious adventure. The magazine folded with the spring 1943 issue.

If the Lone Eagle never achieved the stratospheric success of other pulp heroes, he did remain a newsstand fixture for many years. Much of his popularity can be tied to the realistic details in his magazine's flying sequences. When the Lone Eagle vaults into his Spad, his feet "slam home in the rudder stirrups." He spots enemy planes by holding his thumb against the sun. And his wings "tilt in a split-S curve" when he turns to land. It all sounded just right because his writers had held their thumbs against the sun and had turned their fighting ships into split-S curves.

Most of the novels were ghosted by F.E. Reichnitzer and Robert Sidney Bowen, using the house name Lieut. Scott Morgan. Reichnitzer wrote the early stories. He had been a Royal Air Force Camel pilot in the Great War and had been shot down in Belgium while on a bombing mission and imprisoned at Rasstatt. Once he had been placed before a firing squad and saved only when the commandant had a last-minute change of heart.

Robert Sidney Bowen had left high school when the war began and had lied about his age to join the Royal Flying Corps. The youngest member of the RFC, Bowen went to France as a scout pilot and shot down several German planes and balloons. Later he became a newspaperman, test pilot, editor of Aviation Magazine and finally a prolific fiction writer.

Bowen also created the Captain Danger character in *Air War* magazine, although the series was soon taken over by pulp-hero specialist Norman Daniels. Beginning in 1940 and running through 1944, there were over a dozen Captain Allen Danger novels in all, with titles like Captain Danger's Nazi Hunt," "Captain Danger's Blitzkrieg," and "Captain Danger Over London."

Few of the World War II flying aces were as durable as their Great War counterparts. Two more captains—Captain Combat and Captain V—appeared briefly and then dropped from sight. Captain William Combat was the star of his own magazine, which lasted but three issues in 1940. A Yank-born RAF ace, Combat flew a Hawker Hurricane for the British 42nd Home Defense Squadron. Because of his mother's death at the hand of German flyers, the young American declared a personal war on the Nazi leader. A curiosity of the series is the publisher's reluctance to defame Adolf Hitler. In the novels, the villainous Nazi leader is slightly disguised as Herr Gruber, a middle-aged man with a mustache and a small Van Dyke beard—and is so portrayed in the magazine's illustrations.

Captain V zoomed through seven short novels in *Battle Birds* from August 1942 to September 1943. Created from the flames of war, Captain V once had a name and a position as a minor attaché to the pre-war Berlin Embassy. Indeed, the Gestapo had decided he was too well informed for the comfort of the Fuhrer, so they rigged a fiery plane crash in which he had come close to cremation. Declared officially dead—but reborn as the anonymous ace of American Intelligence—surgeons had given him a new, well-formed but masklike face. Returning to duty as Captain V, he worked in close contact with

British Intelligence and formed his own group of close-knit sky fighters—the V Aces. The V Aces had their own concrete underground hangar and their own Bell P-39 Airacobras, each sleek plane carrying six machine guns and a 37 mm. cannon in the propeller hub.

Captain V was the creation of Ralph Oppenheim, a writer with no flying experience who had produced one of the first air series—the Three Mosquitoes—and, with Captain V, one of the last. It is an ironic fact that none of the flying pulp heroes survived the war they fought in. They flashed and flourished for a brief time between the wars. By 1943, they were hit a one-two blow by crippling paper shortages and a growing disdain for the glorification of fanciful characters supposedly taking part in a very real—and increasingly painful—war.

A slackening of interest in traditional air heroes had been felt almost a decade before, leading the ever-alert publisher Henry Steeger to revamp his mundane *Battle Aces* magazine into *G-8 and His Battle Aces*. In 1935, Steeger tried the same trick with the ailing *Battle Birds* when he transformed it into *Dusty Ayres and His Battle Birds*, a pulp-hero magazine involving a fantasy war of the future, much in the style of his successful *Operator #5*.

Dusty Ayres was dreamed up over lunch—possibly a liquid one—at a 42nd Street restaurant by publisher Steeger and the ubiquitous Robert Sidney Bowen. Their protagonist would be a young man named Dusty Ayres, and he would be instrumental in repulsing a future invasion of North America by a sinister foreign power.

The idea was to plunge the hero into a futuristic war using instruments and weapons still prototypal in the mid thirties:

radar, television, rockets, gas guns, and sleek futuristic aircraft that were sometimes bulletproof and even fireproof.

Dusty Ayres was designed as a pure adventure series, its "foreign" invaders carefully fabricated to avoid any realistic political implications. In fact, realism had little to do with the story line. Set in the near future (probably the forties) the background of the invaders and their curious leader was sketched in the opening paragraphs:

> For three long years all Asia and Europe had been a seething inferno of war; a war started by one man, a man of mystery. Who he was, or from whence he came, no one knew. But like magic he had risen up from an obscure part of Central Asia and screamed his doctrine of eternal vengeance for all forms of government oppression. Nations tottered and fell, and were swallowed up by the great black wave that swept westward. The Black Invaders they became known as, and the man of mystery who commanded them they called "Fire-Eyes," the Emperor of the World.
>
> The name was because of his eyes. They were like blazing pools of flame that looked out from behind a close-fitting green mask… Yes, millions had seen him, and even heard his harsh, cruel voice that could speak every language on the face of the globe, and speak it without a single trace of any other language.

Old Fire-Eyes was a hulking figure dressed in a black form-fitting, bulletproof uniform with snazzy gold shoulder straps. He wore black gauntlets and a black skull cap that came down to cover the nape of his neck. Realizing that he might not have the looks to win a democratic vote, his aim was to take over the world by force.

Not everybody was impressed. In the magazine's editorial column, "Hanger Flying," one disgruntled reader opined: "It's utterly impossible to think of a man like Fire-Eyes even ruling Costa Rica, let alone Asia and Europe."

Be that as it may, the masked invader and his black-clad forces put up a pretty good show. Operating at first from a base in Manitoba, they threw everything from radio-controlled gas rockets to midget flame tanks at the poor old United States. And despite Dusty's heroic interventions, cataclysmic events occurred as his own Dayton Field was destroyed and Atlanta and Roanoke were wiped off the map.

Throughout the series, young Dusty's perpetual eagerness for direct action landed him in hot water with his own superiors but had a telling effect on the flying killer hawks of the black-garbed invaders.

Dusty's perilous adventures were reminiscent of G-8's. Although they lacked the full-throttle horror aspects of The Flying Spy's more outrageous exploits, they had more than their share of exciting air action, captures, escapes, and cataclysmic cliffhangers. In addition, the covers by Frederick Blakeslee were some of the most arresting in the history of air magazines, all detailing futuristic planes and rocket ships.

Blakeslee's cover for "The Red Destroyer" (December 1934) is classic. A massive crimson rocket sliced through Manhattan skyscrapers. Up in the azure sky, biplanes circled. Ant-sized figures raced about on the roofs of buildings, their mouths opened in silent screams as they ran, tripped, fell, plunged hopelessly down the yawning slopes of insubstantial towers slipping liquidly to ruin. It was a surrealistic daymare in vivid reds, blues, and yellows. Pulp Armageddon.

Despite (or perhaps because of) such garnishments, the magazine failed to catch on. In hindsight, it is easy to suggest that Dusty Ayres offered too much fantasy for air-war fans but not enough for science fiction readers. Perhaps the masked Fire-Eyes was simply too absurd a menace to frighten readers already plagued by the Depression and the threat of a real war in Europe. In addition, the nature of the series made it more of an ongoing serial, lacking the monthly change of venue afforded G-8 and other pulp heroes. For whatever reason, Dusty Ayres winged off into the sunset at the end of his twelfth issue.

If *Dusty Ayres and His Battle Birds* was an unusual air-war magazine, Dell Publications came up with one that can only be described as absolutely loopy. *Terrence X. O'Leary's War Birds* was, in fact, so far out—even for the far-out pulps—that it lasted but three short issues before it died of terminal strangeness.

Terrence X. ("sure and the X stands for 'xcillint'") O'Leary was the pugnacious Irish hero of several dozen novelettes that appeared in the late twenties and early thirties in Dell's *War Stories* and Fawcett's *Battle Stories* magazines—making him the only pulp hero to cross the loyalty line between rival publishers. Designed as a clone of that Irish scrapper of the movies, the late, great Victor McLaglen, O'Leary traded bullets with the Boche and punches with his drinking buddy, one Peter Maher McGuffy.

O'Leary's creator, Arthur Guy Empey, was himself a colorful man of the times. Empey had served in the British Army in France during WWI and had been discharged on account of wounds received in the Battle of the Somme. Like his famous character, he also served in the U.S. Cavalry and the tank corps. "Over the Top," a best-selling book based on his war experiences, brought him to Hollywood, where he wrote, produced, and even starred in numerous silent features. When he began writing for the pulps, he was billed as "the world's foremost author of war stories."

In such stories as "O'Leary's Rough Riders" and "That Fighting Irish Son-of-a-Gun," Empey's intrepid alter-ego (with his gang of cowboy Kaiser hunters), was sometimes a cavalryman and sometimes a member of the tank corps. In "O'Leary, Secret Service" (*War Stories*, June 1932) he even joined G-2 as an unlikely spy.

Such was the popularity of the Mighty Mick that Dell drafted him into the air corps in July of 1933, when he appeared in *War Birds* in a story titled "O'Leary, Sky Hawk." For some reason, the double-fisted hero and his battling buddy were even more popular in the air than on the ground. In the new series, the two pals were both air force captains, with O'Leary commonly known as Sky Hawk and McGuffey as Sky Rider.

In stories with titles like "Ghost of the Black Wings," "O'Leary Cracks the Crimson Legion," and "O'Leary, Zeppelin Killer," the indomitable warrior flew against such fearsome foes as The Scarlet Legion, The Black Eagle and The Black Roc. The O'Leary stories were so popular, in fact, that the publisher decided to let him take over the magazine. With the June 1935 issue *War Birds*, America's oldest air-war magazine, became *Terrence X. O'Leary's War Birds*.

It was a bit like allowing the monkeys to take over the zoo. O'Leary and his creator not only shanghaied the magazine but changed its nature entirely. For its brief three-issue run,

Terrence X. O'Leary's War Birds was to achieve dubious distinction as the most bizarre air-war magazine ever published.

Gone were the Fokkers and Heinkels of earlier days. Gone, too, were the Kaiser's pilots who flew them. As the new magazine's editorial so admirably phrased it:

> *We found that, to you, Terrence X. O'Leary represented the spirit of adventure, of dauntless, reckless, laughing courage. You wanted the Sky Hawk pitted against his natural foes— the evil, the scheming, and the vicious. You did not want him forever pitted against a nation with which we had ceased to be unfriendly.*

Noble sentiments. Unfortunately, the characters recruited to replace the villainous Germans came straight from Cloud Cuckoo Land. The first of the new novels, "O'Leary Fights the Golden Ray," introduced Unuk, High Priest to the God of the Depths. Unuk was a mummified, half-nude, 500-year-old madman who, with an earless stooge named Alok, had seized control of Lataki, a hidden island in the South Pacific. With the help of various world scientists—captured and turned into zombie slaves—Unuk devised fleets of air ships, death rays, and other futuristic weapons with which he hoped to destroy a blissfully unprepared North America.

Before O'Leary thwarted his dastardly plans, Unuk did succeed in obliterating great gobs of the United States. The Statue of Liberty was demolished. Half of Cincinnati was laid waste. A large section of Washington was destroyed. Five battle cruisers were blasted into atoms. The Panama Canal was wrecked. Death and destruction rained down on Chicago,

Minneapolis, El Paso, and Seattle. And that was just up to page 31!

In Empey's second superhero opus, "O'Leary, Dyno-Blaster," or "Adventure of the Ageless Men," the vile whip-wielding Unuk returned again, this time armed with such wonders as magic impello stratopedes—produced by his brain-doctored scientist slaves. There was more destruction of American real estate, with O'Leary achieving a last-minute rescue of Washington after making mincemeat of his two hellish foes.

A third, and final, story ("The Purple Warriors of Neptunia") introduced no less a worthy than Umgoop the Horrible—a shark-mouthed, indigo-hued, eight-foot-tall monster whose favorite sport was ripping arms and legs off hapless victims.

It seemed that the bestial Umgoop was the High Priest of the sunken kingdom of Neptunia. Along with a wicked High Priestess called Satania, the horror's main goal was to copy the excellent ideas of Unuk and Alok before him, namely the utter destruction of the United States and the enslavement of the rest of the surface world.

To further his plans, Umgoop even managed to restore Unuk and Alok back to life with the aid of a few drops of "cosmo-serafluo." Each drop of his restorative elixir was produced from the body parts of 1,200 victims, hence the need for all those arms and legs. The Mighty Mick and his battling buddy were also killed and brought back to life in this one. ("I kid you not," as Jack Parr used to say.)

If nothing else, *Terrence X. O'Leary's War Birds* did represent a unique—although misguided—attempt to come up with something a little different in air-war fare. Unfortunately, the magazine's risible plots gave the word juvenile a bad name.

As for those fine boyos, O'Leary and McGuffy, they constantly conversed in a brogue that went out with vaudeville. (In case I have inadvertently made *Terence X. O'Leary's War Birds* sound like a lot of fun, let me assure gentle readers that wading through 50,000-word novels filled with great globs of phony blarney dialect is a bit like swimming upstream through underfed piranha. Each sentence takes a bite out of you.)

With the O'Leary experiment finished, *War Birds* reverted gratefully to its original format. There was one more Terrence X air story cleared from inventory, "The Sky Hawk Screams" (October 1935). After that, the amazingly adaptable warrior returned to his previous scenes of glory—back on terra firma—in both *Battle Stories* and Dell's second series of *War Stories*.

The Mighty Mick's final pulp battles were fought in 1936. This time, he popped up in Ethiopia where, as a major in Haile Selassie's army, he again commanded a cavalry squadron and was known as "The Green Lion of Judah."

After O'Leary's delirious encounters in the stratosphere with Unuk and Alok and Umgoop, Ethiopia must have seemed a relief.

TRAIL OF THE RIO KID

ALTHOUGH THE PULPS are now remembered chiefly for their mystery, science fiction, and horror, far and away the most popular titles in their heyday were Westerns. In his book, *The Pulp Western*, researcher John A. Dinan noted 184 separate magazines devoted exclusively to Western fiction—a list which he admits is incomplete. In magazines with titles like *Blazing Western, Wild West Weekly,* and *Western Raider,* legions of dusty Galahads blasted six-gun trails to pulpwood glory. Vast and forbidding, the landscape of the American frontier produced one of the most alluring blank canvases in popular culture.

Pulp Westerns, with their visions of high adventure and idyllic romance set in that perilous dream world, gloried in the nostalgic appeal of the uncivilized—total escape from anything that might be crowding you. They spoke beguilingly to the homebound reader of men and women with civilization at their backs who were never afraid and never bored.

The pulps were clotted with hundreds of barbed-wire-tough town tamers. Riders of the purple prose ranged from owlhoots with colorful names like Warwhoop Wilson and Guncat Bodman to such recognizable waddies as Hopalong Cassidy and The Lone Ranger. Despite his radio and comic strip fame, The Lone Ranger's own magazine lasted but eight issues while his blatant pulp clone, the Masked Rider (who wore a mask and palled around with a Yaqui Indian companion named Blue Hawk), galloped on for over one hundred numbers. Go figure.

As Western titles proliferated, attempts were made to diversify. Inevitably, many cow-country cavaliers earned the distinction of their own titles. White Eagle—"mightiest of Comanche braves"—was the star of *Big Chief Western*. Popular movie matinee star Buck Jones was the titular hero of the short-lived *Buck Jones Western*. Each issue was based on a particular Jones film, including, The Boss Rider of Gun Creek, Left-Handed Law, and Smoke Tree Range. The Pecos Kid was featured in (what else?) *Pecos Kid Western*.

There were even northern Westerns *(North-West Romances, Real Northwest)* specializing in the adventures of scarlet-coated Canadian Mounties. While the "Northerns" formed a popular Western sub genre, no individual Mountie hero was ever awarded his own magazine.

Street & Smith, proud originators of Doc Savage and The Shadow, attempted Western hero success with their *Pete Rice Western Adventures*, written by staff writer Ben Conlon under the penname Austin Gridley. Pistol Pete was the gum-chewing sheriff of Buzzard Gap, Arizona. His adventures, set in the modern West of airplanes, automobiles, and telephones, were more mystery-oriented than those found in traditional slap-leather wild west pulps. His publishers may have thought they had the makings of another Doc Savage, even employing Doc artist Walter M. Baumhofer to paint splendid Pete Rice covers. Unfortunately, Pete's own magazine lasted a mere 32 issues before his adventures were relegated to the pages of *Wild West Weekly*.

It was left to editor Leo Margulies of Ned Pines' Thrilling Publications to lead the way with the greatest number of long-running single character Western hero magazines. They should be ranked at the top because of reader royalty and the number of issues published.

Described as the Robin Hood of the West, Margulies' the Masked Rider may have bested the Lone Ranger as a pulp hero because, unlike the Ranger, he possessed an intriguing dual identity closer to the publisher's successful mystery man characters The Black Bat and The Masked Detective. He was described as costumed with an all-black outfit complete with cape. The magazine's interior illustrators pictured him that way but cover paintings disappointingly portrayed him in colorful western outfits adorned with a discreet domino mask.

Prompted by reader response to the Rider's success it was soon followed by *Range Riders Western* magazine featuring book-length novels describing the exploits of three hard-riding, fast-shooting range detectives (Steve Reese, Hank Bell and Dusty Trail) presumably inspired by such Saturday matinee movie trios as The Rough Riders and The Three Mesquiteers.

But it was Texas Ranger Jim Hatfield in *Texas Rangers* who was the first of the "Thrilling" sagebrush superheroes to catch on in a big way. Known as the "Lone Wolf" ranger, there were 206 Hatfield novels in all, beginning in 1936 and ending in 1958, an endurance record broken only by The Shadow himself. The character was originated by Alexander Leslie Scott, who wrote the first six stories beginning with the October 1936 number. He named Hatfield in honor of his mother's family. She came from West Virginia, of the famous feuding Hatfields.

Author Tom Curry began contributing to the series in February 1937 ("Lone Star Law") and alternated with Scott throughout the forties, each operating under the fictitious house name, Jackson Cole. As Ron Goulart pointed out in his book, *Cheap Thrills*, it wasn't difficult to spot Leslie Scott's stories from those of Tom Curry. Scott had a grandiose way of opening his stories, like a verbose cross between Zane Grey and James Michener:

> *Starred with silver and banked in jet, the stately River of the Palms rolled toward the distant blue waters of the Gulf... when time and the world were young, it was born amid the crash and thunder of rising mountains. Once the desert through which it now flowed was a shallow sea swarming with strange and ferocious life. The inexorable hand of the ages brushed away the brackish waters of the grey, turbulent sea. The fierce sun of earth's lusty youth dried the reeking sands. The lonely winds that walked the desolate world lifted and shifted the sands, used them as hammer and chisel to carve the stranded islands into weird and grotesque buttes. The monstrous life forms passed away. The mountains grew tall, their cone summit giving place to spire and fang.*

And so on and so on. At a penny a word, Scott had earned lunch money before the story even started.

Another problem with the early Hatfield sagas is the dialogue. Some Western writers of the twenties and thirties considered it necessary to inflict painful cowboy slang and dialect on readers, as if their characters had studied under Gabby Hayes' demented speech coach. Apparently, this was the way you were supposed to talk if you lived west of St. Louis. (Memory tells me that the actors on the old "Lone Ranger" radio show talked like this, even though they all lived in Detroit.) The Tom Curry novels weeded out these faults. Curry wrote in a sharp, pungent style with less emphasis on colorful western lingo. In clearly visualized scenes he wrote of "horsemen galloping like mad centaurs," and "the stinging rap of bullets." Although an Eastern writer who lived in Connecticut, he was a student of Old West history and lore.

When *Texas Rangers*, *The Masked Rider*, and *Range Riders* (featuring the Range Riders trio) proved popular, it was Tom Curry who was consulted by editor Margulies about developing yet another Western hero title—*The Rio Kid*.

The new hero proved so popular that he appeared in 76 featured novels ranging from December of 1939 clear through to May of 1953. The Kid's colorful image blazed across action-packed covers—a powerful figure in blue breeches with a Union army stripe down the side, usually sporting a yellow kerchief.

In creating the character of ex–Union cavalry officer Captain Robert Pryor—the Rio Kid—author Curry initiated a protagonist unusual by pulp standards: a fictional being whose adventures would encompass real events and places and who would move among a supporting cast of historical characters, both famous and obscure. In addition, the author would supply illustrated sidebar inserts detailing the history of each of the real-life personalities involved. These mini histories, often three to a story, involved not just cowboys and outlaws but studies of real-life figures of the great Western frontier ranging from famous generals, governors and judges to native American warriors.

In essence, each of the Rio Kid adventures was in the form of a historical novel. It was a recipe that demanded a lot of research and trouble for a mere half-cent a word—exactly half the rate paid for the more successful Jim Hatfield novels.

Rio Kid author Tom Curry's writing career began when he was 23 and was hired to cover the night beat as a police reporter for the old *New York American*. "I felt I was a free-lance writer and wanted more," he once confided. "I wrote a number of detective stories, and *Black Mask* magazine bought one. Soon I became one of editor Joseph Shaw's regular contributors and my name began appearing in distinguished company—Dashiell Hammett and Erle Stanley Gardner being among the many authors writing for Shaw at the time."

During the late 1920s Curry published 38 stories in *Black Mask* but soon began selling all types of stories, adventure, sports, fantasy, science fiction to a variety of magazines. He became known eventually as a Western story specialist because of his knowledge and consuming interest in the history of the American West.

Under the guidance of Curry and a stable of helpers, the Rio Kid, his horse Saber, and his young Mexican sidekick, Celestino Mireles, fought their way through an endless series of adventures in which they encountered virtually every real-life figure of the pioneer West—not the West that really existed, perhaps, but the frontier battlefield of legend where every man had to prove himself a warrior.

What made the Rio Kid novels of more than passing note was that many of the historical figures made more than a token appearance; they played leading roles in the Kid's ongoing adventures. And Bob Pryor himself was more than a mute witness to history—he was a vital part of it.

Some of the characters appeared throughout the series.

Famed Indian scout Al Sieber aided Pryor in at least three adventures, "The Comstock Lode" (1940), "Arizona Blood" (1942), and "Idaho Raiders" (1946). That cadaverous gun hawk, Doc Holliday, shot and coughed his way through numerous stories. Sometimes Doc was a foe of the kid, at other times an ally. In addition to Holliday, the "The Renegade Senator" (1949) also featured Wyatt Earp, Dutch Henry, Bat Masterson, and even showman Eddie Foy. The Rio Kid story "The Buckskin Militia" (1951) teamed Wild Bill Hickock and Calamity Jane. Hickock made an earlier appearance in "Pards of Buffalo Bill" (1941), along with William F. Cody and Cody's dime-novel biographer, Ned Buntline. Cody returned in "On to Cheyenne" (1946) and "Buckskin Bandits" (1949), along with General Philip Sheridan. "The Comstock Lode" and "The Mormon Trail" (both 1940) featured Brigham Young. And a 1952 adventure, "Rogue's Rendezvous," featured the memorable team-up of Billy the Kid and Jesse James.

There were dozens of other characters recruited from history books, both famous and infamous. The Kid's old boss, General Custer, appeared in the series' introductory novel, "Frontier Guns" (1937), in "Guns of the Sioux" (1940), and in "Riding for Custer" (1941), based on Custer's campaign in Kansas, long before Little Big Horn.

The enigmatic Custer, "magnetic, inspiring, handsome as a blond god" made his final bow in "Bugles on the Bighorn" (1948), in which he fell victim to Sitting Bull's famous "massacre." (If old Yellowhair had wiped out the Sioux, it would have been called a battle instead of a massacre, but that's history, pardners.)

As Custer's chief scout on that fateful day, the Kid not only reported the massed Sioux he spotted only three miles from the vanguard of the Seventh Cavalry but warned the vainglorious Custer about attacking so many foes with but a single regiment. Some facts of history being immutable, it was the Rio Kid's only failure. Even so, the spunky Kid managed to achieve a Pyrrhic victory by intercepting renegade "ambulance" wagons loaded with Springfield rifles, thus preventing Sitting Bull from wiping out the rest of the Seventh Cavalry under Generals Reno and Benteen.

In his book *The Western Hero* (Starmont House, 1989) pulp researcher Nick Carr designed a chronology for the Rio Kid based on the series' generous historical references. As Nick noted, the Kid's mean-spirited, battle-loving horse named Saber must have been the fastest thing on four legs to carry his master to the scene of so many history-making events.

Perhaps some day a book will be written about the Rio Kid's major role in the opening of the American West. Until that day, we have his saga on display in those seventy-six issues of his own magazine, as reported by Tom Curry with the help of a few storytelling pards.

In Curry's novel, "The Comstock Lode" (October 1940), no less a person than former Virginia City journalist Samuel Clemens, already famous as Mark Twain, put forth the suggestion that the Rio Kid story would make good reading:

> "Mr. Rio Kid," Mark Twain remarked, "I would much rather hold your hand than anybody I know! Then I'm safe! I saw you in action the other night and after due deliberation I can say when I want a man to catch a jackrabbit for me, I will call on you."
> Pryor smiled at the humorist.

"It's a pleasure," he said. "But I don't savvy how yuh can write the way yuh do. That seems harder than throwin' a gun. Yuh've got me beat there."

"Nothing to it. All you need do is have someone bring you a big pot of coffee, a pipe and plenty of tobacco. Then lie in bed and shut your eyes and writing comes easy. But, joking aside, you've led a colorful life, Rio Kid. Maybe some day you'll tell your story."

"Maybe one day somebody'll tell it for me," the Rio Kid replied.

Somebody did. His name was Tom Curry.

JUSTICE, INC.

THE YEAR WAS 1939. It was a history book year. War had been declared in Europe but, as troops gathered on the western front and fortifications were strengthened, a strange calm persisted in America.

On the literary front, Steinbeck's *Grapes of Wrath* first saw print, as did C.S. Forester's *Captain Horatio Hornblower* and James Joyce's monumental *Finnegan's Wake*.

On yet another literary front, youthful readers of Street & Smith's *Doc Savage Magazine* thrilled to a special announcement: a new periodical was soon to be published. It was called *The Avenger*—the very name held a ring of excitement!—and the stories were to be written by none other than Kenneth Robeson, "the famous creator of Doc Savage." The new magazine would appear on newsstands August 2nd.

For most of Doc's fans, the wait must have seemed interminable. Finally, the first issue of *The Avenger*, dated September 1939, was dropped in wire-wrapped bundles from distributors' trucks across the continent.

On the cover, a giant, dead face with colorless eyes like ice in a polar dawn stared balefully down at a group of puny humans cupped within the figure's Brobdingnagian hands. It was all the fans could have desired. An inset box announced the title of the lead novel—"Justice, Inc."

The editorial column proclaimed:

> *We give you all the best that is in Kenneth Robeson's magic writing ability: and we give you a character that is the result of long and careful research and study, and not the result of a snap judgment. We have used the experience gained in making Doc Savage so successful, and feel that this new character will be of even more interest to you.*

It was not pointed out, but the interior art was handled by Paul Orban, who was well known for his similar work on both *Doc Savage* and *The Shadow*.

There were other echoes of the publisher's dynamic duo. While Doc was known as the Man of Bronze, The Avenger became the Man of Steel. The Shadow had often been called the Master Avenger; Richard Henry Benson was simply The Avenger—a mysterious being with a terrifying countenance, "dead as wax, motionless as gray steel." Much had been made of The Shadow's burning eyes; The Avenger's were described as "colorless, marksman's eyes, as brilliant as moonstones with a light behind them."

It appears safe to assume that the cancellation of several of Street & Smith's single character pulp magazines and the announcement of The Avenger's birth was no accident. The Skipper, Bill Barnes, and the Whisperer had all failed to capture the audience loyalty generated by their blockbusters, Doc Savage and The Shadow. The Avenger was clearly an effort to form a hybrid of the company's more successful creations.

The magazine had much to recommend it. The Kenneth Robeson byline was a strong plus factor, and with it *The Avenger* made an auspicious debut.

While the publishers exploited the Robeson name to the hilt, the stories were not actually written by Kenneth Robeson nor even by Lester Dent, his tireless alter-ego. They were the product of still another well-known pulpster, Paul Frederick Ernst.

Born in 1902, Ernst had taken up fiction writing in his early twenties. Like many of his pulp confreres, he was a prolific manufacturer of made-to-order potboilers; he frequently employed smooth writing techniques combined with a fine story sense to bring new life to tired themes. Many of his stories in the early science fiction and fantasy magazines *(Astounding Stories, Strange Tales, Amazing Stories)* were of high quality, and he was the author of the famous Doctor Satan series in *Weird Tales*. Later, when pulp magazine markets dried up, Ernst made a painless transition into the more prestigious slick magazines, where his skill with words earned him higher financial rewards.

Writing under the Robeson pseudonym, Ernst put real effort into The Avenger stories. The yarns were well plotted; characterizations were good; there was an unusual amount of attention paid to detail, at least by prevailing pulp standards.

Nevertheless, few derivatives engender strong reader support. The most popular of pulp characters—Doc Savage, the Spider, G-8, The Shadow, Operator #5, the Phantom—were all original creations. The novelty of their concepts, the youthful dreams they evoked, were rightfully stronger than the quality of writing that chronicled their fabulous exploits.

But, if *The Avenger* was a failure as an amalgam, he was at the very least an interesting failure and can perhaps be considered one of the last of the great pulp heroes.

His real name was Richard Henry Benson. He had made his millions by professional adventuring in the days when he was a warm, normal human being, before a traumatic criminal tragedy had transformed him into the dread Avenger.

In his teens, Benson had spotted rubber in South American jungles, led native armies in Java, made aerial maps in the Congo. In his twenties, he had mined amethysts in Australia and emeralds in Brazil, found gold in Alaska and diamonds in the Transvaal. He had done these things so successfully that while still a young man he was very wealthy. As noted before, wealth was almost a prerequisite for pulp heroes, despite (or perhaps because of) the fact that they were all children of the Great Depression. Whatever the sociological implications, there were obvious pragmatic factors: it took real bread to support such crime-fighting appurtenances as souped-up roadsters and high-speed Autogiros.

In the first Avenger story, "Justice, Inc.," Richard Benson, now a world-renowned industrial engineer, boards a Montreal-bound airplane with his wife, Alicia, and their small daughter, Alice. While still over Lake Ontario, Benson returns from a trip to the lavatory to find that his wife and daughter have both vanished. Worse still, no one on the plane will admit to having even seen them previously. When the plane lands, Benson is alone.

In subsequent investigations, Benson finds that both his loved ones have been dropped through a trap door into the icy waters of the lake—victims of a dreadful criminal error. The shock of his loss and the macabre nature of the tragedy combine to paralyze Benson's features, leaving his face as static as a wax mold, white, terrifying, never again to express emotion. Only his eyes could indicate that, "the glints in their colorless depths gleaming like ice under moonlight."

Much was made of The Avenger's unique physiognomy. In "The Smiling Dogs," Ernst/Robeson wrote:

> *His face was dead, like something dug out of a cemetery. The muscles were paralyzed so that never, under any circumstances, could they move in an expression. This dead, weird face was as white as snow—as white, in a word, as you'd expect any dead flesh to be! In the glacial expanse of the face were set eyes so light gray as to seem absolutely colorless. They were like deep slotted holes into which you could peer and get a half glimpse of a world of fog and ice and personal despair.*

Benson's extreme personal misfortune was probably the strongest motivation accorded any of the great pulp heroes. His was a death in life, without the wife and daughter crime had taken from him. Strong-willed, powerful, he is a man of destiny, stalking relentlessly through a desolate world, avenging but never replacing that which had been taken from him.

There is an archetypal scene at the end of "The Frosted Death," in which The Avenger stares emptily at the raging inferno of a shed into which he has lured his foes:

> *The fire lit up his wax-dead face and white hair. Fire that was saving nations from immediate war. The Avenger had succeeded in the greatest venture yet. But as always, success brought no content to his pale and awful eyes. He did not work for content. He knew that was impossible. He worked only to avenge the memory of his wife and daughter, killed by such scum as these—and for whose deaths all other scum should pay.*

The Avenger stories were well-plotted mysteries with mild science fictional extrapolations. As in many of Street & Smith's pulps, the stories often seemed bland when compared to the wildly extravagant melodramas of rival publications. While the Man of Steel could (and often did) save the world from various Napoleons of crime, there was little of the incredible spectacle and macabre variations of such pulp giants as the Spider and Operator #5.

Eschewing the Spider's frenzied carnage, Dick Benson played it his own way—coolly and intellectually. He was the master of the last-minute escape, falling in and out of traps with consummate ease. He made it a policy, as a matter of fact, to allow himself to be trapped as often as possible, this being his unique way of finding out just what the heck was going on.

Mentally, Benson was the equal of Doc Savage—a fellow expert in almost all fields of endeavor, with a mind that was a combination of camera and filing cabinet.

He differed from other superheroes in his physical makeup. Benson was but an average-sized man, just five-foot-eight and weighing barely 165 pounds. Each of those pounds packed superb muscle quality, as demonstrated in most of the stories.

Another of his unique accomplishments related to the tremendous nervous shock that had paralyzed his face. The trauma had left his face in a curiously plastic state. The features could not move of themselves but under prodding fingers they could be molded into any shape desired—and would stay that way until they were carefully put back into place. Hence, The Avenger also became known as Man of a Thousand Faces.

Like most blessings, The Avenger's chameleon-like countenance was not without its drawbacks. His face could never express emotion; and, if pressed out of shape, it stayed that way—a constant menace to him when he went disguised.

If comic buffs believe that Stan Lee was the first to invent super guys with hang-ups, they are simply unaware of such pulp stalwarts as Dick Benson. In one of his adventures, while in disguise, a blow to his jaw flattened and distorted the dead flesh around his mouth. And the flesh simply stayed that way, like putty! A disconcerting phenomenon to be sure.

Nor was The Avenger immune to common errors in judgment.

Once, while disguised as a crew member of a hostile submarine, he was accosted by an old friend of the man whose role he was playing:

> *"Do you remember, Molan," the man asked, "the time in Kolmogne when we went swimming, and you saved my life?"*
>
> *A trap likely. If Benson said yes, the man was apt to say there had been no such occurrence.*
>
> *"I'm afraid I do not," Benson said. "In fact, I do not remember ever having been in Kilmogne—"*
>
> *"Seize him!" the man screamed. "Brocker has a twitching of his right cheek muscles. This man has not. And he does not remember our childhood in Kolmogne."*
>
> *The Avenger had overestimated his man. The question had been a straight one and not a trick.*
>
> *The crew leaped toward him.*

Following Doc Savage's lead, Benson's adventures were never solo performances; he became the leader of a small coterie of people known as Justice, Inc.—a group of people whose lives had been irreparably damaged by crime.

While still tracking down the murderers of his wife and child, the Man of Steel picked up two helpers. First assistance came from a dour Scots chemist named Fergus MacMurdie. MacMurdie's bleak, hard eyes reflected a tragedy similar to that of Benson's; he too had lost his family when protection racketeers bombed one of his drugstores. Like Benson, Mac's tragedy had left him indifferent to the threat of personal death, and he was eager to join The Avenger in a campaign against the scum who preyed on innocent people.

Algernon Heathcote Smith—or just plain Smitty—was a Hercules. He stood six-foot-nine, weighed 285 pounds, and wore a size nineteen collar. Smitty was an electrical engineer who had been framed and unjustly sent to prison for a year. He joined Justice, Inc., after nearly killing Benson in their first encounter, believing that The Avenger had come to arrest him on a false kidnapping charge.

In "The Yellow Hoard," the avenging trio met diminutive blonde Nellie Gray, who quickly became a member of their group. Nellie was the Emma Peel of her day; a blonde grenade of a girl, barely five feet tall with soft blue eyes, she could fling herself like a dainty projectile, scattering men like Indian clubs. She joined Justice, Inc., after Benson and his aides solved the murder of her archaeologist father, saving the old man's cache of buried Aztec gold in the process. Though the treasure was in Nellie's name, it became the equivalent of Doc Savage's hoard of inexhaustible Mayan gold.

Josh and Rosabel Newton joined the group next when Justice, Inc., rescued them from assassins in the mystery of "The Sky Walker." The Newtons were a black couple, unique in fiction of the time in that there was little trace of condescension in Ernst's portrayal of them. An honor graduate of Tuskegee Institute, Josh was often described as a "lithe, black panther," but he feigned Stepin Fetchit docility when it served his purposes. Josh's "protective coloration" was an ironic comment on the image of the black man in the films and fiction of the day.

In later issues, still another member joined the group in the person of Cole Wilson, a young mechanical engineer "with a streak of Robin Hood in him," but the character made less impact.

Headquarters for Justice, Inc., was located on Bleek Street, a short block in New York City. The street was unique in that it was entirely owned by Richard Henry Benson. Three brick buildings opposite a block-square warehouse had been thrown into one, to house his complete laboratory, office, and living accommodations.

Over the entrance was a small sign: *Justice, Inc.*

The many windows in the enormous room on the top floor of headquarters seemed to have Venetian blinds over them. But the slats were not wooden strips and could not be tilted. They were strips of nickel-steel, set at a forty-five-degree angle so no bullet could penetrate the windows. Their ends were embedded in the masonry of the building.

The reason for such paranoid fortifications was that Bleek Street knew few unmotivated wayfarers. Quite often the street's only inhabitants were the ubiquitous baddies who made frequent sallies against The Avenger's fortress.

A closed-circuit television system linked the Bleek Street headquarters with a certain drugstore at Wayverly Place and Sixth Avenue. This was the store owned by Fergus MacMurdie and was perhaps the strangest drugstore in America.

The rear was twice as big as the front and was locked off from the store by a heavy iron door. In this big back room was a double laboratory. Along one side ran all the paraphernalia used by an expert chemist, which modestly described MacMurdie's abilities. Along the other was all the equipment needed by a first rank electrical engineer, and this was used by Smitty.

It was in these locations that Benson, aided by Mac and Smitty, invented and fabricated the scientific equipment and weapons used in their endeavors.

An entire article could be devoted to The Avenger's crime-fighting gadgets. They included: tiny, two-way belt radios (shades of Dick Tracy); bulletproof garments fashioned of special woven, transparent plastic that would turn anything up to a .50 caliber machine-gun bullet; and glass pellets containing a gas with such affinity for oxygen that it volatized instantly, spreading a black, impenetrable pall like instant night. The Avenger could touch a certain spot on his collar and, through the knot of his tie, spout this same inky pall, much the same as an octopus attempting to camouflage its hasty retreat.

The Avenger's automobile deserves special mention. It wasn't much to look at, being a rather dull 1935 model of a well-known, inexpensive make. But it was the favorite automobile of Richard Benson, who was rich enough to order Rolls Royce's in six-packs. It had a top speed of 130 miles an hour—and don't think for a minute that wasn't science fiction. It was bulletproofed throughout and equipped with devices and special little inventions for offense and defense that would have made an army tank officer gasp in disbelief.

When the vehicle was fired upon, powerful springs could ram bulletproof windows into place instantly. A small tube opening just under the breather-cap on the radiator would retaliate with miniature torpedoes of potent knockout gas.

Other, more personal, tools in The Avenger's arsenal included a pair of weapons that he kept strapped in slim sheaths on right and left calf, below the knee. He called one Mike and the other Ike. Mike was a special .22 revolver—so streamlined that it appeared to be a length of blue pipe—with a tiny cylinder holding only four cartridges and with a specially devised silencer on it. Ike was a needle-pointed throwing knife with a hollow tube for a handle, with which Benson could hit a flyspeck from twenty feet.

He tried not to kill but went to elaborate lengths to ensure that criminals would destroy themselves in traps of their own devising. Whatever the merits of such moralistic hairsplitting, The Avenger's machinations did allow Paul Ernst to fashion some fascinating, albeit elaborate, plot structures. If the plots creaked and groaned at times, readers seldom complained, thanks to the magic secret of pulp-fiction writing: pace, pace, pace. Action was spooned out in great dollops. Fans had no time to stop and ponder.

Despite strong action plots and sympathetic characters, the adventures or Richard Henry Benson lasted but some twenty-four issues in his own magazine. For a short time, there was an Avenger comic strip running in Street & Smith's *Shadow Comics*, and even an Avenger radio series carried by Station WHN in New York City and syndicated to other parts of the country.

The magazine had begun with high hopes in September of

1939 but at a time when other pulps were beginning to lose some of their vast audience to the lure of radio, motion pictures, and the new breed of superhero comic book. It started as a monthly and ran that way for eleven issues, through July 1940. Thirteen more issues were published bi-monthly.

In its brief lifetime, the series spanned two distinct eras. Volumes I and II followed the adventures of Dick Benson while his face was still paralyzed from his personal ordeal. This era featured the ominous cover portraits of H.W. Scott—covers that combined foreground action with the brooding face of a giant Avenger.

Beginning with volume III, Dick Benson suffered "a nerve shock of a different sort," regaining his normal appearance. The covers also became more mundane in aspect. These were executed with routine competence by Graves Gladney, Lenosci, and Leslie Ross.

The changes in Benson's physical appearance augured worse things to come. With its third anniversary issue, September 1942, came the sad announcement that the magazine was folding and that the stories would be continued as novelettes in *Clues Detective* magazine. This was the kiss of death that had been accorded such other Street & Smith heroes as Bill Barnes and the Whisperer.

Emile C. Tepperman, pulpdom's favorite takeover specialist, was assigned the continuation of the series in short-story form. Five of these truncated Avengers appeared in *Clues*, with a sixth and final one popping up in the back pages of *The Shadow*. Unlike Paul Ernst's concept, Tepperman's Avenger was a more violent character, shooting to kill rather than incapacitate.

The Street & Smith company was an old family firm first

founded in 1855. Over several generations, they had promoted such characters as Jesse James, Buffalo Bill Cody, Frank Merriwell, and Horatio Alger, Jr. into household names. In the early thirties, with The Shadow and Doc Savage, they had literally invented the pulp superhero. The Avenger was clearly another attempt to produce a national institution. What had gone wrong? The answer lay in the history of the pulp-hero mystique.

During the Roaring Twenties and early thirties in America, organized crime went unchecked. The average man felt helpless. When The Shadow entered the scene in 1931, that same average guy was in the mood for instant justice. The Shadow meted it out with blazing .45s and chilling laughter. When Doc Savage arrived, he carried the fight to global proportions. The Spider started off as still another playboy detective but quickly became enshrined as a ferocious national savior. By the time Operator #5 entered the picture, the North American continent required monthly salvation from incalculable armies of fiendish invaders. Still more demigods rose to join the fray: Secret Agent X, the Whisperer, the Phantom, the Secret Six. Tens of millions of readers thrilled to their exploits. Entire forests were leveled to spread the word. The law may have been helpless, institutions trampled and broken, but this secret army of incorruptible champions would arise—often with only minutes to spare—to restore order and sanity to a universe threatened by madness.

The truth was that by the time The Avenger made his entrance in 1939, he was simply an unnecessary commodity. Because he was second best, he had tried harder. But the timing was all wrong.

The world did not require another good ten-cent hero.

Justice, Inc. / 231

MASTERS OF MENACE

EVERYBODY LOVES A bad guy.

Not in everyday life perhaps, but in the larger-than-life world of vicarious thrills and adventure.

The great heroes of the pulp magazines could never have existed without an unceasing flow of enthusiastic nemesis. There were hundreds of pulp villains—thousands of them—cackling, scheming, dreaming. And barely a dull or uninteresting personality in the lot. Each month, a plethora of magazines shrilled news of their bizarre affronts:

> *From out of the East swings the Oriental mastermind, Shiwan Khan, into New York in another attempt at world domination! The mysterious power of the Orient against The Shadow's automatics as Shiwan Khan attempts to rule the world!*
> *—Shiwan Khan Returns,* The Shadow, *December 1939*

> *Over New York fell the murderous spell of Death's burning stare—and men died in the throes of some terrible, secret, inner fire! Richard Wentworth, alone, as THE SPIDER, dared challenge this astounding attack by a modern Genghis Khan gone mad... this new and fearful crime master who had blanketed Manhattan in the human ashes of his helpless victims!*
> *—Blight of the Blazing Eye,* The Spider, *April 1939*

> *He came from the very fires of Hell to blight the living, and*

he cared not for the cost of his lust! It was G-8 who had to meet this living scourge and match with his human courage and brains a Lust and a Hate and a Scorn for Life such as The Earth Had Never Known!
 —Scourge of the Steel Mask, G-8 and His Battle Aces, January 1937

If the bad guys were almost as popular as the good guys in the hero magazines, it seems inevitable that sooner or later someone should have thought of starring a super-villain in his very own magazine. Oddly enough, that was not to happen until given the sales impetus of an entire new breed of magazine: the weird menace pulp.

The so-called "weird menace" field was conceived in 1933 when Popular Publications' Henry Steeger decided to revamp the ailing *Dime Mystery* magazine. He used as his inspiration the nineteenth-century Gothic romances of Horace Walpole and Ann Radcliffe, combined with the visceral appeal of the legendary Grand Guignol of Paris, a theatrical company that specialized in the realistic depiction of scenes of torture, horror, and bloodshed.

Infused with new blood (literally), *Dime Mystery* emerged as one of the best-selling titles in the pulp field. Under the canny editorship of Rogers Terrill, the new/old magazine was so successful that Popular soon issued two more titles in a sanguinary vein: *Terror Tales* and *Horror Stories*. Rival publishers trailed with *Thrilling Mystery, Eerie Mysteries, Uncanny*, and *Sinister Stories*, among others.

Mild by the unshockable standards of today, the weird menace pulps were considered racy stuff in their time; their stories flirted with sado-sexual themes, and their covers usually portrayed young women in bras and panties (and sometimes less) at the mercies of slavering nogoodnicks.

Even though the stories were seldom as salacious as the covers promised, these few magazines were largely responsible for the low opinion many people held (and still hold) of the entire pulp fiction field. Many dealers sold them under the counter, and New York's Mayor Fiorello La Guardia singled them out when he warned the pulp publishers to clean up their act—or get out of town.

The weird menace yarns usually stuck to twentieth-century settings but paid due homage to such trappings of Gothicism as: threatened heroines, storm-lashed nights, dank castles, Stygian caves, secret passages, and purple prose. Many of the top pulp fiction writers (Hugh B. Cave, Ray Cummings, Arthur Leo Zagat, and Norvell Page) churned out stories for this subgenre. The writing was formulaic stuff, similar in many ways to the Gothic romance market, although decidedly more colorful.

The covers were great, though, especially if you had a taste for the preposterous. Who could resist such titles as "The Corpse Wants Your Widow," "Our Host, The Madman," "Mate for the Thing in the Box," "The Werewolf of Wall Street"—and, my favorite, "The Corpses' Christmas Party."

It was only a matter of time before someone came up with the idea of combining the appeal of the single character pulp-hero genre with the weird-horror pulps. The first such hybrid burbled out of its cauldron in February of 1935.

Its name was *Doctor Death*.

In fact, Doctor Death had been previewed a year earlier in a series of four novellas by Edward P. Norris in Dell Publishing

Company's *All Detective*. With the February 1935 number, *All Detective* became *Doctor Death*, thus inaugurating the pulp field's first full-fledged villain magazine.

Like all of the single character villain pulps to follow, Doctor Death failed to capture readers' fancies, and the magazine lasted only three short issues. But what issues they were!

The first full-length Doc Death novel was called "12 Must Die," and it was credited to a writer with the single cognomen of Zorro—who was not Johnston McCulley's famed Robin Hood of California but simply the pen name of a pulpster with the unprepossessing name of Harold Ward. Ward, who died in 1950, was a newspaperman, songwriter, and theatrical press agent, who had achieved some success in the early pulps. He was one of the mainstays of the legendary *Black Mask* when it began its life in 1920 and was a regular in the equally legendary *Weird Tales* magazine prior to his work on Doctor Death.

Ward was never a full-time fiction writer but wrote nights and after work, typing rapidly with two fingers. Unlike many pulp pros, he never submitted first draft material, preferring to rework patiently until he was satisfied. It is amusing to think that the man would write such terror-filled manuscripts as "The Shriveling Murders" and "The Gray Creatures" was also the author of some 200 Tin Pan Alley songs of the soft, mushy, sentimental variety—the kind wherein the singer informs his beloved that "under a moon is a good place to spoon some night in June." Who knows? Doctor Death may have been Ward's revenge on a public that lapped up such stuff.

The character of Doctor Death as expounded by Ward in "12 Must Die," is certainly one of the wackiest, most entertaining, villainous creations in the history of the pulps.

The world's greatest occultist, ex-dean of psychology at Yale, Doctor Death (or Doctor Rance Mandarin as he was once known) was described as a white-thatched, cadaverous figure with a thin face, hooked nose, and weirdly glaring, deep-set eyes. If a movie had been made of Doctor Death back in the thirties the part could have been played to perfection by Ernest Thesiger, the late, great character actor who portrayed the wonderfully nutty Dr. Pretorius in Universal's *Bride of Frankenstein*.

A habitué of caves and underground places, the old man was a human fungus who appeared to have an affinity with the earth itself. It is this affinity perhaps that made him one of the world's leading but most misguided amateur ecologists. Despite the author's assurance that "maggots of madness" were chiseling into the old man's brain like feasting woodpeckers, Death was portrayed almost sympathetically as a half-crazed, old dotard who, deprived of his Messianic tendencies, was probably content to while away his days, and especially nights, in his gloomy caves, caring for his fungi. His one fatal flaw was that he was sincere—a sincere fanatic, that is.

Like John Brown, he believed that he had a mission—that an all-seeing Creator had placed him on this earth to accomplish certain goals and that the mantle of sanctification made it impossible for him to commit a wrong. (Perhaps no one is a villain to himself. Mob boss Al Capone once bragged that all he wanted to do was bring a little happiness into the world.)

In the name of righteousness, Doctor Death had made himself master of the black arts: necromancy, sorcery, metempsychosis, demonology, divination—you name it. Backed up by regiments of zombie stooges, dissolution rays, antigravity flying machines, and gelatinous, vermin-gray primal earth forces, the dedicated doctor waged a concerted attack upon 4,000 years of civilization.

To destroy the plutocracy of science and in hopes of returning everything to a virginal state, Death selected as his target the world's leading scientists and began to destroy them one by one. Using methods both weird and singular, he delivered his ultimatum to a reeling society:

> *The wheels of industry must stop. Scientists must cease their work. All patents in the United States Patent office must be destroyed. The cities must be emptied, and men must return to the soil. Eventually I intend to wipe out all cities as I have destroyed the aircraft plant of the men who disobeyed my commands. To do so now would cause the deaths of many innocent people, and I have no quarrel with the common man. I intend, therefore, to give the cities time to purge themselves before I blast them to dust. Two weeks from today, on August twenty-fourth, unless I see that steps have been taken to carry out my commands, I strike again. The national capital will be crumpled into dust and the dust scattered to the four winds of heaven. Following that, another respite of two weeks will be given. Then I strike for the last time. When I finish, not a plant of any consequence, not a machine, not a building of importance will be left in the hemisphere.*

Tough talk! But old Doc Death had the wherewithal to back it up.

Arrayed against him in his fight for the Good Life were a handful of recurring characters, principal among them being Jimmy Holm, the ostensible hero of the piece. Jimmy's biography was true to the great pulp-hero tradition. Orphaned at an early age, his guardianship had been placed in the hands of the man who later became mayor of the great city. A millionaire many times over, Jimmy distinguished himself by his studies in chemistry, psychology and the occult—and later, after traveling extensively, had surprised his guardian by requesting a position in the city's detective bureau.

Jimmy's friend and superior was Detective Inspector John Ricks, a grizzled, honest "copper" who had clubbed and fought his way from a routine beat to the position of the head of the greatest detective force in the world. Ricks and Jimmy are joined in their battle against Doctor Death by Nina Fererra, Mandarin's own beautiful niece who comes to recognize the extent of her uncle's madness.

Later, in a remarkable secret meeting held in a small town on the east coast, Franklin D. Roosevelt himself forms an organization known as the Secret Twelve—a dozen influential figures all concerted in their fight to curb Doctor Death's exaggerated socialistic tendencies—headed by the President of the United States and with Jimmy Holm as his managing director.

In the meantime, the object of the Secret Twelve's vigilante justice was operating from a hideout only a quarter of a mile from Lake View cemetery, connected to it by a cavern once used as a burial ground by the ancient Mound Builders. A perfect spot for Doctor Death to function. It was here that the old fiend collected and stacked like cordwood hundreds of dead bodies in his recruitment drives for zombie armies.

"I am anticipating the future," he bragged to Jimmy Holm. "When the time comes that all mechanical activity ceases, there

will be a need for additional labor. It will be hard for man to adjust to changing conditions. Nor is it the Creator's desire that humanity should become a race of slaves. These Zombies, then, must do the drudgery."

Like many of pulpdom's mad villains, Doctor Death had the natural pride of an originator. It was his fatal flaw. Just when he should be concentrating on the primary task of eliminating his chief antagonist, he took time out to justify his actions or bragged about his genius. The consequences of such foolish techniques were that "12 Must Die" ended happily for society with Doctor Death temporarily routed, his headquarters—and with it all his infernal apparatus—burned to the ground. Nina was awarded the congressional medal by a grateful President and she and Jimmy announced their wedding plans.

But wait. One of the President's secretaries handed a wire to Jimmy, who glanced at it and then passed it on to the President to read aloud.

CONGRATULATIONS ON YOUR APPROACHING WEDDING. TAKE WARNING: GOD GAVE ME THE RIGHT TO DESTROY AND THE WEAPONS WITH WHICH TO WORK. THE WORLD MUST BE SAVED FROM ITSELF AND I AM THE INSTRUMENT. I GO, BUT SOON I WILL RETURN.
—Doctor Death

Return he did, and only a month later, in a story called "The Gray Creatures." That one began with Death's kidnapping of Nina and his consequent flight to Egypt in a scheme designed to bring civilization to its knees through instant overpopulation. Aware of the countless millions of Egyptians buried in the past whose bodies had been preserved through mummification, the diabolical doctor envisioned bringing to life hordes of men and women who had walked the earth thousands of years before Christ. He pictured a world inundated by living corpses, every spot as thickly settled as New York City.

Needless to report, he was eventually foiled in his scheme—but only after a dozen cliff-hanger scenes of chills and thrills. The novel ended with Doctor Death crushed beneath an avalanche of rock in far-off Egypt.

Doctor Death epic number three, "The Shriveling Murders," began with a remarkable scene in which President Roosevelt called together a special meeting of the Secret Twelve. With trembling fingers, the President removed from his briefcase a small shoebox done up in brown wrapping paper.

"This arrived at the White House by special delivery late this afternoon," the President whispered. "Look!"

He lifted the lid. In the box was the tiny figure of a man, perfect in every detail, yet smaller than a newborn infant.

It was the body of the Vice President of the United States.

But that was only the beginning. The President proclaimed a state of dictatorship. More great men shrank right out of their clothes. There was a lovely but sadistic Egyptian princess; voodoo rites in the Louisiana outback; horrific doings beneath an asylum for the homicidally insane; poisoned postage stamps; the theft of Cagliostro's secrets from the Library of Congress; and last but not least, Doctor Death's final confrontation in the gloomy caverns on the little island in the middle of his beloved swampland.

Meanwhile, over at *Weird Tales*, the legendary magazine (under the editorship of the equally legendary Farnsworth Wright) was undergoing some lean days. Circulation was down—despite its fame, the magazine at the best of times was seldom far out of the red—and Wright was concerned that the new weird menace pulps, *Terror Tales* and *Horror Stories,* might be draining off some of his old-time readers. In retrospect, it seems doubtful that this was so, because *Weird Tales* had long established its reputation as a quality vehicle for literate tales of imagination and the supernatural. The so-called weird menace pulps, on the other hand, appealed blatantly to less sophisticated readers who did not demand writing above a cliché level and who, in fact, preferred mundane explanations for supernatural trappings.

Wright attempted to appeal to both factions when in August of 1935 he introduced a new series character to the pages of The Unique Magazine. That character, Doctor Satan, is included within the scope of this investigation not because he was ever honored with his own magazine but because he was obvious blood kin to Doctor Death (they may have attended the same medical school) and because he was linked to the supervillains yet to come.

Loyal *Weird Tales* readers must have been startled when they witnessed Margaret Brundage's cover for that landmark issue. Her painting featured a masked figure dressed in an outlandish devil's costume, complete with horns and a scarlet cape. The cover blurb announced: "Meet the sinister and mysterious Doctor Satan—the world's weirdest criminal."

If the character on the cover appeared to be dressed somewhat ludicrously, it was not because Ms. Brundage embroidered the author's initial description of Satan's habiliment:

> *The figure looked like one robed for a costume ball, save that in every line of it was a deadliness that robbed it of all suggestions of anything humorous or social.*
>
> *Tall and spare, it was covered by a blood-red robe. Red rubber gloves swathed the hands. The face was concealed behind a red mask that curtained it from forehead to chin with only two black eyes, like living coals, showing through the eyeholes.*
>
> *Lucifer! And to complete the medieval portrait of the Archfiend, two horned red projections showed above the red skullcap that hid the man's hair.*

While Doc Satan may not have looked like your average pulp maniac, his actions certainly qualified him for that elite brotherhood. In the editorial pages of that debut issue, Wright somewhat nervously announced:

> *We await with eager interest your verdict on the stories about Dr. Satan, the first of which is published in this issue... To those of you who are afraid that Weird Tales will degenerate into just another detective magazine, we definitely promise that it will not do so... If the stories about Dr. Satan and Ascott Keane—the world's greatest criminal and strangest criminologist—are ordinary detective stories, then we do not know a weird story when we see one.*

There was little danger of the astute editor not recognizing a weird tale when he saw one. In the first story, titled simply "Doctor Satan," sides are drawn. The hero of the piece was a criminal investigator named Ascott Keane (love that name!), a man who had "raised a hobby of criminology into an art that passes genius." Keane was clearly patterned after Sherlock Holmes, that Victorian archetype whose hawk-visaged face and steel-trap mind were seminal influences on many a pulp hero.

The investigator was accompanied by his "secretary and companion," beautiful Beatrice Dale, while Doctor Satan was backed up by a monkey-like man named Girf and a legless giant named Bostiff, proving once again that a man can be judged by the company he keeps.

In the first story, hints are given as to Satan's real identity: that of a rich man, still young, with a family name known to everyone in America, a man jaded with purchased thrills who had made a study of super science and the occult to become the world's leading criminal.

Doctor Satan made his criminal debut with the aid of a little science and more than a soupçon of the occult. He began by blackmailing and then destroying millionaires by his unsettling use of a species of Australian thorn bush. Altered by the malefic doctor's botanical skills, the thorn bush seed, a tiny thing that floats in the air, was first inhaled by the victim and then roosted itself in his brain before flowering a mere hour or two later.

When the doctor found his scheme threatened by criminologist Keane, he trotted out his second little surprise: a destroying voodoo flame first compounded in temples along the Nile some 5,000 years ago. Keene counteracted with the green paste, which the old priests used against the consuming flame of their enemies.

"I'll not underestimate you a second time," Doctor Satan

warned. "The death shrub—the blue flame—you are armed against those. But I have other weapons."

The Mephistophelian inventor unleashed his other weapons in the string of seven novelettes that followed: "The Man Who Chained the Lightning," "Hollywood Horror," "The Consuming Flame," "Horror Insured," "Beyond Death's Gateway," "The Devil's Double," and "Mask of Death."

Doctor Satan's arsenal included: static electricity bombs, Cretan voodoo dolls, a time diverter, occult dragons, and a deadly, crystalline lightning tube. One of the arch-fiend's choicest pieces of blackmail machinery involved an atomic ray, which he used to realign the molecular structure of skin. Beaming the ray from a movie studio light, he was able to change the world-famous faces of Hollywood stars into grinning skulls—and right in the middle of a take.

As the series progressed Ascott Keane followed Doctor Satan into the realm of death itself, discovered that there was an actual hell—and had cause to wonder if his red-cloaked foe was in fact the incarnation of Old Scratch himself.

The Doctor Satan stories were all turned out by Paul Ernst, a popular and prolific writer whose name was a staple in the weird menace subgenre and who later wrote The Avenger novels under the famous Kenneth Robeson byline. In addition, Ernst was already well known in the pages of The Unique Magazine. One of his non–Doctor Satan stories, "The Way Home" *(Weird Tales,* November 1935 as by Paul Frederick Stern), is considered a near-classic in the field.

Ernst's Satan yarns were all competently written and are still fun to read, but it soon became evident that loyal *Weird Tales* readers wanted no part of the formula.

"Glad you left out Doctor Satan," one indignant fan wrote in the magazine's letter column. "We readers can struggle along very nicely without him. A super detective against a super crook has no place in a magazine devoted to *Weird Tales*."

Fearful that more old readers would be repelled than new readers attracted, Wright could only concur, and the series was peremptorily dropped.

Stimulated by the advent of the Doctors Death and Satan, the folks at Popular Publications (who started the whole thing when they revamped *Dime Mystery*) decided to come up with a villain magazine of their own. They used as their model Sax Rohmer's immensely successful creation, Doctor Fu Manchu.

Entire books could, and should, be written about the Yellow Peril theme which was prevalent in the literature and theatre of the West in the first half of this century. No matter what depths of ignorance and paranoia it sprang from, the menace of the Yellow Peril certainly added thrills and chills to literally thousands of motion pictures, plays, books, magazines and even comics. Today it is a quaint footnote in the history of pop literature—an era of adventurous menace that a more tolerant and more sophisticated society can no longer endorse.

Sax Rohmer more than any other writer brought world fame to London's Chinatown in the East End Limehouse District. In Rohmer's day, the area was a badly lit maze of alleyways where opium dens actually flourished and cutthroats really stalked. It was there, in 1911, that young Arthur Henry Ward recorded his first glimpse of Mr. King, Chinatown's uncrowned ruler of crime.

"I knew that I had seen Doctor Fu Manchu!" Ward said. "His face was the living embodiment of Satan." That same year,

Ward, writing under the pseudonym Sax Rohmer, finished the first of the Fu Manchu thrillers that would bring him lasting fame and would influence the entire body of popular literature for years to come.

Rohmer was not the first to exploit the Yellow Peril theme (a good decade earlier some of M.P. Shiel's novels were of the Oriental-hordes-invading-the-West type), but he certainly did it with more style and with decidedly more impact on the mass collective unconscious. Furthermore, he added his own wrinkle: not just an individual menace, but a secret international organization consisting of criminal types representing all races and countries.

Small wonder that Popular's first all-villain pulp should be titled *The Mysterious Wu Fang*. In 1935, when the Wu Fang magazine made its debut, the name of Fu Manchu was already a household word; the Fu Manchu books were best-sellers, and they were usually serialized in such prestigious slick magazines as *Collier's* and *Liberty*. If the public confused one character with the other, the confusion could only aid the sales of the humble pulp magazine.

Oddly enough, the name Wu Fang was not completely unknown at the time of his pulp magazine debut. As early as 1915, Arthur K. Reeve, creator of Craig Kennedy the Scientific Detective, had featured an Oriental mastermind of that name in his Kennedy novel, *The Romance of Elaine*. The villainous creation was carried over into the Pathe serial version starring serial queen Pearl White.

Silent movie audiences must have responded to the thrill of the Yellow Peril because Wu Fang became Miss White's own saffron menace in a number of early chapter plays. In one such thriller, *The Lightning Raider* (1919), he was portrayed by Warner Oland, a Swedish actor who later graduated to playing Fu Manchu himself as well as the decidedly non-villainous Charlie Chan.

For a few years, there was even a British Wu Fang; his adventures as related by Roland Daniel appeared first in *The Thriller* magazine and in such books as *Wu Fang* (1929), *Wu Fang's Revenge* (1934), *The Son of Wu Fang* (1935), and *The Return of Wu Fang* (1937). The character Wu Fang also turned up in comic strips (notably Dan Dunn, Secret Operator 48) and in comic books as well. Unlike Sax Rohmer's menace, old Wu seems to have been in the public domain, a sort of unlicensed yellow terror.

Doing their best to add to the identity crisis, the publishers of Wu Fang obtained the services of illustrator John Richard Flanagan, a fine commercial artist who had illustrated all of Sax Rohmer's stories in *Collier's* from 1929 to 1935, as well as the American book edition of *The Mask of Fu Manchu*.

Known alternatively as the Emperor of Death and the Yellow Dragon Lord of Crime, the mysterious Wu Fang was described as a tall, gaunt figure with sloping shoulders; his mouth was pinched and narrow, but the upper part of his face above the hideously gleaming green eyes widened to a forehead of great brain capacity. He usually wore a yellow silk robe embroidered across the front with a dragon—and was thus depicted in Jerome Rozen's excellent cover paintings.

Rozen's depictions were true to the mood of the Wu Fang stories, which in turn reflected the entire Rohmerian netherworld of secret passages, dank caves, trap doors, Egyptian tombs, poisonous creepy-crawlies, and the ubiquitous hordes of leering acolytes.

When publisher Henry Steeger first decided to do a Fu Manchu–type magazine, he chose as his writer Robert J. Hogan of *G-8 and His Battle Aces* fame. Hogan was no stranger to themes of Oriental menace, having successfully transplanted a Chinese villain—the infamous warlord, Chu Lung—into the Master Spy's adventures on the western front during World War I. Editorship of Wu Fang was handed over to young and pretty Edythe Seims, who was also a veteran of the G-8 magazine.

Under Hogan's guidance, Wu Fang emerged as a worthy godson of the notorious Devil Doctor. Like his prototype, he operated at first from Limehouse London, but the ever-lasting contest between Wu Fang and his heroic adversaries soon spread around the world.

Playing the Nayland Smith to Wu's Fu Manchu was Val Kildare, former number one investigator of the United States Secret Service. The hero of the original Fu Manchu books, Nayland Smith, was British through and through—a character based, in turn, on Sir Arthur Conan Doyle's Sherlock Holmes. Val was, of course, American, but on occasion he reveals his literary ancestry with such Anglicized exclamations as "Jove, what a pity."

One of the *Wu Fang* magazine editorials even went so far as to compare Val directly to the great detective of Baker Street:

> *Out of sheer modesty we concede that Mr. Kildare has not yet attained the prominence of Sherlock Holmes. But being younger, we are convinced that he can not only think as clearly, but can run faster and fight harder than the distinguished gentleman from Scotland Yard (sic).*

Aiding Kildare in his battle against the sinister symbol of the night was young Jerry Hazard, a newspaper reporter. Jerry was eventually crippled and retired voluntarily from the fray in favor of a two-fisted explorer and archaeologist named Rod Carson.

Their wily nemesis played it safe by employing hundreds of helpers, although he preferred the company of female slaves. Old Wu was unlucky in love, however—he thought that whips made up for caresses. As was often the case in pulp melodrama, his number one aide, a beautiful young lady named Mohra, fell in love and ran off with Jerry Hazard. Later still, Wu's tall blonde helper, Tanya, began making eyes at Rod Carson. No wonder Wu was mad.

Ever faithful to him were such staunch buddies as Zaru the beast man, who was part ape, and Djigas, who was described as the most repulsive of Wu's agents. Djigas was keeper of the Death Beasts—a poisonous menagerie of vipers, spiders, bats, and scaly mini monsters that combined the worst features of the lizard, the toad, and the rat.

Wu employed these and other little pets throughout a series of seven fast-paced novels beginning with "The Case of the Six Coffins." He was killed off in his sixth caper ("The Case of the Black Lotus"), but the following month saw him resurrected from his glass sarcophagus. That yarn ("The Case of the Hidden Scourge") sent the saffron scourge packing off to Baghdad, hot on the trail of electrical secrets first developed by Nebuchadnezzar when he illuminated the ancient hanging gardens. Nebuchadnezzar's secret suggested a plan whereby one man (guess who?) could fry every person on earth who uses electricity.

True to format, the Hidden Scourge ended with wily Wu once again in shackles, his shocking schemes short-circuited.

"It is written," Wu Fang cooed through his thin, cruel lips, "that defeat is often nearest when victory appears to come."

The Dragon Lord of Crime was to have the last word. His statement was the last one uttered in the final issue of the magazine.

It is not certain whether the *Wu Fang* title was discontinued because of poor sales or because Sax Rohmer may have finally balked at the use of a name so close to that of his famous creation. In any case, the folks at Popular Publications must have retained faith in the idea of an Oriental menace magazine; after a mere two-month breather, they introduced a similar title—*Dr. Yen Sin.*

Yen Sin, as portrayed on Jerome Rozen's cover, looked suspiciously like his predecessor, Wu Fang. In fact, the cover was commissioned for the eighth Wu Fang novel, "The Case of the living Poison," which was announced but never issued. It seemed to matter little, since both characters were based on the identical model—Fu Manchu.

The editor of the new magazine was Ken White. Interior illustrations were handled by Ralph Carlson, and the novels themselves were written by pulp writer Donald E. Keyhoe— the same man who as Major Donald E. Keyhoe was to become well known as the author of five best-selling "fact" books on UFOs.

Keyhoe shifted the scene from London's Limehouse to Washington, D.C. It is a Washington that must have seemed foreign to Americans living in the year 1936: fog-shrouded, mysterious, deadly, with dark doings in places both high and low. (This was forty years before the Watergate conspiracy; Yen Sin probably ranks as the most prophetic pulp to precede John Campbell's *Astounding Science Fiction*.):

> *Fog, like a sinister cloak, had swept in from the Potomac, enshrouding Washington in its clammy folds. By nine o'clock, the Capital lay buried under an ocean of drifting mist, the light of Pennsylvania Avenue only blurred yellow spots in the almost impenetrable gloom.*
>
> *Unseen cars crawled along the famous thoroughfare, the hoarse blasts of their horns muffled in the evil-smelling murk. Shadowy forms moved like phantoms in the fog.*
>
> *But there was one shadow that did not move.*
>
> *Almost invisible in the blackness of a shop entry, stood a motionless figure. Except for its low, harsh breathing, it might have been a dummy—a wooden figure placed there to draw attention to the trinkets in the window. But the window was dark, and the shop was closed.*
>
> *Minutes passed, and still the shadow did not move. There was something more than ominous about that crouching form. It was as though Death itself lurked there in the fog, inexorably waiting.*
>
> *Just once, the man's arm lifted. For an instant, blurred light from the nearby restaurant fell on a dark-skinned hand, on a curious silken noose gripped between powerful fingers. Then the hand was jerked back, and the strangler's cord was swiftly hidden from view...*

From those opening paragraphs, we are plunged into an unrelenting world of night, a universe dominated by mystery and murder—and even worse. Burmese blowguns poke from raised coffin lids. Innocent-seeming chair covers conceal Dacoit stranglers. Beams of emerald flame cut through walls and windows. Torture chambers beneath the Potomac. Tibetan corpse-flowers. Mummies that sing. Corpses with their heads sewn on backwards. It's the formula as before, straight from the special world of magic and menace that only Sax Rohmer could have inspired.

Doctor Yen Sin, also known as the Crime Emperor and the Invisible Peril, was more or less interchangeable with other Oriental menaces (one can postulate a medical college somewhere in Kwan Chow that specialized in graduating Evil Doctors *magna cum laude*). His eyes were a de rigueur green, although sometimes his pupils enlarged like hypnotic black pools—bottomless, malignant. Yen's symbol was a cobra. He was taller than most Chinese—an expert might have traced the Manchurian blood which coursed in his veins—and his feline grace was accentuated by the silken folds of his mandarin costume.

Fortunately, the good guy of the piece, Michael Traile, was considerably more interesting than most. Traile was known as The Man Who Never Slept, predating Lawrence Block's, *The Thief Who Couldn't Sleep*, by several decades.

Traile had been the youthful victim of a hasty brain operation by a Hindu surgeon. His horrified parents had discovered after the operation that the surgeon had damaged the lobes of the brain controlling the function of sleep. An Indian Yogi had saved his life by teaching him the art of relaxing his body completely, even though his mind would ever be awake.

"That's the reason for my hobbies—my studies—my eternally

keeping busy," Traile once confided to his adventurous sidekick, Eric Gordon. "Be thankful that you can lie down, close your eyes, and shut out the world for a few blessed hours. I have never known a single instant of forgetfulness in twenty-seven years!"

Traile's functional apartment contained no bedroom, thus frustrating Yen Sin who, like Fu Manchu, made a habit of springing surprises on sleeping adversaries. Instead, the apartment was a maze of exotic weapons, gun cases, lamps, swords, carvings, and curios from scores of countries. The objects were like monuments down the long vista of sleepless years, even to the language books on his table—reminders of Traile's endless search for new challenges to ward off the desolation of endless nights.

While most of us would consider his affliction a blessing—he had his nights free to read and bone up on all the world's knowledge—Traile himself considered it his Achilles' heel. He had an imperative need for recharging his vitality by frequent rest periods; prolonged action without a yogalike relaxation would bring on a state of exhaustion terrifying in its sudden effect. He knew that not even sheer agony, not a stunning blow, could blot out his wakeful brain. Death was the only sleep he would ever know.

Despite this intriguing hero-with-a-hang-up, the new magazine was even less successful than its predecessor. The career of the Crime Emperor was terminated after three brief forays into print. (Sales were not the only reason; publisher Steeger has since related that he yanked the magazine off the stands when someone pointed out that Yen Sin sounded like a sexual reference in Yiddish.)

As in all the supervillain magazines, the series had no resolution. At the end of the third novel, Doctor Yen Sin remained still at large. Somewhere in the Valhalla of pulp villains, Wu Fang and Yen Sin must still exist, plotting their evil schemes, dreaming their insane dreams.

Two of the strangest and most puzzling of all pulp magazines were *The Octopus* and *The Scorpion*. The magazines lasted but one issue each, and one was really a follow-up to the other. For years, pulp historians believed that both issues were written by Norvell W. Page (under the pseudonym Randolph Craig), the super-imaginative chronicler of the Spider's turbulent tribulations. Small wonder, since both The Octopus and The Scorpion raced with Page's brand of manic invention and overheated melodrama. But researcher Robert Weinberg has since revealed that payment checks for both stories were made out to the husband-and-wife team of Ejler and Edith Jacobson, Page's fellow specialists in the weird menace field. If Page did write both novels, it's possible that the Jacobsons were paid to retool his Octopus character into the equally sinister Scorpion—surely the most bizarre mutation in fictional history. To clarify earlier ruminations regarding authorship of the Octopus/Scorpion stories, the original writer is now believed to be the prodigious Arthur Leo Zagat, one of the acknowledged masters of the weird menace yarn. It was Zagat's work that the Jacobsons may have reworked to suit editorial specifications.

The first and only issue of *The Octopus* (listed on the contents page as volume 1, number 4 for reasons that only pulp publisher's accountants understood) contained an editorial feature that attempted to explain something of the magazine's new slant on villainy:

> *"The pages of man's history are crowded with strange and awesome legends,"* the editorial began, *"weird, unauthenticated tales of monstrous beings and eerie happenings. Of them all, perhaps the most fantastically grewsome (sic) is the little-known legend of the 'Purple Eye.' All the evils of mankind (so runs this legend) can be blamed upon the men with purple eyes. During every great social catastrophe in history, purple eyes have made their appearance as harbingers of destruction... Randolph Craig—an author of national reputation who has assumed this nom de plume for the purpose of this series—has, in the pages which follow, revived this figure out of ancient legend. He has made of him a modern super-criminal who, for protective purposes, has assumed the name of The Octopus. And he has given him all those truly weird and terrifying powers which modern science can bestow upon a great intellect."*

Other than that outré historical footnote, there is no more attempt to explain who The Octopus is or what fuels his insane rage. He is the consummate, interchangeable master villain: a madman willing to destroy human society in order to dominate it.

Physically, The Octopus would draw second-takes in any crowd, even in today's liberated milieu. He is described as a weird, sea-green thing with four suction-cupped, weaving tentacles above hideously malformed legs. He wears a small, pointed mask; beneath the mask a purple light glows and behind the light, two gigantic luminous eyes.

If The Octopus himself was a little strange, he was hardly more so than his chief antagonist. The hero of the book was a young millionaire philanthropist named Jeffrey Fairchild.

Like many other pulp heroes, and especially those created by Norvell Page, Fairchild is not content with one simple identity. In fact, not even two distinct identities are good enough for him. Within a few pages of the story opening, Jeffrey was revealed in a weird triptych personality split. At least part of the time he was Jeffrey Fairchild, son of the late Dr. Henry Fairchild, who had achieved medical fame and a sizable fortune before his death. Jeffrey, as administrator of his father's estate, had been instrumental in the erection of the Mid-City Hospital and in the further allowance of the large sums necessary for the hospital's upkeep.

Jeffrey's own younger brother, Robert Fairchild, was a longtime patient in Mid-City Hospital; the youth's body had been permanently crippled by ruthless criminals. It was from that traumatic incident that Jeff's interest in crime fighting had started.

His brother's illness, both physical and mental, had taught Jeff that healing must go deeper than he had imagined. With the use of a grey wig and makeup in order to pose as the trusted old Doctor Skull, he sometimes had been able to fight more battles for the poor in his slum neighborhood than confining his skill solely to the struggle against disease.

It was Jeff's third identity that led the reader to suspect the lad's own sanity, for in an even greater effort to root out the malignant growth of crime in the community body, he assumed the role of the dreaded Skull Killer. The legend of the Skull Killer had flared to life when three insurance policy racketeers were found one by one, in various lonely corners of New York, with raw outlines of skulls burned into their foreheads. The weapon used had been a metal stamp fashioned in the shape of a skull; in the middle of the stamp was a single steel spike. The tooth of the skull had been used like the exacting thunderbolt of an ancient god, and when the victim fell, he bore the Mark of the Skull as a death sign.

In the underworld, the Skull Killer—like the Spider before him—was a dread legend, and the mark of the Skull was known as a declaration of war to the death. Among the police, he was regarded benevolently, although each fresh killing brought assurances from the commissioner's office that the Skull Killer would shortly be brought to justice.

As a man trained to heal rather than injure, Jeffrey was aware that his work as the Skull Killer was violent medicine, but he also believed that there were times when nothing short of radical surgery could keep the patient alive—the patient in this case being society itself.

As noted, this theme of ruthless vigilante justice was a popular one in the pulp magazines of the thirties. It was a theme that popular entertainment would return to with the advent of such controversial films as *Death Wish* and *Dirty Harry* and in a rash of pulp-inspired paperback novels along the lines of Don Pendleton's best-selling "Executioner" books.

What made the thirties stories drastically different from their modern counterparts was the imaginative scope of their plots, inspired no doubt by the flagrant schemes of their larger-than-life villains. The Octopus, for instance, was clearly no semi-sympathetic Sicilian father figure. Instead, he was the genuine article: a real honest-to-God, pulp-fiction maniac.

Consider as evidence this opening vignette in "The City Condemned to Hell." Gentle old Doctor Skull (Jeffrey Fairchild) had taken in a woman who was found battered and half crazed, the victim of an inexplicable assault that left her almost drained of blood. Then the good doctor discovered—to his horror—that his patient had no pulse or heartbeat and that her blood was of the temperature and approximate consistency of seawater! And she moaned repeatedly something about an octopus....

The scene in question began when Doctor Skull heard a scuffle behind the curtains that veil Mrs. Purvins from the rest of Ward Seven. He brushed past the curtain and finds:

> *Mrs. Purvins' mouth was fastened like a suction pump on the nurse's bosom, and in the staring grey eyes there was stark, maddened hunger!*
>
> *Dr. Skull seized his patient's shoulders, his muscular fingers pulled against that sucking, intractable force even as he gasped at the hideous strength of those hungry lips... Then, with a soft woosh, he pulled her clear.*
>
> *The nurse dropped like a dead weight, with a three-inch circle of raw muscle bleeding over her heart, and even more terrifying in its implications, he saw the shredded torn remnants of part of her uniform on the floor!*
>
> *The thing that had been his patient turned its shining inhuman eyes on the doctor. Suddenly it reared—not on it legs, but with a swift upward surge that seemed to involve every molecule of matter in its body. He felt the white surgeon's jacket torn from him as though it were cheesecloth and suddenly he understood why the nurse had been unable to give alarm when she had been attacked.*
>
> *The thing's clammy hand slapped against his mouth, jammed into his throat, nearly suffocating him, while with the swiftness*

of a striking snake, that terrible mouth fastened on his shoulder, its suction rending his skin, tearing with intolerable pain at the muscular flesh beneath.

He lunged desperately with arms and legs—felt himself free, and gasped for air. He cried out then, trying to call for help as his staring eyes saw his erstwhile patient rear up at the window, and with a peculiarly undulating movement slip outside. He staggered after it, his fingers clutching the sill as the Thing descended the fire escape with unbelievable rapidity... And then he saw something else that momentarily caused him to forget his pain, and his horror.

As the Thing passed the third floor, a snakily prehensile arm whirled a net from a window, trapped the creature that had been Mrs. Purvins and pulled her back inside the hospital.

And that, he knew, was one of the windows opening from the maternity ward!

What in the name of reason is going on here?

Well, it seems that our friend The Octopus had created an army of atavisms—once ordinary men and women who had millions and millions of years of evolution lopped off their heritage. They had suffered some kind of dreadful sea change. And now, as the city slept, they came crawling from their subterranean sanctuaries to perform the tasks set out by their octopod mentor.

Entrenched in the very heart of Manhattan, in a new skyscraper citadel aptly called the Victory Building, The Octopus beamed out a purple arm of death—an ultraviolet ray—to sweep away his enemies. Each night a dreadful cavalcade—malformed creatures that once were human—poured forth from their secret places as if summoned by the awful beam.

New York City was in a state of siege, the first pawn in a master plan for world conquest.

As in most pulp character novels, things get a lot worse before they get better. The Octopus beamed in on Jeff's beloved Mid-City Hospital, demolishing the building entirely. Within a few lightning-paced chapters, some eight million innocent victims had been destroyed (you got a lot of spectacle for your dime in those days). What's worse, Jeff's alter-ego, Doctor Skull, was condemned as their murderer.

All's well that ends well, however—as another famous hack writer once said. By the time page sixty-three rolls around, a bewildering array of plot complexities had been resolved, The Octopus and his fishy minions had been routed, and Jeff had taken over as the new owner of the once infamous Victory Building. He planned to turn the edifice into a haven for the sick and injured, a logical substitute for his devastated Mid-City Hospital. Considering the number of sick and injured by this point, one could only hope that it's a mighty big structure:

> But The Octopus—that incredibly evil personality who had been the skyscraper's first master—would his presence really be gone forever from the place he lorded? Jeffrey recalled those old legends of the Deathless One, and he couldn't swear that the man was dead. It had been impossible to identify all the mangled bodies after that dreadful revenge.
>
> Jeffrey sighed. He had done his part in the freeing of this city; he could only continue to do his part in the interests of its welfare. If sometime in the unpredictable future that essence of evil threat-

ened once more to test its malignant, deadly powers, the new owner of the Victory Building would have to do his part again...

Poor Jeff didn't have long to wait. Precisely two months later, his specialized services were required once again in what appeared to be a new magazine—*The Scorpion*.

Despite the magazine's disclaimer, The Scorpion was really our old friend The Octopus wearing a new fright mask. The lead novel, "Satan's Incubator," was an obvious rewrite of what was to have been the second Octopus story, with all references to The Octopus altered to that of The Scorpion. All the other major characters remained the same.

Physically, the cowled figure of The Scorpion appeared to be more human than the tentacle-waving Octopus—if it hadn't been for a birthmark extending from his forehead to his chin. Black and as clearly outlined as a shadow at noon, the disfigurement was the exact replica of a scorpion. While the super fiend's stigmata is less grotesque than in his previous incarnation, his brain is honed to even greater nastiness.

This time, the chastened but wily madman had discovered the benefits of working within the establishment. Operating through the city administration itself, he had somehow fashioned a huge base beneath Manhattan, the symbolic entrance to which was the city's main garbage incinerator. A fleet of Scorpion-controlled garbage trucks rumbled out into the city's streets each night, each one equipped with the latest in hellish gadgetry: hypnotic brain rotors capable of turning ordinary citizens into packs of murder-maniacs.

"Last week," announced a Scorpion henchman at a secret coun-

cil meeting, "we had three trucks making rounds in the city, equipped with four brain rotors each. Even with that meager equipment we were able to bring several score new subjects a day to The Scorpion. Now, we have fifty trucks ready to start as soon as the new rotors are put in. Six of them will be equipped with one multiple brain rotor capable of transforming twice as many subjects as the old-type engine, in one-tenth the time."

American know-how in action! Furthermore, The Scorpion had the ruthlessness to see that his newfound slaves stayed in line. You think you're familiar with nastiness? Witness this scene in the master fiend's incinerator headquarters; The Scorpion was addressing his lieutenants:

"What you are about to witness will sharpen your faculties immensely," he promises. "You, Gordon, you were a veterinarian once. I want you to perform an operation on this man Dugan. Take him into the inner room and amputate his legs. Be careful about it—I want him to stay alive and in good appetite. When he comes to, if he requires a fluid diet, offer him broth brewed from his own legs. Nothing else. As soon as he can stand it, take off the arms. Those four chunks of meat should have enough nourishment to last him a week. If he wants something solid, fry him a piece of his own ham."

How's that for nasty?

Fortunately for the citizens of Fun City, Jeff Fairchild is around in his guise as the villain-hating Skull Killer. As in the previous Octopus novel, the plot of "Satan's Incubator" contained enough elements for a dozen normal stories. It combined an outrageous sense of melodrama with the pulp writers' knack of making the preposterous believable. Well... almost believable.

Suffice it to say that by the time the final chapter rolled around, much of New York City was in ruins (again), and the good guys were about to pull themselves phoenix-like from The Scorpion's funeral pyre:

> *The city would be as it had been before except for a thousand empty places that had been filled before these two days of horror. How long would it be that way? No man could have survived who remained below ground during that terrific explosion—but was The Scorpion a man, and no more? For the leader of the Purple Eyes could not die, the old legend had stated—and everything else in the legend had proven true.*
>
> *Jeffrey touched the Stamp of the Skull Killer in his pocket. If the city was attacked some time in the future, that was the only answer he knew.*

The stamp of the Skull Killer was to remain in Jeff's pocket because no other issue of *The Scorpion* ever appeared. Perhaps the bizarre two-faced villain and his tripartite protagonist were too far-out even—for the wild and woolly pulps.

Perhaps readers simply did not take to magazines that honored criminals in their titles.

In any case, the quick death of The Octopus/Scorpion brought an end to the all-villain pulp magazines. It was the bad guys' last hurrah.

Today, these magazines are among the scarcest of surviving pulps. Depending on title and condition, they fetch inflated prices from dealers in paper collectibles—an interesting fact considering what must have been reader resistance to laying out the original cover price: a modest ten cents.

Not counting the Doctor Satan stories in *Weird Tales*, there were only five pulp villain titles ever published—fifteen novels in all. The entire subgenre came into existence and perished forever with those fifteen issues.

Various archfiends would continue plaguing the great pulp heroes right up until the final gasp of the pulps themselves. But never again would a villain have a magazine all to his very own.

The publishers had learned the bitter lesson which their readers already knew:

Crime Does Not Pay.

LOST CITIES AND HIDDEN JUNGLES

IMAGINE A WORLD in which Tarzan of the Apes had never existed. Even if you could, who would want to live in such a dreary place? Of all the great pulp heroes, Tarzan is incontestably the most universally renowned, even among those who have never read a book of any kind.

In the mid forties, in the lingering summer dusk, there was barely a street in our neighborhood that was not punctuated by sudden falsetto impressions of Johnny Weissmuller's fearsome jungle yodel. Known to youthful literati as the "Victory Cry of the Bull Ape," it was a sound effect as familiar to my generation of kids as a mother's call to dinner.

Like Dodge City, Pacific battlegrounds, and the red planet Mars, Tarzan's jungle was never far from us. We swung on ropes, pretending they were vines, and loped down city laneways grunting UNGAWA! to faithful elephants, just out of sight. And in the steamy summer evenings, we tossed in crumpled sheets, imagining ourselves in jungle tents.

What fabled riches, lost races, and bizarre life forms inhabit such uncharted regions of the earth? That's a question that causes few to lose much sleep nowadays. The jungles of the world, a luxurious girdle around the equator, are themselves threatened by man's desire to turn everything into parking lots as he steadily forecloses on his own future.

Happily, it was not always so.

One of the joys of reading pulp fiction is to be able to take a time trip back to a more innocent age (was it only just a number of decades ago?) when the world seemed still unformed, and we could imagine vast miasmic places untrammeled by camera-wielding tourists and hard-eyed men in business suits—places suffocating with impenetrable vines and parasitic creepers masking cities of stone and ancient civilizations. If our view of native races was naive and even ignorant, so was our comforting vision of a natural world too immense to be plundered, too remote for all its mysteries to be revealed.

This was the untamed jungle of the imagination that a failed businessman named Edgar Rice Burroughs liked to dream of at the end of vexing days. Stuck in sweltering Chicago traffic, Burroughs comforted himself with visions of a splendid alter-ego who did not have to cope with crowds, clients, or the problems of raising a family. Dressed only in a loincloth and with a knife between his teeth, he could zip his way from one end of Africa to the other without even touching the ground. He'd swing on vines in a jungle Eden. What a way to go!

Not being a business success, Burroughs began to put his dreams to paper. "Most of the stories I wrote," he later admitted, "were the stories I told myself just before I went to sleep."

Such a story was *Tarzan of the Apes*, scribbled in longhand on the backs of old letterheads.

"I did not think it was a very good story," he confessed years later, "and doubted if it would sell."

He was wrong. ERB (as he would become known to his legions of admirers) sold his jungle yarn to Munsey's *The All-Story Magazine*. Subtitled "A Romance of the Jungle," it was published in full in the October 1912 issue, where it caused an immediate sensation. A hardcover version, published two years later, sold over a million copies, not counting later reprint editions. Flushed with success, Burroughs worked rapidly to put more of his vivid dreams on paper—stories about Mars and Venus, the Wild West, detectives, lost cities and prehistoric monsters, tales of the Moon and of Pellucidar at the earth's core—nearly seventy books in all, published in thirty-one languages—as well as an impressive 322 pulp magazine credits. But it was Tarzan who would remain ERB's most famous creation—one of the indelible figures in the history of popular literature.

Burroughs published twenty-three more Tarzan books in his lifetime, most of them appearing first in such top adventure pulps as *Argosy*, *All-Story Weekly*, and *Blue Book*. None of the novels were stylistic masterpieces, but Tarzan himself achieved a literary permanence because he tapped a universal human myth—that of the Noble Savage, Rousseau's "natural man" personified.

Following the runaway success of the Tarzan books, movies, comics, and radio shows, producing Tarzan-type characters became a growth industry in the pulps. Otis Adelbert Kline, a Chicago-based writer long considered Burroughs's chief rival and slickest imitator (excluding Burroughs himself), came up with "Tam, Son of the Tiger" for *Weird Tales*, "Jan of the Jungle," and "Jan in India" for *Argosy*, all takeoffs on Tarzan. Kline's Jan of the Jungle was raised as a chimpanzee boy—in Florida, of all places—but did his Tarzan thing in the jungles of South America and India in order not to clash with the Ape Man's African franchise.

There was talk of a Burroughs-Kline feud, but little substantiation. The truth is that imitation is the sincerest form of flattery, and Kline was an acknowledged fan of Burroughs. Besides, wasn't Tarzan himself a derivation of Kipling's Mowgli, transported holus bolus from India to Africa? (Although a magnificent tale spinner, ERB knew little about the Dark Continent, managing to relocate one of Kipling's Indian tigers in the process.)

While he was the greatest of the great pulp heroes in terms of worldwide fame, Tarzan never did achieve his own magazine. That honor would be left to a mere four of the Jungle Lord's brusquely named competitors: Matalaa, Ka-Zar, Ki-Gor, and the lovely—but even more unlikely—Sheena, Queen of the Jungle. Before these swingers arrived on the scene, there were any number of less-prominent tryouts.

While manufacturing Tarzan clones, writers strained to come up with exotic locations that would not impinge on Burroughs' Congo. Morgo the Mighty appeared in a serial of that name in *The Popular Magazine,* beginning in August 1930. Morgo was a Tarzan-type who inhabited bizarre caverns in the bowels of the Himalayas. Morgo's author, one Sean O'Larkin, supplied his hero with jungles of fungus and an army of flying bat men companions named Bakketes.

Not to be undone, Walter A. Tompkins (writing as Valentine Wood) produced Ozar the Aztec, who appeared in a number of stories ("Ozar and the Jade Altar," "Death Drums of Ozar," "Ozar and the Plumed Serpent") in Street & Smith's *Top Notch* in 1933. Known as the sky king of the Aztecs, Ozar was really Larry Sterling, captured as an infant in the mountains of Mexico by a lost tribe of Aztec Sun God worshipers.

William L. Chester's Kioga, the Snow Hawk, was a popular staple in *Blue Book* from 1935 to 1938. Kioga did his tree-swinging as far from Tarzan's turf as could be imagined—marooned as a youth in a strange land north of the Arctic Circle. Called Nato'wa by the ancestors of the American Indians who still lived there, the island was made habitable by warm ocean currents and a ring of still-active volcanoes. His parents killed by savages (a sacrificial prerequisite in the jungle god business), young Kioga was raised by their Indian friend, Mokuyi, from whom he learned the English of his fathers as well as the Indian arts of hunting and fighting. He was joined in his subsequent adventures by a pet bear, Aki, and a silver-coated puma, Mika.

Many Burroughs fans who have read the Kioga series consider that they are the only ones who can measure up to ERB's better Tarzan novels for imaginative scope and narrative sweep. Kioga's further similarity to Tarzan was enhanced by the fact that *Blue Book* illustrator Herbert Morton Stoops was assigned to delineate both characters for the magazine.

A further Kioga/Tarzan connection was introduced in 1938, when Republic Pictures produced a twelve-chapter serial based on the initial Kioga novel, *Hawk of the Wilderness*. A first-rate production, the chapter play starred a leanly muscled Olympic athlete named Herman Brix, ERB's own choice as the ideal Tarzan type.

THE JUNGLES OF the Malay peninsula were the setting for Sangroo the Sun God, who appeared in the first issue of Clayton's short-lived *Jungle Stories* in August 1931. The character, written by J. Irving Crump, appeared in at least one other story, "The Trumpeting Herd," which was featured in the October 1931 number. Crump left the pulp field shortly after to write daily radio dramas for the late-afternoon cereal set. (Both he and the legendary Talbot Mundy worked on Jack Armstrong, the All-American Boy, that national institution sponsored by Wheaties, "breakfast of champions.")

Kwa of the Jungle, raised among apes in Africa, proved to be an uninspired Tarzan copy. He appeared in a half-dozen stories in Standard's *Thrilling Adventures* in 1932 and 1933 but gathered no fan club. The same might be said for the likes of Avar *(Fantastic Adventures)*, Tharn *(Amazing Stories)*, and Toka *(Fantastic Adventures)*. These three, along with Manly Wade Wellman's Hok *(Amazing Stories)*, were part of a phalanx of Cro-Magnon Tarzans nurtured by editor Raymond Palmer of Ziff-Davis Publications, who had a thing about cavemen. What attracted him to them was that they sold magazines—especially when those magazines bore covers painted by J. Allen St. John, the master artist most closely associated with Tarzan himself.

Robert Moore Williams's Jongor ("Jongor of Lost Land," "The Return of Jongor," "Jongor Fights Back") also appeared in *Fantastic Adventures,* but proved a cut above the rest, if only because of his interesting milieu—a modern-day dinosaur-infested land in the middle of Australia's great desert.

Jongor's Lost Land was a world that was not only lost to mapmakers but lost to time as well. Here, a gray-eyed young giant rode out on dinosaurs, fought leather-winged pterodactyls, and waged war on the Murians—a lost colony of degenerate monkey-men from ancient Mu. Because anything that ever existed on earth might still exist in Lost Land, it was a premise open to endless variations. Even so, only three Jongor stories were ever published, and these over a ten-year period.

One of the irksome factors in the jungle Adonis image was that the hero invariably had the wherewithal to battle bull apes but appeared to lack the testosterone sufficient to raise a five o'clock shadow. Robert Moore Williams dismissed this anomaly with a brief mention of Jongor's bearded face. Even so, the illustrators continued to depict his cheeks as bereft of fuzz as a granite statue.

One of the Jongor illustrators was the aforementioned J. Allen St. John, whose striking cover for the first Jongor novel has been credited with setting new sales records for Ziff-Davis, thereby saving *Fantastic Adventures* from threatened cancellation. Most of the caveman stories that appeared in Jongor's wake were created specifically to encourage new Tarzan-like paintings from the estimable Mr. St. John.

Not surprisingly, the Tarzan myth became a merchandising craze in the gray days of the Great Depression when Americans need to escape reality increased and their faith in the "benefits" of civilization decreased. It seemed inevitable that some enterprising publisher would finally offer a Tarzan-type in his own magazine. The first of these, Bob Byrd's Ka-Zar, not only achieved his own title, but had it named after him.

Ka-Zar was introduced in October 1936 in a novel titled "King of Fang and Claw." The story was well crafted but hewed tediously close to Burroughs' initial concept. A ritualized child-of-the-jungle origin was dusted off: John Rand, his wife Constance, and infant son, David, crash in a light plane in the heart of the Congo two degrees south of the Equator. Mother dies (to no reader's surprise) and father becomes mentally unbalanced when conked on the head by a falling tree.

Lost Cities and Hidden Jungles / 273

Raised in the wilderness by a lunatic father, young David realized that a kid has to have some kind of pals, so he made friends of the jungle beasts. On one occasion, he saved Zar the lion from a treacherous bed of quicksand. When young David's father died in his arms from a murderer's bullet, the mighty lion adopted the grief-stricken boy and took him to his own jungle lair. There a pact of brotherhood was sworn. The boy ceased to be David Rand and become instead Ka-Zar, brother of Zar the lion. He even learned to speak the universal language of the beasts, a kind of jungle Esperanto.

In his second adventure, "Roar of the Jungle," Ka-Zar encountered the opposite sex in the person of beautiful Claudette, slave to a banished Indian rajah who had set up a kingdom (complete with harem) in the Congo. Ka-Zar saved Claudette from the rajah's Fate Worse Than Death but, in an ironic twist, lost the girl because he was unable to communicate with her. He spoke only the language of the beasts.

While ostensibly a bimonthly, the third (and final) issue, retitled *Ka-Zar the Great*, did not appear until June of 1937. It was an improvement on the first two plots in that it dealt with that reliable theme beloved by both H. Rider Haggard and ERB, "The Lost Empire." In this case, the lost people were descendants of ancient Egyptians who ruled an inaccessible valley in the manner of their ancestors. The citizens of Khalli must have picked up something from the Romans as well since there is one scene in which Ka-Zar was tied to a block in an arena to be fed to a wild lion. The lion turned out to be our old friend Zar, who gave his jungle brother an affectionate greeting, much to the crowd's disdain.

While Ka-Zar lasted only three issues as a pulp hero, he had a longer life in the comics. In 1939, Ka-Zar pulp publisher Martin Goodman produced a comic book titled *Marvel Comics,* after his science fiction pulp *Marvel Stories.* Kazar and his faithful beast brother popped up in Goodman's comic as backup acts to the likes of the Human Torch. They were reinstated in 1965 in the Marvel Comics line as jungle peacekeepers in a sort of Antarctic Pellucidar.

Matalaa, the White Savage, created by E. Hoffman Price, appeared in the lead novel spot in each issue of *Red Star Adventures* magazine. While not strictly a jungle swinger, he fulfilled the pseudo-Tarzan image by sticking to Burroughs's tried-and-true noble savage formula. Christened Warren Steele, Jr., he was orphaned when shipwrecked with his parents on a reef off a tiny South Pacific island. Raised by natives, and renamed Matalaa, or Eye of the Sun, because of his red-gold hair, the youth was taken under the wing of an old witch doctor, Poi Uto, who instructed him in things no other white man had ever learned. Matalaa fought evil Asiatics, renegade whites (usually Dutchmen), pearl poachers, and even a typhoon, but he was downed by his own publisher when his magazine was cancelled in 1940 after a mere four issues.

In truth, there was only one pulp jungle hero who would prove as popular as Tarzan—at least in number of return engagements. His name was Ki-Gor, known to friends and crocodiles alike as the White Jungle Lord.

Ki-Gor swung along the arboreal routes in every issue of Fiction House's *Jungle Stories* (no relation to Clayton's earlier title). The new *Jungle Stories* maintained quarterly publication from winter 1939 to spring 1954, producing fifty-nine Ki-Gor novels in all—a respectable record for any vine crawler.

Because he wasn't the first jungle kid on the block, Ki-Gor had to try harder. Most of his adventures bore titles of undisciplined invention: "Cobra Queen of the Congo Legions," "Safari of the Serpent Slaves," "Monkey-Men of Loba-Gola," "Voodoo Slaves of the Devil's Daughter," "Warrior Queen of Attila's Lost Legion," "The Beast Gods of Atlantis," "Slave Brides for the Dawn Men," and so on.

Flamboyance was the norm in T.T. Scott's Fiction House publications. But when it came to their pulp and comic magazine logos, the company favored bare bones titles: *Action Stories, Fight Stories, Frontier Stories, Planet Stories, Wings.* They couldn't afford the best stories or the top writers, so they concentrated on other features. The action-packed Fiction House covers, identified by a colophon inset in a bull's-eye target, invariably exhibited lightly draped females in attitudes of peril. Those parts of the covers not taken up with sexually tinged violence (admittedly a miser's portion) were overprinted with manic titles designed to reach out and punch the newsstand browser.

Even the story blurbs crackled:

> *The jungle seethed with terror. Devilish rumors flew the vine-route: Ki-Gor was doomed! The vile Wandarobo, hordes of stunted beast-men, had trapped the blond stalker... And copper-haired Helene, the tree-telegraph whispered, would die beneath the cannibal moon!*
>
> *Into the soulless domain of the gray apes; into the jungle city of Dargh-Abar—where man was slave and beast was king—stormed a wrathful Ki-Gor to pit muscle and guile against the brute strength and simian cunning of a power-mad ape army.*

> *In the heart of the juju forest... in an island city... the strange V'Lorians murdered in the night. Only Ki-Gor, great White Lord of the Jungle, could face that unworldly horde and hope to win. Yet within his heart was not the will to fight—for Helene, his golden mate, was no longer at his side. She was among the living dead in an unmarked grave.*

From the foregoing hyperbole, astute readers will note that Ki-Gor was (a) blond, (b) married to a redhead named Helene, (c) kept busy rescuing said Helene from menaces ranging from giant snakes to pygmy cannibals.

Ki-Gor was the son of a Scots missionary, Robert Kilgour, who was killed by natives so that his son could grow up lion-thewed and command his own pulp magazine. This happened offstage in the first Jungle Lord story, "King of the Jungle."

In the best pulp tradition, author John Murray Reynolds began that introductory story in the middle of cliff-hanger action. Helene Vaughn, a twenty-five-year-old society aviatrix, is winging her way across equatorial Africa when the engine of her small plane splutters and dies, and she is forced to crash land in a patch of open grassland.

> *Suddenly from just behind her, very close and somehow threatening came a soft sinister rustle of leaves. Quickly she turned her head, and the warm blood in her veins turned cold. Not more than a dozen paces away was a great sable jungle cat. A black panther, sleek and cruel.*

But, hey, this is Ki-Gor country. A naked, brown form shoots from the trees directly onto the panther's back. One of the jungle man's arms slides around the panther's neck, the other stabs a long-bladed knife between the beast's ribs. This is the dynamic scene that top pulp artist Norman Saunders portrayed on the historic cover. Helene was portrayed in full flying suit with aviator's cap and goggles—the last time she would appear clothed in public.

That first Ki-Gor story was not very long, only twenty-two pages, but it set the stage for future action. In it, Ki-Gor not only meets the woman who will become his mate but also gets some worthwhile on-the-job training while rescuing her from native tribes, a giant ape, and Arab slave traders. As in all subsequent issues, *Jungle Stories* delivered what it promised: a magazine packed with stories about the jungle. Its back pages would be routinely filled with yarns about treasure hunters, witch doctors, explorers and head-hunters, along with copious supplies of treacherous jungle bullies. The magazine's publication would be sporadic—mostly a quarterly, occasionally bimonthly, and sometimes skipping an issue altogether—but for sixteen years it would remain a jungle fan's cornucopia.

So why did Ki-Gor succeed when dozens of Tarzan-types did not? Despite those wild covers and even wilder story blurbs, the answer lies in the stories themselves and in the fact that there were so many of them. What Tarzan fans wanted was not variations on a theme, but more Tarzan adventures—and lots of them. Ki-Gor was not a dawn-world cave man or a modern day Arctic native. To all intents and purposes, Ki-Gor was Tarzan—an amalgam of Burroughs' literary creation with the more familiar (and comfortably simplistic) movie version.

To set up Ki-Gor as a surrogate for fans who couldn't get enough of Tarzan, a hefty amount of detail was lifted from

ERB's own books. Like Tarzan, Ki-Gor was a man who moved backwards on the bitter trail of evolution. King of the predatory jungle, he fought crocodiles and apes, befriended elephants, and ruled the jungle with his mate like Adam and Eve before the fall. While Ki-Gor's eyes were a blazing blue in his origin story, they soon turned gray—a shade Ki-Gor's pseudonymous authors no doubt picked up while cribbing from the Master.

Like most nostalgiacs, Burroughs was fond of ancient civilizations. To keep the Tarzan stew bubbling, he had his hero mix it up with a lost colony of Atlanteans, various cities inhabited by the descendants of Amazons, ancient Romans, and even a lost race of Mayans in the Pacific. Ki-Gor's scribes took ERB's fantastic elements to their limits with stories not only of lost cities and civilizations but horrendous battles with prehistoric thunder dragons, ant-men, talking apes, zombies, sea serpents, stunted beast-men, and humans turned into gigantic monsters.

The surprise in all this is not that so many of the stories are repetitious and hackneyed but that so many of them are energetic and entertainingly preposterous in the best pulp-hero tradition.

Today, *Jungle Stories* is considered one of the more collectible of pulp-hero magazines, a feat made complicated by the magazine's bewildering inconsistencies. There are three pairs of issues bearing the same cover but different novels inside; six other pairs of issues share the same cover and identical titles, but the stories are all different; two other novels, "Ki-Gor and the Gorilla Men" and "Nirvana of the Seven Voodoos," although bearing different titles, covers and interior illustrations, are identical stories. If this isn't confusing enough, many of the stories have little connection to their titles, including one listed as "Cromba has a Thousand Spears" on the cover and "Zomba has a Thousand Spears inside." In addition, dates and volume numbers on the spines often do not correspond to similar information on the content's pages.

Editors responsible for this jungle-style stew included Malcolm Reiss (sometimes labeled as general manager), W. Scott Peacock, Jerome Bixby and Jack O'Sullivan. Authors of the Ki-Gor series are harder to pin down. John Murray Reynolds wrote only the first story, the one with his name on it. Writers who labored under the subsequent John Peter Drummond house name included Stanley Mullin, Dan Cushman, and top mystery writer Robert Turner (who wrote the February 1943 novel, but not the fall 1950 story, which had the same title and cover). Fiction House artist Murphy Anderson believes that Scott Peacock was alternating on the novels with an unnamed Florida writer. When Peacock became editor (summer 1944), he wrote all of the lead novels until he left the editorial post the following year.

The White Jungle Lord's writers may appear guilty, at best, of a condescending attitude toward native Africans, but the truth is that they were reflecting a stigmatization of racial types long accepted in popular literature, both in and out of the pulps. To Ki-Gor's credit, his two closest jungle pals were both black—N'Geeso, Chief of the Kamazila pygmy tribe, and the giant Tembu George—once known as George Spelvin of Cincinnati, United States. George was a former Pullman porter and ship's cook who had become a Masai chief in the M'balla tribe of the East Congo. Both men are portrayed as intelligent, brave, humorous, and ferociously effective in battle. They are the Monk and Ham to Ki-Gor's Doc.

While both Ki-Gor and Tembu (meaning elephant) George were usually armed with shovel-bladed Masai spears and little

N'Geeso with a darkly polished blowgun, the giant George was known to go into battle packing a .45 automatic "equalizer" in a holster on his waist.

Like Tarzan and Jane before them, Ki-Gor and Helene were married with official church blessing ("Ki-Gor and the Cannibal Kingdom," summer 1940). During the series, the Jungle Lord's blue-blooded mate gradually developed from a spoiled social butterfly into a pelt-draped equal of the Jungle Lord. One of the later stories enthuses:

> *Helene Vaughn had been a beautiful woman when she first came to the jungle—but now, after many moons of the swift, yet simple life in the island home, of chase and tree-top travel through the wide bush, of the freedom of a scanty two-piece leopard-skin garment, she was more than just beautiful. She was lithe and strong now, although completely a woman. She curved in the right places; her legs were long and clean, and her bosom was evident, shapely and firm.*

Talk about redundant! All you had to do was glance at one of those cover paintings and you knew that such descriptions were superfluous. As some have pointed out, the covers of Fiction House magazines were often the best part. The company continued this tradition when they entered the comic book field in 1938. Ki-Gor and Helene were carried over into *Jungle Comics* in January of 1940, but their names were changed to Kaanga and Ann for reasons unexplained. All else was identical, including a pygmy friend named N'Geeso.

Another Fiction House comic, *Jumbo Comics*, featured the exploits of a she-Tarzan named Sheena. Although it is true that Fiction House created hundreds of characters for their long-running comic line, none made the impact that Sheena did. Because she was better looking, sexier, and tougher than her competition, she appeared in eighteen issues of her own magazine, one 3-D comic, and all 167 issues of *Jumbo Comics*. Small wonder that the company decided to try her out in her own pulp title in 1951. Alas, her comic fame did not carry over to a pulp audience and her book died with that single issue. A final Sheena story was carried in the last issue of *Jungle Stories*, but it was a case of too little too late. Although the single issue of her magazine is considered eminently collectible, the leopard-skinned Sheena and her jungle consort, Bob, did not have a significant role to play in pulpwood history.

The final issue of *Jungle Stories* was dated spring 1954. Before his magazine disappeared, Ki-Gor was alone among the great pulp heroes, the last of his fictional breed. Perhaps he outlived his rivals because of the enduring legacy of his literary precursor, the immortal Tarzan. Ki-Gor, like dozens of Tarzan acts before him, had been an idealized identity figure for any reader who ever answered Sir Arthur Conan Doyle's classic description of "the boy who's half a man or the man who's half a boy."

Edgar Rice Burroughs, the man who practically invented jungles, died in his sleep in 1950 at the age of seventy-four. Newspapers all over the world reported his passing and millions of readers felt the loss as if they had known him. Not only did Burroughs make the grade from pulp magazines to books, but he had become one of the most influential authors of all time, thanks to his enthralling daydream of a youth raised in the jungle by apes.

> *"The power of imagination is all that differentiates the human mind from that of brute creation,"* ERB once wrote in defense of so-called pulp literature. *"Without imagination there is no power to visualize what we have never experienced and without that power there can be no progress."*

THE ROAD TO ZERO

THE GREAT PULP heroes were a phenomenon of the Great Depression. During the giddy thirties, every pulp publisher had at least one super guy among his titles. But for every Doc Savage or Spider, there were hundreds of hungry want-to-be heroes, masked and muscled symbols of hard times and youthful expectations, all reaching for the brass ring of popular adulation.

Some characters achieved the dignity of their own magazines, their names slashed across covers in vivid reds and yellows. But for every hero with a title of his own, there were hundreds of other characters—often more unusual—who helped fill the short-story quotas. Some series ran for years, although not always in the same magazine. Others appeared briefly and were dismissed.

The detective pulps alone featured uncounted numbers of idiosyncratic oddballs and also-rans. Robert Leslie Bellem's private eye, Dan Turner, who operated out of *Spicy Detective* (renamed *Hollywood Detective*), was once burlesqued by the famous humorist S.J. Perelman, but Turner's own adventures were parody enough. Dan spent most of his time either bashing someone or getting bashed, and he had a colorful way of describing things. (The guns in his yarns never barked or even spat—they sneezed: *Ka-chow!*)

While Dan is best described as the stereotypic private eye, dozens of other detectives and their writers took pains to be different. Street & Smith's *Detective Story Magazine* was the home of Thubway Tham, a lithping (pardon: lisping) pickpocket who preyed on those in need of a little humility. *Detective Story* also harbored The Crimson Clown, another streetwise Robin Hood. The clown stole from rich baddies to give handouts to the poor—minus his commissions of course—while disguised in the full regalia of a circus clown.

Thubway Tham and The Crimson Clown were but two of the mystery men invented by the prodigious hero maker, Johnston McCulley. Over three decades, McCulley introduced a host of roguish pulp characters, including The Thunderbolt, the Man in Purple, Black Star, Captain Fly-by-Night, Don Renegade, The Whirlwind, and even an early version of the Green Ghost.

His most famous creation, of course, was Zorro, that dashing caballero from L.A., who was first introduced to the pulp world as early as 1919. In the forties and early fifties McCulley was still cranking out Zorro stories for the magazine *West*. To prove he was a bona fide pulp hero and not some movie dandy, the magazine Zorro wasn't content to scratch his famous "Z" trademark on furniture and costumes—he slashed it on startled faces with three incisive sword strokes.

If The Crimson Clown's makeup was a little strange, it was no more so than Frederick C. Davis' eccentric Moon Man *(Ten Detective Aces)*. The Moon Man was policeman Stephen Thatcher, who prowled the night wearing the unlikely rig of a long, black cloak and a fishbowl helmet made of one-way Argus glass. One must suspect hero Thatcher's mental acuity because just a single crack of the glass and his loony disguise would have been shattered for all to see.

Davis' Moon Man was not the usual vigilante hero, but

another Robin-Hood-type who robbed villains of their loot to give to the poor. Depression-era readers must have approved of the theme because the mystery man's suspenseful exploits ran from 1933 to 1937 for a total of 38 stories.

Black Mask, the most famous of all detective pulps, was not without its share of continuing characters, ranging from Dashiell Hammett's Continental Op to Frederick Nebel's Tough Dick Donahue. But it was a companion magazine, the spunky *Dime Detective,* that really played up its ongoing series. Throughout the thirties and well into the forties, under the expert guidance of editor Ken White, *Dime Detective* continued to sell because of its dynamic tough-guy heroes. Most were unusual, and more than a few were downright preposterous, but they did their job in commanding reader loyalty. They ranged from John K. Butler's two-fisted, hard-luck hacker, Steve Midnight, who drove the night streets of Los Angeles in his Red Owl taxi, to William Barrett's Needle Mike, the alter-ego of playboy Ken McNally, who enjoyed dressing down as a sleazy habitué of the Badlands to run a tattoo parlor as a front for his crime-fighting proclivities.

Not to be outdone by rival eccentrics, *Dime Mystery* once featured an outrageous number of characters known posthumously as the "defective detectives." They included Nat Perry, the Bleeder, a hemophiliac crime fighter to whom a single scratch might mean death; Peter Quest, a blind detective; Dan Holden, who was deaf; and private eye Calvin Kane, whose deformed body made him look like a refugee from a sideshow attraction.

Jules de Grandin, one of the most popular pulp detectives of them all, stalked the pages of *Weird Tales* for twenty-five years and nearly one hundred adventures. The mercurial little French sleuth was an occult version of Agatha Christie's Hercule Poirot. He and his aide, Dr. Trowbridge, practiced spook-busting in a New Jersey town called Harrisonville—which was the geographic rallying point for more fiends, ape-men, devil worshippers, vampires, sorcerers, and generally creepy goings-on than any other place in literary history.

There were, of course, hordes of other characters who rose to challenge the rule of the great pulp heroes. Some of the challengers commanded their own titles, along with their own devout fans, before succumbing to the ruthless odds against them.

The venerable Nick Carter left dime novels for the pulps back in 1915, when he appeared in the premier issue of Street & Smith's *Detective Story Magazine*. He graduated to his own magazine in 1933, which ran for three years until June of 1936. But old Nick couldn't compete with his publisher's own dynamic duo—The Shadow and Doc Savage.

Doc and The Shadow were tough acts to copy. Even their own publisher bombed out trying. Street & Smith's Cap Fury was a seafaring roughneck groomed to be a tougher, sexier version of Doc. He appeared in his own short-lived title, *The Skipper*, and then was relegated to the back pages of Doc's own magazine, where he continued doing battle with pirates and other aquatic scum.

The Whisperer was designed to be a Shadow type but also experienced a short run. He wound up as an addendum back in the final folios of the magazine he sought to imitate. He was an interesting character, though. A brash and stocky police commissioner with a taste for violently clashing clothes,

James "Wildcat" Gordon assumed the strange gray guise of the Whisperer in order to deal brutal justice to criminals the law could not touch. The colorful Wildcat made his transition into the Whisperer with the aid of a drab gray outfit and a pair of odd dental plates that, when inserted, lengthened his upper lip and made his jaw freakishly pointed. The plates also caused him to speak in a low, weird whisper.

His publishers must have liked the bizarre Whisperer because they revived his magazine three years after its original cancellation, and it ran for another ten issues before becoming yet another victim of wartime paper shortages.

One of the more obvious attempts to emulate The Shadow was The Green Lama, a character who appeared in fourteen issues of *Double Detective*. The stories were written by Kendall Foster Crossen under the pseudonym Richard Foster. He was the editor of Munsey's *Detective Fiction Weekly* at the time and was requested to come up with a Shadow-like hero to stimulate sales of the publisher's ailing companion magazine.

Like The Shadow, the emerald-robed Green Lama boasted Far East origins. Also, like The Shadow, he had several alternate identities, notably that of wealthy Park Avenue playboy Jethro Dumont as well as that of a disguised Buddhist priest, the Reverand Dr. Charles Pali. As Jethro Dumont he spent ten years in Tibet, studying under the lamas and becoming a fully ordained priest in the Lamaist sect of Buddhism. Returned to America, he realized he could spread the basic doctrines of Tibet by fighting violent crime with the use of magic, disguise, and radiating electrical shocks through his fingertips.

Unlike The Shadow, and most of the other great pulp heroes, the Buddhist superhero never carried a gun, believing "this would make me no better than those who fight me." He wore no mask but garbed himself in a monk's hooded robe with a red whiplike scarf around his neck which he used as a weapon. Because of his fondness for green, "one of the six sacred colors," Jethro Dumont was dubbed The Green Lama. Author Crossen had created him as The Gray Lama but was dissuaded by artists who needed color for their cover paintings.

The only successful single character pulp title published by A.A. Wyn's Ace Magazines was *Secret Agent "X,"* which enjoyed a healthy run of forty-one issues over five years, beginning in 1934. Known as "the Man with a Thousand Faces," the secret government operator Agent X was another disguise whiz who, unlike the Phantom, had no identity of his own. Faced with a chameleon-like hero sans personality, the stories tried harder to excite. Bearing such titles as "Legion of the Living Dead," "Brand of the Metal Maiden," "Claws of the Corpse Cult," and "Kingdom of Blue Corpses," X's adventures were certainly titillating enough, even if his authors were guilty of formula filching from more successful rivals.

Allegedly a crime-fighting detective, many of "X"s adventures veered into the path of science-fiction, weird menace and outright horror. Like The Shadow, Agent X disguised himself with numerous aliases. Like Doc Savage he employed non-lethal gadgets of defence including darts concealed in a cigarette lighter and a tear gas bomb in the stem of his wristwatch. Like the Spider and Operator #5, the faceless and unsung Agent X routinely saved society from crazed scientists, masked villains, and armies of the ungodly. Amid such an atmosphere rife with truly depraved foes, monstrous crimes and grim death devices, the only humor to be found in *Secret Agent "X"* was the publisher's blatant invention of the name Brant House as a "house name" to mask the magazine's true authors.

Paul Chadwick initiated the "X" saga under the Brant House pseudonym. He ghosted many of the early novels before being joined by pulp hero specialists Emile C. Tepperman and G.T. Fleming-Roberts.

In Paul Chadwick's "Hooded Hordes" (October 1934) a dread secret society known as The Defenders of the American Constitution (DOACS) threaten to bring the nation to its knees through riots, bombings and crime spread from State to State in a miasma of murder and destruction. In April 1935 Emile Tepperman contributed "Talons of Terror," in which the vampiric Dr. Blood littered the city with the dried, bloodless husks of what once were humans. Not to be outdone, G.T. Fleming-Roberts wrote of the evil Emperor Zero in "Brand of the Metal Maiden" (January 1936) Described as "a master of murder music," Zero's unwilling music pupils danced a mad rhythm into their graves. As they danced, they aged and became withered mummies in silks and satins and modern dinner coats.

Frederick Davis, who wrote the Moon Man series, contributed several stories to the back pages of the Secret Agent X magazine. Five of his shorts featured the enigmatic character named Ravenwood who was an occult detective raised in the mysterious ways of the Far East—shades of the Green Lama.

Popular Publications failed to copy the success of their own *Spider* magazine with a late arrival titled *Captain Satan*. The good Captain took his cue from the Spider by dealing swift justice with his guns, then leaving his mark of "Satan" on his victim's foreheads. Described as "a new figure among the tough guys of literature," Captain Satan operated with the assistance of a coterie of helpers. Bearing such names as Doc, Kayo, Soapy, Sledge, and Happy, they may have sounded like Snow White's Seven Dwarfs but were, instead, a loyal band of masked ruffians known as the Ambassadors from Hell. Unlike Doc Savage's crew or The Shadow's agents, Satan's Ambassadors had a high mortality rate. Within the span of the series, several of them bit the dust, followed by the magazine itself with its fifth issue.

And so it went. Through the pages of the pulps the garish parade flowed: hordes of masked, cowled, caped, and variously disguised crime-fighting geniuses dedicated to bringing law, order, and tranquility to the land, even if they did leave the streets corpse-littered in their wake.

But every parade must have an end.

While the pulps enjoyed unprecedented profits during World War II, the growing cost of wood-pulp paper, combined with the gradual erosion of their entertainment market by comic books, paperbacks, radio, the movies—and later—television, conspired against them. The hero pulps took the first blows when wartime readers began rejecting their brand of outright fantasy in favor of stories reflecting a world closer to the one in which they lived. The more extravagant pulp icons either disappeared or lost much of their superhuman powers, elbowed out by the relatively mundane figures of the coming TV age: private eyes, cops, and cowboys. As their sales softened, the watered-down heroes remaining saw their monthly exploits slip back to bimonthly and even quarterly issuance. Only a few of the character pulps limped on through the late forties and into the final days of the pulps themselves. They were increasingly out of place in a literature turned slavishly realistic.

Harry Steeger, who had created the Spider, G-8, and Operator #5 back in the glory days, made a nostalgic bid to extend pulp heroism a little longer when he brought out the *Captain Zero* magazine in late 1949. The initial cover promised much, from its dramatic logo to a lead story titled "City of Dreadful Sleep."

Even the story blurb rang with the zest of halcyon days:

> *Three sinister slay-rides turned a giant metropolis into a city patrolled by terror... helpless, save for one man—the fabulous Master of Midnight, whose strange cloak of invisibility was, at the same time, a gift of the gods—and a curse of the Devil!*

The only problem was that the Master of Midnight really was a zero. His name was Lee Allyn—not too impressive compared to such bell-ringing monikers as Richard Wentworth, Lamont Cranston, and Richard Curtis Van Loan. Even worse, Lee was just a little squirt—only five-feet-four—bland of personality, uncoordinated under stress, and blind as a bat without his glasses. If he'd been forced to fill out a pulp-hero job application form, he surely would have flunked the test.

What happened was that editor Alden Norton had instructed author G.T. Fleming-Roberts to produce a pulp character with more human characteristics. Earlier, Fleming-Roberts had brought a sense of sophistication and humor to the adventures of his magician sleuth The Ghost. With Captain Zero, he turned the conventional pulp hero upside down. Because of an atomic experiment gone wrong, Lee Allyn became invisible every night at midnight and snapped back to visibility each morning at dawn. But he had no control over it. It just happened. "It's an affliction—not an asset," the poor guy pointed out.

As Captain Zero, Lee really tried to be a good crime fighter, but he lacked the expertise that came so naturally to the super guys of the thirties. His author had trapped him in the real world—our world—where nothing went smoothly. Wherever he walked, someone was always noticing his footprints from depressions in the grass or carpets. He couldn't carry a weapon because weapons weren't invisible. Because his eyeglasses would also reveal his presence, he substituted contact lenses, but the light kept striking them, alerting cops and crooks to his presence. He even had to bum rides because how long could a driverless car go unnoticed? And since he was on the job all night as Captain Zero, he barely dragged himself to work each day.

It sounds like parody but, with Fleming-Roberts at the helm, it was just good-natured entertainment. The Captain Zero novels all had busy, intricate story lines featuring suspense, realistic action, good characterization, and a terse writing style. But old-time pulp readers, perhaps anticipating a return to the imaginative mayhem of The Shadow or the Spider, were less than enthusiastic about the new brand of realism. And more sophisticated types were put off by cover depictions of the Master of Midnight as a giant robed figure with electrical discharges sizzling from his fingers. For whatever reason, the *Captain Zero* magazine was terminated with its third issue. With it died pulp fiction's Heroic Age—not with a bang, but a whimper.

When the pulps perished from neglect in the mid fifties, it

was the end of a way of writing and a way of dreaming. Many pulpsters never escaped from their penny-a-word ghetto. Some of the old-timers graduated into the "slicks" or family magazines. Others found work in comic books, and many, like John D. MacDonald, Elmore Leonard, and Louis L'Amour, emigrated to the paperback field, where publishers welcomed their hard-earned ability to tell a good story and make the story move. Still others drifted out to Hollywood to work in movies and TV. Ironically, they were fueling the very mediums that had killed the pulps by imitation.

In their variety, the pulps attempted to supply something for almost every age and taste. While such quality titles as *Argosy* and *Blue Book* commanded the loyalty of mature readers, the demographics for *Captain Future* and *Operator #5* were weighted heavily with the male youths who answered all those back-of-the-book ads for acne relief and Charles Atlas' body-building secrets. Author Will Murray once pointed out that it is an axiom of popular literature that if you write for the young and touch their young lives, they will never forget you. Perhaps this is why the single character pulp-hero magazines are among the most warmly remembered today and the most avidly pursued by collectors of yesterday's ephemeral treasures.

Time is taking its inevitable toll on the crude paper, glue, and staples that bound together those summer-sweet dreams of masked phantoms and bronzed geniuses. But, to their once-youthful readers, the great pulp heroes live on in the theater of the mind, where nothing once loved is ever forgotten. It is there where bronzed Doc's trilling whistle still echoes through impossible green jungles; where the Spider and The Shadow—midnight's twins—still perch on timeless skyscraper eyries, black cloaks billowing like giant wings, their chilling laughter even yet filling the mind's ear with mystery and excitement.

Thanks for the memories, super guys.

CORRESPONDENCE

THIS EDITION OF *The Great Pulp Hero*s is dedicated with gratitude to the multitude of pulp magazine authors, artists, editors and publishers who entertained readers so extravagantly in years gone by.

While doing research for this book I recalled with fondness one line of fiction magazines. The Popular Publications colophon (two back-to-back letter Ps) identified some of the most exciting magazines ever published: *Operator #5, Adventure, Terror Tales, G-8 and His Battle Aces, Dime Detective, The Spider, Ace G-Man Stories, Black Mask.* The list could go on and on.

We had no knowledge of publishers or editors back then but as a devoted reader I became aware of the familiar Popular Publications business address—205 East 42nd Street—from whence emerged wondrous thunderbolts of pulp magazine action. How amazing then to send a letter off to that address in 1971 (a decade and more after the demise of the pulps) and receive a prompt reply from Henry (AKA "Harry") Steeger, the legendary creator and publisher of those spectacular magazines.

That initial letter was the beginning of rewarding correspondence and eventual friendship with Steeger and many of the other creative individuals who had pioneered in the unique world of pulp fiction. The following are a few of the letters received.

POPULAR PUBLICATIONS, INC.
205 EAST 42ND STREET
NEW YORK, N.Y. 10017

HENRY STEEGER
PRESIDENT

September 30, 1971

Mr. Don Hutchison
147 Leacrest Road
Leaside, Toronto
Ontario - CANADA

Dear Mr. Hutchison:

I enjoyed your letter of September 4th very much.

Publishing and editing the Pulps was indeed most pleasant and profitable and, looking back at them now, is nostalgic, to say the least.

The Operator 5 series was, indeed, written by Frederick C. Davis but, whether or not Emile C. Tepperman had a hand in it, I don't know. Our Mr. Al Norton, an editor at that time, is presently away on vacation but when he returns I'll be glad to ask him to search out his memory.

Norvel W. Page was the writer of The Spider series but I'm afraid I do not have any biographical data. It's possible that Mr. Norton might be able to dig this up for me as well as the other information. I expect him to return in the next two weeks and will quiz him at that time.

Kindest regards - and good luck with your work.

Sincerely,

Henry Steeger

HS:ls

Popular Publications Inc. 205 East 42nd Street, New York 17, New York

MURRAY HILL 9-4900

November 23, 1971

Mr. Don Hutchison
147 Leacrest Road
Leaside, Toronto 17, Ontario
Canada

Dear Mr. Hutchison:

Please excuse the delay in replying to your letter of September 14th, which Mr. Steeger gave me some time ago.

Yes, Frederick C. Davis and Emile C. Tepperman both had a hand in the OPERATOR FIVE series. I just can't tell you which stories were written by each, but I do know that both were the authors of the stories.

I shall have some dope on Norvel W. Page for you later. I know I will because I am trying to prepare a comprehensive history of the pulps and a one time acknowledgment of Page is promised to fill you in his contribution to the pulps.

If you don't hear from me in a few weeks, please write me again and I will try to keep you in mind, if it doesn't escape me.

Sincerely yours,

ALDEN H. NORTON,
Editor

AHN:ad

Frederick C. Davis
6940-A Sunset Drive, Apt. 2-A
So. Pasadena, Florida 33707

8 December 72

Dear Mr. Hutchinson,

    Operator #5 was fuller of surprises than I ever suspected until recently. When I gave birth to him I endowed him with attributes which made him, as you say, a superman, but I never dreamt he would show an ability to survive this long.

    I was amazed and flattered to hear so favorably from Ron Goulart and Robert K. Jones and Nick Carr, but your lead article in Captain George's Whizbang is by far the highest compliment of all, and I can't see how it can ever be topped. You are truly a thoroughgoing student of the series, and I'm greatly impressed by the accuracy of your perceptions and deductions. And also grateful indeed for the copy you sent me.

    I can't help wondering why it was so hard to track down the facts about the Operator #5 stories---almost everybody in the business at that time knew who was producing them---although I do understand Harry Steeger's later confusion, and the intervening decades are enough to dim anyone's memory, including mine.

    Your checklist of Operator #5 titles gives me a clue as to how far along I carried the series. I remember writing Attack of the Blizzard Men and possibly Scourge of the Invisible Death provided it deals with cosmic rays. The 1936 titles suggest Emil Tepperman's work. Your analysis of the footnotes may confirm this.

    You may have wondered why I decided to bid Operator #5 farewell. There were several reasons. One, suitable ideas were becoming increasingly hard to dream up. Two, I was sadly underpaid---$500 per story, about half my word rate with other pulp publishers and with other magazines of the same publisher. Three, I was feeling the strain of my heavy work load. While writing Operator #5 I was also turning out more than an equal number of words for other markets---among these, the long-running Moon Man series, a novelette every month, for Ten Detective Aces.

    I never read any of the Operator #5 stories after I stopped writing them, which accounts for my ignorance of The Purple Invasion. (I never read any of the Doc Savage or Shadow stories either.) I had had a surfeit of him and I was busily putting my nonworking time into the pleasure of dating a lovely girl whom I later married and who still later presented me with a son whose name is neither Jimmy nor Christopher.

Of course I knew Tepperman by name as a fellow writer, but I never met him personally and there was never any communication between us concerning Operator #5. Judging from your account of the tremendous scope of The Purple Invasion, it seems to me that he deserves the greater share of the credit for the long-lasting interest in Operator #5.

Please feel free to quote this letter in full or in part. If I can be of any further help, I'll be glad to hear from you again.

Reminiscently yours,

Fred C Davis

POPULAR PUBLICATIONS, INC.
205 EAST 42ND STREET
NEW YORK, N.Y. 10017

HENRY STEEGER
PRESIDENT

February 6, 1973

Mr. Don Hutchison
147 Leacrest Road
Leaside, Toronto 17, Ontario
Canada

Dear Mr. Hutchison:

Al Norton no longer works for Popular Publications but has turned over to me your letter of December 4th about Norvell Page.

Unfortunately we have no data on Page. He was a very colorful character who enjoyed identifying himself as the Spider, his lead character. I remember frequently that he would appear in the office in a black cape with red lining and a big black floppy hat, and on his finger he wore a Spider ring. We sold Spider rings for several years and developed it into a very brisk trade. Outside of this information, I really have no other.

Sincerely yours,

Henry Steeger

HS:lbt

HENRY STEEGER
301 EAST 79TH STREET, 11A
NEW YORK, NEW YORK 10021

October 4, 1987
(Dictated but not read)

Mr. Don Hutchison
585 Merton Street
Toronto, Ontario M4S 1B4
CANADA

Dear Don:

Yes, of course, I am well acquainted with your name. I know you are in the group of Pulpsters and that you are president of it and that you are a good friend of Wooda Carr and I know of your active interest in the pulp era and all the work you've done in connection with it.

I was delighted to receive a copy of your G-Men Years introduction. Needless to say, I enjoyed it enormously. It's extremely well done and you've covered a multitude of angles that makes a good collection of information on the subject. It produced a great deal of nostalgia and pleasure in me as I read your wonderful piece. Now I can hardly wait for the book. I am most anxious to have it in my collection and I congratulate you on your splendid accomplishment. It will add a very worthwhile chapter to the annals of pulp publishing and will help people in future years to learn more about the field than they would have otherwise. There is only one small correction in the introduction - small, that is, to you but large to me. When we started Popular Publications in late 1929 I was in my mid-twenties not, as you say, in my mid-thirties. I'm old enough as it is without adding another decade and, besides, I don't know if I'll be able to play tennis every day when I'm 10 years older.

Please pardon the delay in answering you. I wanted to do so right away but I've been so bogged down with work I haven't had a chance to get to my mail. I run a large hospital unit in New York and have a magazine group that continues publishing, together with other interests that keep me constantly involved.

HENRY STEEGER
301 EAST 79TH STREET, 11A
NEW YORK, NEW YORK 10021

Mr. Don Hutchison   - 2 -   October 4, 1987

It was a pleasure to hear from you and I hope that all goes well.

With kindest regards,

                                        Sincerely,

                                        Harry

HS:lbt

NORMAN DANIELS
6107 VILLAGE 6
CAMARILLO, CALIFORNIA 93010

21 September 1987

Dear Don:

My good friend, why are you not engaged in writing for a career? The quality of your word-handling in this introduction certainly indicates you have the ability to do whatever you please in this field.

That out of the way, I do admire all you good folks who are trying to provide old pulps with a place in history. I have always believed these gaudy and blood-and-guts stories once helped youngsters to learn and enjoy reading. Those kids were surely a far cut above what our schools are producing today. Yet, with the advent of radio and TV, how can there be any competition? I know from experience. I did enough of those two mediums.

It does seem to me that there is some revitalization of interest in the pulps these days, mainly through the efforts of people like you and those in Pulpcon. The traffic in old copies doesn't begin to match that of the comics, but...maybe some day.

My wife Dorothy and I had the pleasure of a visit from Al Tonik and Joe Lowendowski last week. It was nice to see them again. We were able to introduce them to Allan Grossman, a pulp devotee, who had been trying to find us for years--and he lives practically in our back yard. Only one town away. Allan's claim to fame, in my selfish opinion, arises in the fact that he has every copy of the BLACK BAT series I created and wrote so many years ago. I also created other series characters, all of which lasted several years.

Back to Al, Joe and Allan. The three of them engaged in spirited dialogue re the pulps, educating me in the quality of both the writing and art work. I must admit the art work predominated, but it was all interesting.

The jacket blurb enclosed, you may edit or change as you please, but it's a delight to have you use it. And if there is any way we can be of help in any further matter, you have only to ask.

Best,

Norm

NORMAN DANIELS
6107 VILLAGE 6
CAMARILLO, CALIFORNIA 93010

May 20, 1988

Don Hutchison
585 Merton Street
Toronto, Ontario
Canada M4S 1B4

Dear Don:

    Thank you for your informative letter and I'm pleased to hear that your THE SUPER FEDS is near publication. I'll be delighted to see a copy.

    Your chapter on the PHANTOM is, of course, highly interesting to me and it might be interesting to you if I tell you that the publisher Frank Havens really had a live counterpart. His name was Marcus Goldsmith. He had some kind of financial interest in New Pines' outfit, though I believe it was only in regard to the PHANTOM. I also believe that he thought of himself as Frank Havens. In his opinion, the PHANTOM was the best crime magazine in existence. Mr. Goldsmith was extremely wealthy and one of the finest gentlemen I ever had the privilege of knowing.

    He discussed each synopsis with me in detail, sometimes in his Manhattan apartment, a luxury residence if ever I saw one. We got along fine. Other writers who worked with him, hated him. He would nit-pick and was not easy to please. However, he certainly enjoyed his role in the PHANTOM and he could dream up some mighty hard revisions which I learned how to simplify.

    He would invariably pick a section in the middle of the book which he didn't like and give me his idea of how it should be done. So I used to write the book in its entirety, just as I felt it should be, give him the manuscript with an inserted middle part weak and absurd. He would pick that part to pieces and instruct me how to improve it. I'd simply remove the inserted part, replace the pages already written. He was always completely satisfied. How the other writers handled him, I don't know, but I assume they met with the same reception I did.

    As a matter of interest, I was rummaging in the garage the other day and I discovered a completely forgotten record book of mine of the early pulp days. Both my wife Dorothy and I believe that it seems impossible to have written exactly one thousand pulp stories ending in 1943, but it's all there. I wrote many more pulps after that, but the idea of more than a thousand stories either makes me feel very old or very tired, though I'm not.

    After the pulps, I did a lot of radio, even a Canadian soap opera on CBC. I did live TV, filmed TV and finally found a final haven in paperback books. In this field, Dorothy and I had 256

NORMAN DANIELS
6107 VILLAGE 6
CAMARILLO, CALIFORNIA 93010

- 2 -

books published. I wonder how many pulpwood trees were felled to provide all that paper.

As I recall, I originated the series characters of the MASKED DETECTIVE, CANDID CAMERA KID, THE CRIMSON MASK and, though I can't call them to mind at this writing, many others. But of them all, THE BLACK BAT was my favorite, mainly because the characters seemed so real to me. In fact, one of the characters, a detective, was patterned after a real life police chief. I carried that series through eleven years with the exception of the final book.

After all that work, we have box after box of file copies of our paperbacks, but of pulp magazines practically none. My mother-in-law, who was always trying to help people, discovered a bedridden man who loved to read pulps. All our file copies were stored in her attic at the time and she delightedly bundled up the hundreds of magazines and presented them to the sick man. It gave him happiness, she said. Maybe it did, but he died of tuberculosis and everything in his room was burned. All those pulps must have made a beautiful blaze. So the few we have, we managed to scrounge from friends.

Both Dorothy and I are very happy with the resurrection of the pulps in the form of history and the endeavors of people like you to perpetuate them and give them a place in the field of writing. For this, you have our profound thanks. If there is any way we can be of help, please call on us. And thanks again for the book we are going to receive.

Sincerely,

HENRY STEEGER
301 EAST 79TH STREET, 11A
NEW YORK, NEW YORK 10021

June 9, 1988

Mr. Don Hutchison
585 Merton Street
Toronto, Ontario M4S 1B4
CANADA

Dear Don:

I am just recovering from 11 days of celebrating birthdays, anniversaries and alumni associations and am still riding along on cloud 9, or maybe even 10 or 11, and finding it difficult to concentrate on returning to my everyday tasks. However, writing you is a pleasure and recalling all of the wonderful pulp paper days is in itself a celebration. I was unable to answer your letter sooner because of all of the out of the ordinary activities but I must say I derived enormous pleasure and gobs of nostalgia from reading your letter and your wonderful article on G-8. You have really done a most sensitive and clever analysis of Bob Hogan's work and it goes without saying I reveled in every word of it. It recalled some many happy occasions. When I read your inspired study of Bob Hogan I think back on what type of person he really was. Bob was never complicated or burdened with any of the restrictions of the academic world. He invented everything from his own fertile imagination. To look at him you would say this is the last person on earth who could be an author. As you recalled, at one point in his writings I must admit his face did look a little bit "horse-like." He had a long thin face and he was a very thin gangling type of person put together really with steel wire rather than glue. He had sort of pale washed-out eyes and thinning hair but was most active physically and, of course, his fertile mind never stopped for a moment dreaming up dramatic situations. He was most uncomplicated; he was really one of the simplest people you could ever hope to meet, with an enormous sense of the dramatic and the magic of a born story teller. Erudition was not part of Bob's life, either. He was in every way a very simple person, lived in a simple little home and

HENRY STEEGER
301 EAST 79TH STREET, 11A
NEW YORK, NEW YORK 10021

Mr. Don Hutchison   - 2 -   June 9, 1988

had a rather simple life because there was not much time for anything else. I believe he had a daughter and, of course, I know he had a wife who helped him with his work and he had very little time for anything else but putting together his yarns. 200,000 words a month was, I believe, his basic production, as you say, but I'm sure that other work crept into that schedule as well.

Bob was also, as you might suspect, a born talker. He could rattle along just as fast and dramatically as he did on his typewriter, but it was all down to business and all planning for future issues of how to make the best of what he had done. He loved talking over his characters and his plots and we spent a great time doing just that.

Incidentally, I worked with the authors and the artists on every single cover we ever published. That was my essential duty in getting each issue started. Nobody else **ever** did any of the covers, so, no matter how horrific they might now seem, I at least was responsible for them. And I believe, as I told you, we worked on these covers as though they were fine Swiss watches, sending them back over and over again to the artists to improve. There were grumbles but never any real refusals. Fred Blakeslee, the cover artist, was a man of similar ilk, with a simple home life and with a driving desire to paint the air covers which he did, I think, to perfection for our audiences.

As you say, Bob was accustomed to spending a great deal of time at his home in New Jersey and also a good deal of time down in Florida and I'm sure, as you say, most of it was spent working on his stories. He was not a scholarly type of person and he was not much interested in going to the theater or to the galleries or any similar cultural activities because he didn't have time for them, so his conversations never ranged along these lines but he loved nothing better than telling me about new evil doings of his villains and also of the great heroics of his heros.

HENRY STEEGER
301 EAST 79TH STREET, 11A
NEW YORK, NEW YORK 10021

Mr. Don Hitchison   - 3 -   June 9, 1988

Two other flyers of the same era, O. B. Myers and Sidney Bowen, were also frequent visitors to the office and worked just as hard as Bob although, of course, with lesser production -- and each of them had stories in almost every issue of our flying magazines. Ralph Oppenheim was also a regular and produced a series called "The Three Mosquitoes" which was extremely well known but really blasted my concepts one day when he admitted he had never been near an airplane in his life and that his stories were put together in a fiction factory supervised by him. By contrast, Bob Hogan did all his own work and when he came to town we did as we did with the others -- we closed up the doors and celebrated with lunch or whatever else was fun and we kidded around and just had a great time, none of it connected with putting magazines together except for the particular author involved.

Edythe Seims had the office next to mine and was our most competent editor starting from the very beginning. I must admit I "stole" her from the Dell Publishing Company and she was the editor of all our books for a long time. Edythe was not part of these meetings which were more on the masculine side like squatting down on the floor and shooting craps, or getting boiled on martinis or whatever else, and having a great old time. The whole thing was more fun than I can possibly have imagined. I had returned from two semesters of study at the University of Berlin and from a degree at Princeton and was ready to enter the world of thoughtful publications. However, a friend of mine, Ernest W. Heyn, subsequently editor of Popular Science, had a sister who knew George Delacorte, head of the Dell Publishing, and through her we got jobs as editors there and were given a book to edit called "Famous Story Magazine" for which we re-translated translations of famous stories. This was sold to Golden Book Magazine ultimately and we were then transferred to pulps. After about two years of that I figured I knew enough about publishing to go into business for myself -- and that's

HENRY STEEGER
301 EAST 79TH STREET, 11A
NEW YORK, NEW YORK 10021

Mr. Don Hutchison   - 4 -   June 9, 1988

how it all began. Obviously, I didn't know anything at all and we were just plain lucky to be able to survive the first couple of years.

I will, of course, be more than delighted to help you in any way I possibly can so please call on me as often as you wish. You have a most sensitive feeling for the work you do and it is done with an excellence of style and thought most admirable. I really get a very big kick out of it.

Yes, my wife and I will be at Pulpcon and will look forward to seeing you there. I'm delighted to read that you will be on hand. Wooda Carr has given my wife the name "Mrs. Operator 5" and since she joined me in our work for the first few years, and even devised the name "Popular Publications" for us, she will enjoy Pulpcon and I'm certain everybody will be very happy to meet her. We just had our wedding anniversary, by the way, our 60th, but can still walk without crutches and, in fact, I'm looking forward to my game of tennis tonight which is usually played several days a week, as long as I am able to stand up.

I can't say enough in praise of your manuscript. It was a joy and a delight and I had the time of my life reading it. It was so sensitively and capably done and I know you will have a book which will help future generations of students understand what our era was all about. Thanks again for sending it and if you wish me to return it, please advise.

Every best wish.

Sincerely,

Harry

NORMAN DANIELS
6107 VILLAGE 6
CAMARILLO, CALIFORNIA 93010

July 29, 1988

Mr. Don Hutchison
585 Merton Street
Toronto, Ontario,   M4S 1B4

Dear Don:

    I'll do the best I can in response to your letter re: anecdote on the Black Bat. Many years ago Leo Margulies asked me to come up with a series to be in competition with The Shadow. I concocted the set-up which, without change, became The Black Bat. I called it The Tiger. It seemed a natural since Tony Quinn's face was scarred from an opening sequence in the first book. The scars on his face, resembled the markings on a Tiger's. However, as it was going into Black Book Detective, Leo decided to change the title of the character to conform with the magazine and so, to blend with Black Book, he renamed it Black Bat. I suspect that was what they were after anyway.

    So far as interference with plot, layout, characterization, I was given carte blanche and nobody ever interfered. I don't recall a synopsis reject. I wrote all of that series over a period of eleven years. I was paid exactly what Gibson was paid and raised when he was raised. The final Black Bat was taken over by a new group (pulps were rapidly fading then). They wanted to load the story with sex and I wasn't about to comply. They loaded it, I understand, and it was the final book.

    Another interesting thing came about a few years ago. I learned, from a good source and backed up with physical proof, that one of the largest publishers in Germany had reprinted every Black Bat without changing character names or the entire set-up. I was informed that when they used up the English written books, they went on with the series and eventually (this is difficult to believe) nine hundred Bats in all. I took this up with our British after learning this. He could obtain no information, nor could our German agent who bemoaned the great waste. Of course, I never owned any rights anyway, but I do think, if the nine hundred mark is true, that must have set come kind of record for a series character. Incidentally, this same publishing house bought the German rights to about fifty of Dorothy's paperback Gothics, so we weren't going to complain too much. Nothing to be done anyway. A chap in Greece has also published a number of Black Bats and Phantoms in miniature form and in English, but he's a friend of mine now and he isn't doing this to get rich.

    As to the question of real-life relationships with characters in the Black Bat, that of McGrath was based on a Captain of Police named George Kelly, who was the most perfect example of a police officer I ever knew. He was a very close friend of mine.

NORMAN DANIELS
6107 VILLAGE 6
CAMARILLO, CALIFORNIA 93010

- 2 -

Other than this--maybe one more--one time when they were ready to go to press with a Black Bat, Dorothy and I were finishing it in a hurry. As I took it out of the typewriter, she would edit and copy each page. Suddenly, a storm took out all electricity. We spent most of the remainder of the night writing and editing and copying in candlelight, but we got the script in on time.

That was another thing we had a reputation for--when there was a hole in a book about to go to press, we were called in and given the assignment with the understanding we had 24 hours to get the copy in. I think we accomplished it most of the time. I do recall there was a magazine called Ten Detective Aces and in one printing all ten stories were mine under ten different names. They were good old days all right. We really never suffered in the big Depression of the 30s.

I do recall I was given a full head of steam on all of the series characters we developed and those we took over. And it all ended with an amazing suddenness when everything folded and threw us into radio, then TV and, finally, pocketbooks.

Dorothy and I enjoyed most of it, but I will say that when we decided to retire, we did it without one iota of sorrow.

Anything else we can do, just ask. It's fun to see the old days resurrected with all the fanzine publications and we're delighted to help this effort in any way we can. We're also looking forward to reading THE SUPER FEDS.

Best,

Norm

Dear Don:

You'll notice that, in certain paragraphs, Norm used the pronoun "we". He's a modest chap. I want to state, in all honesty, that my only contribution to his pulp writing was to edit and copy his stories.

However, in so doing, I learned how to carry a story and later, book lengths. I also wish to say that whatever I know about writing, I learned from him. He always discussed his plots, characters and story continuity with me.

Sincerely,

Dorothy

```
                        HENRY STEEGER
                301 East 79th Street, 11A
                    New York, N. Y. 10021
```

                                              November 29, 1987

Mr. Don Hutchison
585 Merton Street
Toronto, Ontario M4S 1B4
CANADA

Dear Don:

Needless to say, I enjoyed your letter very much and am delighted to have you use any excerpts from me you care to have. Please use anything you feel might be helpful.

Don't worry about the age problem. It didn't really bother me when I first read it in ECHOES. I realized the mistake existed at that time and I would have let it go entirely if it hadn't cropped up again as it has in your book. When the magazine came out I was younger and it didn't bother me but now that I'm older I have to watch the age business so that I don't appear to be too much of an antique!

Speaking of age, I am so glad you have Huch B. Cave on your list of endorsements. The amazing part to me is that Hugh B. Cave was one of our major writers and to me was one of the best we had -- and yet, here he is, still as active as he could possibly be. He must have been a mere child in his mother's arms when his first story came to him and I'm sure he could barely toddle along when he began typing it out.

I play tennis several times a week and still play a very active game, but I begin to sense signs that this isn't going to go on for too much longer. I keep track of my competitive value by what the score turns out to be and when the score is on the negative side I'll begin to think about giving it up, although it'll be a bad day when that day comes along!

It's too bad we don't have a training ground for young authors any longer. The pulps were such a wonderful way for young men to develop their skills in writing and still get paid for it at the same time. I never minded the least bit when we handed a good author along to a so-called slick publication because I

HENRY STEEGER

Mr. Don Hutchison   - 2 -   November 29, 1987

figured we'd gotten his best and most vital stories on his road to fame. I guess, with the advance of all technologies, people wanted something a little finer than the paper on which the pulps were printed and they wanted the pages trimmed and they wanted a package that looked a little neater. Well, they got it but they also lost a regular monthly collection of the best stories written anywhere. You couldn't buy any fiction any finer than the material we printed in ADVENTURE Magazine. Maybe some day we might have a revival of the pulps in a more modern manner. Your book may help to accomplish that.

                                                    Every best wish,

                                                   Harry

HS:lbt

www.ingramcontent.com/pod-product-compliance
Lightning Source LLC
Chambersburg PA
CBHW032018230426
43671CB00005B/126